THE ART OF LIFE AND DEATH

EXPLORES HOW THE WORLD
APPEARS TO PEOPLE WHO HAVE
AN ACCUTE PERSPECTIVE ON IT;
THOSE WHO ARE CLOSE TO DEATH.

BASED ON 20 YEARS OF
WORKING ALONG SIDE ~~[scribble]~~
PEOPLE DYING OF HIV/AIDS
IN NEW YORK.

HAU
BOOKS

www.haubooks.com

THE MALINOWSKI MONOGRAPHS

In tribute to the foundational, yet productively contentious, nature of the ethnographic imagination in anthropology, this series honors the creator of the term "ethnographic theory" himself. Monographs included in this series represent unique contributions to anthropology and showcase groundbreaking work that contributes to the emergence of new ethnographically-inspired theories or challenge the way the "ethnographic" is conceived today.

THE ART OF LIFE AND DEATH

RADICAL AESTHETICS AND ETHNOGRAPHIC PRACTICE

Andrew Irving

Hau Books
Chicago

Cover, © 1998 Albert Velasco, *Spectre*, pencil drawing on paper. *Reproduced by permission from the artist.*

Cover and layout design: Sheehan Moore

Typesetting: Prepress Plus (www.prepressplus.in)

ISBN: 978-0-9973675-1-5
LCCN: 2017934090

Hau Books
Chicago Distribution Center
11030 S. Langley
Chicago, IL 60628
www.haubooks.com

Hau Books is marketed and distributed by The University of Chicago Press.
www.press.uchicago.edu

Printed in the United States of America on acid-free paper.

This book is dedicated with much love to the person who encouraged and taught me to be curious about the world: my mother, Olive Beryl Irving.

Table of Contents

List of Figures

Acknowledgements

First and foremost I would like to extend my deepest gratitude and appreciation to all the people in this book who consented to share their lives with me. Without you the book would simply not have been possible. Meeting and working with each of you has been one of the most important experiences of my life. Thank you also to all my friends and colleagues who read, gave comments on, or otherwise inspired the following chapters; to the Economic and Social Research Council of the United Kingdom and the Wenner Gren Foundation of New York who funded this research; to all the staff and volunteers at Visual AIDS; to the wonderful editorial team at HAU Books, including two anonymous reviewers, for their invaluable advice and dedication to bringing out the potential of this work.

The book draws on some of my material that previously appeared in the following publications:

2009. "The color of pain." *Public Culture* 21 (2): 293–320.
2010. "Dangerous substances and visible evidence: Tears, blood, alcohol, pills." *Visual Studies* 25 (1): 24–35.
2013. "Into the gloaming: A montage of the senses." In Transcultural montage, edited by Rane Willerslev and Christian Suhr, 76–96. Oxford: Berghahn Books.

The research for this book was supported by grants from the Economic and Social Research Council of the UK (RES-000-22-4657) and The Wenner Gren Foundation.

The limits of the world

This is not the book I wanted to write—indeed, perhaps no book whose main subject matter concerns death and disease can be described as a book that someone *wants* to write—but the circumstances of the world sometimes dictate otherwise, and over time stories about the lived experiences and imaginative lifeworlds of persons living under the shadow of death began to fill the blank pages. As such, *The art of life and death* attempts to understand how the world appears to persons who are close to death and who are confronting their own mortality and nonexistence after being diagnosed with a terminal illness— namely, those diagnosed with HIV/AIDS in New York City. *The art of life and death* also pertains to persons living with other illnesses or under conditions of uncertainty and disruption. When living under such circumstances, the contingencies of life and death are made explicit on a frequent, often daily, basis. Many taken-for-granted beliefs and practices are called into question or undergo reevaluation and adaptation as people learn to understand themselves and the workings of their bodies in new, sometimes radically different ways. A typical day may include complex cycles of emotion, hope, doubt, uncertainty, joy, and reflection, together with periods of mundane activity, as people adjust to their new circumstances. Often, the world is seen with a renewed and different intensity, as the influential playwright Dennis Potter described when interviewed on live television while he was dying from cancer: "Things are both more trivial than they ever were, and more important than they ever were, and the difference between the trivial and the important doesn't seem to matter" (Potter 1994).

In presenting an experience-near ethnography of life and death, the following chapters attempt to bring to life the ongoing and often unseen transformations in knowledge and understanding that occur when living with existential uncertainty: transformations in self identity and body image; transformations in long-standing religious and moral commitments; transformations in everyday social roles and relations; transformations in the perception of time, existence, and nature; and last but not least, transformations in the type of imaginative and emotional lifeworlds people inhabit when confronting death or attempting to negotiate a new life.

"Before there was wonder at the miracle of life," Hans Jonas (2001: 8) wrote, "there was wonder about death and what it might mean." For while it is obvious that life cannot exist without death and vice versa, the question of how life and death are so thoroughly conjoined and yet differentiated is still to be answered. Moreover, from the very first panvitalistic impulses, where everything in the world was understood to be animated and alive, to broader existential questions about the meaning and purpose of life, it is more often death rather than life that in the first instance calls for an explanation. For Jonas, "the *problem* of death is probably the first to deserve this name in the history of thought. Its emergence as an express problem signifies the awakening of the questioning mind long before a conceptual level of theory is attained" (2001: 8). It is a problem that has remained active throughout history and continues to test the combined knowledge of science, religion, and culture, generating multiple (often conflicting) reasons concerning the purpose of death and how it has become incorporated into life. Meanwhile, from the perspective of individual persons confronting their own mortality who have become acutely aware of their temporality and contingency, there exists the daily challenge of how life and death are negotiated in specific moments as a particular kind of social, familial, religious, or moral being.

There are commonalities and discrepancies found within most life events and experiences, which tend to become intensified and exacerbated in relation to the processes of death and dying. These pertain both to the species and what Gregory Bateson ([1936] 1958) termed the *ethos* and *eidos* of the social group, that is to say, the shared emotional, moral, and cognitive norms that bind persons together or differentiate between them. For Bateson, these are not immutable, are subject to moral variation over a person's lifetime, and possess substantial latitude within and between societies. Nevertheless, these provide a collective mechanism through which persons come to reflect on and understand themselves not only as humans or as social and cultural beings but also as a particular individual with a particular life biography; that is to say, as a finite, mortal human being who is situated in society and history but who can also live, act, and imagine the world in a different way.

This involves the person in an ongoing process of interpretation and understanding through which the constitution and contingency of life is frequently made explicit and persons contemplate their past, present, and future in relation to the many other possible lives they might have ended up living. The actual and alternative life courses someone imagines provide an emotional and moral framework of interpretation and understanding. As such, a person's thoughts, dreams, and imaginaries of a life lived otherwise are not immaterial fantasies or abstractions but are constitutive of embodied being and understanding. The events that comprise our lives are continually being relived, reimagined, and retold so as to interpret and reshape experience or inform future action. This is the idea of life as an unfinished, ontogenetic process grounded in the contingency of being and world: a being who is born onto a particular soil with a particular social, economic, and gendered status—and whose life course is subject to random events, luck, and happenstance—which are all negotiated and understood in the context of ongoing social and moral relations, practical activity, and the wider forces of the global political economy (Irving 2017). Often, it is in those moments of realization wherein the contingencies of life and death are most intensely experienced, spoken about, and reflected on, that we can also trace a history of philosophical, religious, and anthropological inquiry itself.

For William Barratt ([1958] 2011), the modalities of subjectivity and personal inquiry that emerge in the face of contingency mark a decisive transformation in existential understanding that is reflected at the level of the history of thought. Whereas many disciplinary approaches and schools of thought have asked the question, *what is a human being?*, it requires a further existential shift to ask, *who am I?* For Barratt, the first question presupposes "a world of objects, a fixed natural and zoological order, in which man was included; and when man's precise place in that order had been found, the specifically differentiating characteristic of reason was added" (2011: 95). By contrast, the questions *who am I?* or as pertinently *why me?*, *what will become of me?*, and *who am I among?* have their origins in a more vital, if obscure, realm of uncertainty and inquiry located within the lives of the questioners themselves, which for Barratt often betrays a personal sense of dereliction and loss that goes beyond the impulse to define human beings and social groups or categorize them within a broader scientific, biological, or anthropological order.

Moments of subjective transformation and personal questioning might be generated, for example, in times of affliction, liminality, schism, and communitas (Turner 1969, 1982), a falling out of the world or ongoing experiences of existential disorientation (G. Becker 1997; Al-Mohammad 2016), changes in perception generated by movement and shifts in identity and belonging (Kondo 1990; Jackson 2013) or incongruities and contingencies that "cannot simply be 'writ away' through contextualization" (Crapanzano 2015: 160; see also Crapanzano and Jackson 2014). Such moments of personal and critical reflection regarding life and death can be strategically cultivated—for example, through religious practice and contemplation, ritual events, or therapy, self-analysis, and introspection—or else might emerge unbidden and spontaneously within the flow of people's mundane everyday experience and interactions. Whether embedded squarely within quotidian life or seen from the margins, it involves a smaller or larger scale movement in which a person comes to reevaluate their habitual orientation and understanding of themselves, others, nature, the universe, and the gods, thereby turning the question of *who am I?* into an ethnographic question about life and its relationship to death.

Death poses an intractable problem not just for individual persons but also for families, societies, and cultures, often locating them near the limits of knowledge, emotion, and understanding. Attempts to come to terms with death, including comprehending the boundaries between the living and the dead or imagining what happens to the person afterward, stretch back to the origins of humanity, as evidenced by a wide range of funeral and death-related practices. There is also clear evidence that burial and death rituals were not only central to early human societies but also to Neanderthals (Mithen 2006), who demonstrated a similar awareness of mortality beyond the more straightforward realms of reflex, instinct, and self-preservation.

Nietzsche already alerted us to how humanity, although part of the animal world, can no longer understand itself as just another species within nature due to our efforts to know and understand ourselves ([1882] 1974). As a consequence, human beings have loosened the bonds of nature, challenged the gods, and created the conditions for our own peculiar anxieties about death and dying. Charles Taylor summarized the problematical nature of the species: "Man as a living being is not radically different from other animals, but at the same time he is not just an animal plus reason, he is a quite new totality; and that means that he has to be understood on quite different principles" (Taylor 1979: 19).

In becoming such, human beings have not only questioned the meaning and purpose of existence but have been confronted by the problem of how to reclaim life in the knowledge of death and nonbeing. Stories of death and dying have been told through culture and history and have provided an essential means for passing on as well as challenging personal, moral, and religious understandings. With the advent of art and writing it became possible to signify and share thoughts and feelings about death in new and more durable ways. To date, a vast body of work has accrued on a subject that has troubled and inspired generations of poets, writers, and artists, alongside prophets, philosophers, and scientists. In this, it is possible to discern the stirrings of a different kind of self (Taylor 1992) and the generation and transmission of new forms of knowledge and moral practice whose realization takes the form of persons aware of their own individuality and agency but also their shared fate and status as finite, mortal beings.

DEATHLY ENCOUNTERS

From medical and legal perspectives, there are a number of different ways of defining death—from the cessation of breathing and the heartbeat to notions of brain death, where the brain stem is no longer functioning but the majority of the organism remains alive (Lock 2004; Kastenbaum 2011). Strictly speaking, the human body is not even a singular entity—or for that matter entirely human—but an amalgamation of many different organisms. Consequently, although death may mark the cessation of consciousness, life continues at the level of cellular activity and metabolic processes (Mims 1999). As the twenty-first century progresses, the borders between life and death are becoming increasingly complicated, not just through the copresence of different, often contested, social, religious, and biomedical understandings but also through technological advancements, organ transplants, the use of genetic material, and new developments in brain and computer science that are trying to establish direct communication between our brains and computers, and exploring how consciousness might be downloaded, stored, and distributed.

Death presents an equally thorny problem to the humanities and social sciences, and at times there is little consensus between different disciplines. While philosophy, psychology, and psychoanalysis gravitate toward universal themes and explanations, anthropologists focus on the diverse social, cultural, and religious practices that mediate death and maintain the continuity of the social group. As such, anthropological approaches try to understand the many and varied beliefs and practices that shape people's perceptions and do not focus solely on the destiny of the individual or the shared phylogeny of the species but on the common and discrepant ways human beings understand life and respond to death. Although individual people die, society, culture, and humanity endure through the handing down of language, knowledge, and moral perspectives between generations, necessitating a comparative ethnographic understanding of how death is negotiated through different social institutions, cultural traditions, and religious practices.

When approached ethnographically, it soon becomes apparent that there are as many ways of dying as there are of living, in which case emotions such as fear, dread, and anxiety—which are often seen as elemental or universal in medicine, psychology, and psychoanalysis—may have more to do with specific cultural epistemologies and ways of being than the human condition *per se*. However, the variety of responses and attitudes toward death both *within* and *between* societies shows how death can neither be reduced to a specific social, religious, or moral perspective nor to a timeless and universal truth. Albert Camus alerted us to the error of mistaking the intensity of one's feelings and emotions for a shared social characteristic, or by extension, one of humankind. No matter how strongly someone may feel about death or how committed an individual or social or religious group is to a particular perspective or worldview, it does not mean it is shared by others or possesses universal validity.

There is as much variation within a person's life as there is between persons. "Anyone who turns his prime attention to himself," wrote Michel de Montaigne in *Of the inconstancy of our actions*, "will hardly ever find himself in the same state twice" (2003: 377). "We are entirely made up of bits and pieces, woven together so diversely and shapelessly that each one of them pulls its own way at every moment. And there is as much difference between us and ourselves as there is between us and other people. '*Magnam rem puta unam hominem agere*' [Let me convince you that it is a hard task to always be the same man]" (Montaigne 2003: 380). This does not make a person's ideas, emotions, and presuppositions about death *wrong* but it does make them personal, situational, and socio-historical, highlighting how death is a complex, polythetic phenomenon that encompasses multiple modes of experience and understanding. As such, death can no more be defined by a particular sociological, anthropological, or medical model than the death-related practices of a given person, social group, or historical period define it in perpetuity for all humankind.

Death lies at the very foundations of society insofar as many important social and cultural phenomena—from language, religion, and education to art, medicine, and science—have their origins in the attempt to transcend individual finitude and ensure life and knowledge are transmitted between generations (Bloch and Parry 1982). Indeed, "without mortality, no history, no culture—no humanity" (Bauman 1992: 7), reinforcing how death is not simply a destructive presence but also a creative life-force that also gives rise to social, cultural, and religious forms that provide meaning and purpose in the face of the body's eventual demise (Robben 2004; Kaufman and Morgan 2005; Hallam and Hockey 2006). The knowledge of our eventual death—alongside the capacity to imagine a range of possible outcomes, including reincarnation, an eternal afterlife, the disintegration of self and consciousness, or one's constitutive atoms and molecules being dispersed across the universe—sets humans apart from other species. As the anthropologist Ernest Becker wrote shortly before his own death from cancer:

> The essence of man is really his *paradoxical* nature, the fact that he's half animal and half symbolic. We might call this existential paradox the condition of *individuality within finitude*. Man has a symbolic identity that brings him sharply out of nature. He is a symbolic self, a creature with a name, a life history. He is a creator with a mind that soars out to speculate about atoms and infinity, who can place himself imaginatively at a point in space and contemplate bemusedly his own planet. This immense expansion, this dexterity, this ethereality, this self-consciousness gives to man literally the status of a small God in nature, as the Renaissance thinkers knew. Yet, at the same time, as the Eastern sages knew, man is a worm and food for worms. This is the paradox: he is out of nature and hopelessly in it; he's dual, up in the stars and yet housed in a heart-pumping, breath-gasping body that once belonged to a fish and still carries the gill marks to prove it. His body is a material fleshy casing that is alien to him in many ways—the strangest and most repugnant way being that it aches and bleeds and will decay and die. Man is literally split in two: he has an awareness of his own splendid uniqueness in that he sticks out of nature with a towering majesty, and yet he goes back into the ground a few feet in order blindly and dumbly to rot and disappear forever. It is a terrifying dilemma to be in and to have to live with. (E. Becker 1997: 26)

Illness, misfortune, and uncertainty frequently reveal gaps in knowledge and generate questions that distance persons from their familiar understandings of themselves or the world (Reynolds-Whyte 1997). As such, the encounter with illness and mortality is not just a medical, religious, or ethical problem but a profoundly ethnographic one insofar as persons from all social and cultural backgrounds can be found reflecting on the reasons for their illness, searching for meaning, or interrogating the moral purpose of their life. When a question first comes to mind, it rarely stands alone but is distilled from and embedded within an entangled mass of related questions and uncertainties (Collingwood [1940] 2002). People's expressions of uncertainty and contingency—as embodied in questions such as *why me?*, *what should I do?*, *what is happening to me?*, *what's going on?*, or simply *why?*—are all common questions forged out of simple words but often exist beyond the realm of medical science and religious explanation. People ask questions in many different ways—rational, rhetorical, angry, pleading, speculative, in dreams, in prayer, and in dialogue with others— which are not always an ultimate quest for truth but an attempt to get through the night and make the world livable again. Consequently, although questions are often a means for seeking answers they are also a pragmatic strategy for opening up a dialogue, seeking solace, or creating stability in a context of misfortune and uncertainty.

Questions are not disembodied but are located "within our life, within our history: they are born there, they die there, if they have found a response, more often than not they are transformed there" (Merleau-Ponty 1968: 104). As such, a question is located at the boundary of the known and unknown world and needs to be understood as a particular kind of embodied inquiry grounded in the questioner's practical concerns and life circumstances. People's questions disclose a specific bodily experience and moral understanding of the world and might be asked during times of uncertainty, hope, suffering, pragmatic need, or the realization of life's transience. They are typically formulated and expressed in language to a range of human and nonhuman agents—including oneself and others, medics, and religious representatives, as well as wider society, God, and the universe—for particular reasons, such as to seek knowledge, create obligations, express anger, to find meaning and cathartic relief, justify a way of being, or simply to obtain a response and acknowledgement.

The act of questioning encompasses social, cultural, and moral presuppositions that are embedded within a specific form of life (Wittgenstein [1953] 2009) and articulated in particular contexts: for example, a home, hospital, a bar, or church. This brings a range of other persons into the realm of some-one's personal and emotional experience, including friends, family, and medical professionals, illustrating how illness creates a shared social, cosmological, and medical context of knowing and understanding that is rarely confined to the individual but constituted between persons in places. Although the questions people ask emerge from a shared set of social concerns and presuppositions, they can also reveal significant personal and moral differences that individuate and distinguish people's experiences and understandings of illness, including how persons negotiate disruption, pain, and uncertainty.

The act of questioning is predicated on preexisting knowledge and under-standings of the world insofar as "every inquiry is a seeking. Every seeking gets guided beforehand by what is sought" (Heidegger 1962: 24). For example, ask-ing God for help presupposes a particular understanding and interpretation of God's character and discloses a specific social, moral, and existential worldview. When seen in the field, the questions people ask during times of crisis and distress invariably confirm, modify, or challenge established understandings of the world. However, there are also many occasions when questions remain un-answered or unanswerable. To repeatedly put one's faith in medical science and remain sick or ask God, "*why me?*" and receive no answer, exposes an emotional and existential dislocation between person and world. As such, the questions people ask often articulate a moment in which the limits of existing knowledge and understanding are made public and are not only directed toward particular agents or discursive forms—for example, religion or science—but toward the fact of being alive in *this* body, in *this* time, and in *this* place.

TIME, FINITUDE, AND PHENOMENOLOGY

The original intention behind *The art of life and death* was not to investigate illness or death but to explore the perception of time in response to a prob-lem Maurice Merleau-Ponty identified toward the end of *The phenomenology of perception*: "The problem is how to make time explicit as it comes into being and makes itself evident, time at all times underlying the notion of time, not as an object of our knowledge, but as a dimension of our being" (Merleau-Ponty 1992: 415).

This places Merleau-Ponty in a long line of thinkers, including Edmund Husserl, William James, Henri Bergson, and Martin Heidegger, who have attempted to understand time not as an abstract philosophical concept but as part of embodied life and experience: a problem that becomes even more challenging when considering the diverse character of people's lives in different societies and across historical periods. Although time is a precondition for life, experience, and action, it is notoriously elusive and frequently recedes from conscious awareness when immersed in everyday concerns and activities. At the very point one attempts to understand or direct attention toward time, its character is transformed and thus perceived differently. As Augustine of Hippo (354–430) famously lamented, the more we try to comprehend what time is, the more distorted and mysterious it becomes:

> For what is time? Who can easily and briefly explain it? Who even in thought can comprehend it, even to the pronouncing of a word concerning it? But what in speaking do we refer to more familiarly and knowingly than time? And certainly we understand when we speak of it; we understand also when we hear it spoken of by another. What, then, is time? If no one asks of me, I know; if I wish to explain to him who asks, I know not (Book Eleven: XIV).

Without time there would be no sentience, no life, no death, and no social existence insofar as human beings are formed as persons, think, act, and inhabit the world in time; carry out their domestic and working lives in time; and experience moods, feelings, and emotions in time. Although time is invested in all the senses of sight, sound, taste, touch, and smell—and is the medium through which perception, knowledge, and understanding emerge—it cannot be perceived in itself and is instead discerned in things such as rhythm, movement, the passing of the seasons, and bodies that grow, age, and die. In the ancient Greek tradition, before the concept or word for time even existed, the primary focus was on the phenomena of *change* (Lloyd 1976). Why did crops ripen and people get old and die? Why did flowers wither and animal flesh rot while rocks endured? That is to say, what was the animating force that lay behind the visible and sensory properties of change and transformation?

Such concerns were already present before the dawn of Socratic philosophy and can be found in the myths and legends of the ancient Mediterranean where the titan Chronos lived on the horizon at the furthest edge of the world (Turetsky 1998). Chronos fathered a number of sons and daughters and in some accounts ended up eating his own children, thus furnishing a graphic example of the past devouring the future. The implication here seems clear: time is simultaneously a creative and destructive phenomenon that is necessary for birth and life but exists beyond the sphere of human influence and understanding. The world and its contents are brought into existence by time—including life, consciousness, and the body, which cannot exist in stasis—but ultimately all things that are born into the world end up being devoured by the very same phenomenon that enabled them.

Time always needs an *other*. That is to say, time can only be conceptualized in terms of difference and understood in comparative terms. Thus, human time is contrasted with the time of trees, rocks, the planet, Gods, eternity, and the universe. Or as Johannes Fabian (1983) argued, the time of one "culture" is defined in relation to other cultures, so that different ways of being—for example, hunter gatherers—are erroneously described as belonging to the past while other societies are seen as modern. However, perhaps the most persistent and significant of others has been the phenomenon of death insofar as experiences and understandings of time stand against the human organism's fundamental mortality and finitude. Consequently, a number of influential philosophers—including Heidegger, Emmanuel Levinas, and Jacques Derrida—have ventured that death presents the ultimate otherness, which for Heidegger is intrinsically "nonrelational" (1962: 303) and for Levinas diminishes us to a state of sobbing and infancy (1996).

Such conceptualizations reveal an overly static phenomenology of death, typically couched in Western notions of fear, dread, and anxiety. Importantly, they do not accurately reflect the experiences and understandings of the men and women I worked with, whose orientations toward death would change within and between situations: during times of illness, when drunk, when playing music, when walking, when looking at the ocean, or when laughing. People's moral actions and concerns about death are as much concerns about life (Parry 1994) and the dominant sense that emerged from my fieldwork was that in many ways death is quite straightforward and instead it is *life* that is extraordinary in its otherness: life in its infinite variety and multiplicity, life in relation to illness, time, and the body, life in contrast to what is imagined to exist beyond death. For a life with HIV/AIDS is a life continually *made strange* and retains the capacity to enchant or surprise. Or shock.

Many social-scientific and philosophical theories about time have focused on the idea of time as a linguistic or cultural construct, while other approaches, including some that draw on physics, argue it is an illusion or deny it exists at all (see Turetsky 1998; Birth 2012). Regardless of its ontological status, time as a collective social phenomenon is measured by a wide range of quotidian, ritual, and mechanical means that provide frameworks for structuring society and coordinating action, ranging from the daily organization of work and leisure to shared social events and ritual occasions that mark the passage of time, such as birthdays, anniversaries, and commemorations. Such modes of social organization provide the primary materials for the anthropology of time, and there is a substantial literature concerning the different ways of structuring time across the world's cultures (Gell 1996; James and Mills 2005).

Far less common are anthropological studies "with the people in," which bring a sustained ethnographic and phenomenological focus to people's lived experiences of time. An ethnographic, fieldwork-based approach to time does not hinge on whether time is real or illusory but on how temporality is disclosed in people's lives, thoughts, practical activities, and concerns. Consequently, a key aim when beginning this book was to turn Merleau-Ponty's phenomenological problem of temporality into an ethnographic question by placing it directly into the field and working alongside persons for whom the passage of time was made explicit, often on a daily basis. For the persons I worked with, life was encountered as overtly temporal following the diagnosis with HIV/AIDS; they thereafter not only found themselves face to face with death but also the subject of a burgeoning social, national, and political crisis. Consequently, by paying close attention to people's situated perceptions and embodied understandings, a key aim of this book has been to identify people's lived experience of time, as framed by an ongoing condition of mortality and finitude, in an era of rapid social, moral, and political change.

From a phenomenological perspective, time begins and ends with the lived body, which provides the foundational conditions for thought, experience, and action and is the medium through which knowledge of time emerges for us as individuals and as a species. As we cannot step outside our bodies—outside the flow of life and action—people's perceptions of time are continually recast from the standpoint of finite bodies embedded from moment to moment in a world of memory, action, and the future. And while the body-in-action is not the only means for establishing the grounds of understanding, it offers the best starting point for exploring how perceptions and experiences of time and space are generated during periods of health and illness.

Approached ethnographically, it is possible to identify the common and idiosyncratic ways persons engage with time and mortality, not as a representative member of a particular society, social category, or humanity as a whole but as an individual person living under specific conditions of illness and uncertainty, who is subject to different moods and emotions, and who lives with incomplete knowledge about themselves and the world. As such, my intention is less to explain experiences of time in terms of shared social structures or overarching cultural models but to try to catch those moments when an explicit temporal awareness emerges within a person's situated actions and expressions of being a body continually engaged in the world.

BODIES IN ACTION: THE CONTINGENCIES OF LIVING AND DYING

The human body is a site of considerable commonality and difference. Whereas running a mile for some people is an enjoyable, life-affirming experience, for other people it is a painful, interminable ordeal that leaves them struggling to breathe or conceive of anything outside the moment. Each day presents numerous ways of coordinating nerves, lungs, muscles, and metabolism with specific emotions, moods, and trajectories of thought and memory, all of which have the potential to generate different experiences of being a body-in-the-world, reinforcing how perception is not determined by phylogeny, action, or social context alone and that people do not engage with the world through identical bodies or shared states of being and belief.

In fact, "normal" bodies do not exist in any tangible or empirical sense—instead they are produced by statistics, averaging out differences and dividing bodies into classifications of normal and abnormal—to produce normative bodies that act as the mark against which other bodies differ or fall short of (Hacking 1990; Butler 1999). For Georges Canguilhem ([1943] 1991), bodily life is grounded in action and movement (without which the organism would cease to exist) and occurs in environments that are diverse and in a process of change. Normality, when understood as a mode of life, as opposed to an outcome of normative forms of classification, encompasses the entire range of the organism's many and varied adaptations to changes in their own body and the surrounding environment, with the consequence that definitions and experiences of health and sickness are neither completely predetermined nor reducible to normative measures and statistical averages. "Especially in humans, health is precisely a certain latitude, a certain play in the norms of life and behaviour. What characterizes health is a capacity to tolerate variations in norms on which only the stability of situations and milieus—seemingly guaranteed yet in fact always necessarily precarious" Canguilhem 2008: 132). Or in Paul Rabinow's summation of Canguilhem's work: "Life is not stasis, a fixed set of natural laws, set in advance and the same for all, to which one must adhere in order to survive. Rather, life is action, mobility and pathos, the constant but only partially successful effort to resist death" (Rabinow 1994: 17).

From Canguilhem's perspective, it is no more normal to be healthy than it is abnormal to be sick: both are constitutive of people's embodied experience and ongoing negotiation of life. It is a perspective that is developed anthropologically in Veena Das and Clara Han's (2016) consideration of how life and death are interwoven into the fabric of experience—for example, in the way that certain Buddhist practices see life and death as working together within each moment. "What if we took such ways of conceptualizing the relation between life and death as present not only in exotic practices," they ask, "but also in concepts generated from the experiences of everyday life and its perils" (Das and Han 2016: 1)? Human beings only exist on this earth in a perceiving, sensing, and embodied form before death transforms us into a lifeless corpse (Fink 2016). An embodied awareness of what it means to be alive in the moment and in the world, and the different possible forms this might take, is not just linked to instantiations of anomaly, disruption, or illness but might also be heightened, for example, when listening to music, in love, or walking in the street.

The world that the living body inhabits and acts in is not pregiven (Al-Mohammad 2016; Pina-Cabral 2017) but is constituted and disclosed from moment to moment through the different senses. The body's sense organs produce and reveal contrasting properties: whereas the eye sees a world dominated by stable entities and emplaces objects in space, sound is more amorphous and unfolds over time, while touch is localized and highly sensitive to movement. Combinations of smells, sights, sounds, tastes, and textures continuously impress themselves onto the nervous system, but at the very same time a person transforms and modifies the environment through their thoughts, movements, and actions. As such, both the perceiving organism and inhabited environment are in a process of constant change and adaptation through which life and personhood is individuated and expressed.

In his works, *Life, death, and the body in the theory of being* (1965) and *The phenomenon of life: Toward a philosophical biology* (2001), Hans Jonas, who along with fellow Jewish students Emmanuel Levinas, Hannah Arendt, and Henri Marcuse studied under Heidegger, considered how life continually adapts and attunes to new or changing environmental conditions—for example, in the way that trees and plants are capable of sensing sources of light and water or responding to temperature and soil conditions—which for Jonas, provides an empirical starting point from which to build a phenomenological account of organic life and serves as the basis of two related projects. The first, following Heidegger's ambiguous relationship with Nazism, concerned an investigation of how Being or *Dasein* in its broadest sense, relates to ethics, and the second attempted to formulate a schema for the analysis of biological life forms that was consistent with modern scientific understanding. In tracing the flow of life from unicellular organisms through plants and flora to animals and human beings, Jonas notes how plants and trees are driven by metabolic needs, accompanied by diurnal and seasonal rhythms and environmental responsiveness. In animals, these metabolic needs are combined with motility, perceptual and sensory awareness, and emotion, and in the case of human beings, encompasses self-reflexive capacities including thinking, imagining, reasoning, and moral and ethical understanding.

As such, for Jonas, life is precarious and contingent because of its dependence on metabolic processes and exchanges with a mutable environment. Simply to be in the world is to exist in a conditional state that necessitates different kinds of action. For humans, action incorporates within it an ethics—for example, through the choices we make, the ways we move, how we express ourselves and speak to other people, or relate to plants, animals, material things, and the planet. This is not to conflate action with ethics or an attempt to ascribe a value judgment on the particular ethics that are lived and performed as good or bad. Instead, it is to assert that ethics has as its starting point our animal condition (MacIntyre 1999) and to recognize the complex intertwining of ethics, contingency, and action that shapes a person's past, present, and future relations and existence in the world. No account of ethical and moral life is possible independent of biology or that does not consider the forms of life available to us as animals with specific metabolic needs and the cognitive capacity to remember our infancy, contemplate the future, and conceptualize different ways of being and acting in world (MacIntyre 1999).

"In a word, ethics concerns existence" (Lambek 2015: 18). Consequently, in asking, "where is the ethical located?" Lambek argues it is most clearly found and manifested in our everyday actions, social relations, and linguistic practices rather than in a separate realm of philosophical and religious discourse. "The task is to recognize the ethical dimension of human life—of the human condition—without objectifying ethics as a natural organ of society, universal category of human thought, or distinct kind of human practice" (Lambek 2010: 10).

As an intrinsic component of human activity, the ethical is always situated in relation to alternative, sometimes conflicting, possibilities and life choices that shape our continued being-in-the-world (Lambek 2015), which for Immanuel Kant ([1800] 1963), coalesces into the pragmatic query, *what should I do?*

The existential question of how to live amid the exigencies and ethics of action is often characterized in terms of a conflict between divergent forces, for example, good and bad, faith and reason, individual and society, life and death, and often takes cross-cultural form in the relation between *fate* and *free will* (Malik 2015). The sources of fate might be variously understood in terms of smaller or more powerful gods; biology, phylogeny, and genetics; social structures, class, and habitus, et cetera, while free will might take the guise of creativity, inspiration, and agency; resistance and opposition; independence and individuality. More straightforwardly, those areas of action in which the person has no choice or control do not relate to ethics, unlike those areas where the person has some movement and latitude. A further implication is that our being-in-the-world is contingent and incorporates numerous possible presents and futures whose character remains open and undetermined, and that there is always some form of practical and contiguous connection (as opposed to merely conjectured or abstract association) between life and death.

 A striking example of the critical role of contingency in establishing the contours of life and death can be found in William Barratt's account of the French scientist and mathematician Blaise Pascal. Born into a wealthy family, Pascal struggled with illness throughout much of his childhood and adult life. By his twenties, he had introduced important new ideas in mathematics, geometry, and physics that laid the foundations for much modern theory. Pascal had already been working on gambling, chance, and concepts of probability when his father broke his hip in a serious accident on the ice. Pascal witnessed what he regarded as his father's miraculous recovery from a condition that could otherwise be fatal. Then, on November 23, 1654, Pascal experienced an ecstatic vision and intense religious awakening that by many accounts followed a profound brush with chance a few weeks earlier. Pascal was out driving his six-horse carriage across a bridge over the Seine when his carriage lurched, the door was thrown open, and Pascal was almost flung to his death. So powerful were these events that he wrote a document about his experience and sewed it into his coat, secretly transferring it and re-sewing it whenever he changed coats, so as to keep it as close to him as possible at all times. The document served as a perpetual reminder of the proximity of life to death, not just in terms of how life is perpetually shaped by chance, contingency, and random events but also in terms of how nonbeing and uncertainty are imminent within the structure of all human existence. Thereafter, Pascal dedicated much of his thinking to understanding the role of contingency, arbitrariness, and oblivion in shaping existence and long before Heidegger and Sartre introduced their ideas concerning human contingency and nothingness.

> The arbitrariness and suddenness of this near accident became for him another lightning flash of revelation. Thereafter he saw Nothingness as a possibility that lurked, so to speak, beneath our feet, a gulf and an abyss into which we might tumble at any moment. No other writer has expressed more powerfully than Pascal the radical contingency that lies at the heart of human existence—a contingency that may at any moment hurl us all unsuspecting into non-being. Death does not arrive punctually by appointment. (Barratt [1958] 2011: 117)

The contingencies of life and death are shaped by structural, political, and ecological factors, and incorporate within them a range of associated and ancillary understandings whose meaning varies across linguistic communities in relation to concepts such as freedom, empowerment, causation, destiny, providence, natural and divine justice, the necessity of nature, and various other forces associated with luck, chance, and providence (Crapanzano 2015). As *subjects of luck* constituted between personal and impersonal aspects of fortune and fate—and as realized through different social and culturally grounded modes of interpretation and imagination—people's recurrent interactions and engagements with the contingencies of life can be seen as events, much like a roll of a dice, whereby "the cosmos is engaged and challenged to reveal itself" (da Col and Humphrey 2012: 15). Partly anticipatory and partly remedial, it is a process of engagement where the conjoined forces of contingency and necessity do not exist as absolutes beyond the sphere of agency but are personalized and reshaped through action wherein humans can exert some influence over these forces up to and including luck, nature, the gods, and the universe (da Col and Humphrey 2012).

Here an affinity can be found between philosophical, theological, and ethnographic approaches in which there is no radical separation of person and world, ethics and action, contingency and necessity, illness and health, or even living and dying: they are all necessary conditions of life. Echoing Paul Stoller's work among the Songhay (2005), Das and Han (2016) consider how life involves responding to an ever-changing world that requires negotiating and anticipating different possible presents and futures. For the Songhay, the paths of life are perilous and phenomena such as sickness, death, and bad luck are unavoidable. However, the forces of fate are not all encompassing and as such invocations and divination enable anticipatory or remedial actions that allow persons to adjust their life course to make it more livable. Following Canguilhem and Wittgenstein, Das and Han similarly draw attention to life as an ongoing process of adaptation and transformation, including those moments when anomaly shifts to disease in which a person's embodied responses to life events cannot always be specified beforehand in the way "that the scale of the human body or the range of the human voice cannot be determined in advance but must be found in each case" (see Das and Han 2016: 17).

This shifts the anthropological focus away from the more stable or enduring patterns of sociality, relationality, and moral action, toward the precarities of life and death as generated by fluctuating global markets, unexpected and revolutionary events, biopolitical developments, and advances in biology, technology, and medicine. A key implication, beyond the established idea that politics, economics, and ethics are inseparable from the sphere of life, is the more radical assertion that the social is not foundational and does not form the ground of all being. Instead, the social is itself seen as a provisional and precarious activity that is not necessarily pregiven and needs to be worked at rather than assumed.

This reminds us that all academic theory is founded on a series of epistemological and "absolute presuppositions [that] do not need justification" (Collingwood [1940] 2002: 44), which for anthropology encompasses concepts such as society, relationality, and context, which need to be recognized as modes of disciplinary analysis rather than determinants of people's lives. As such, "if we take the problem of individuality—or variation—instead as a starting point for the mutual inflection of biological and social norms, 'context' begins to appear in a different light" (Das and Han 2016: 16). For disciplines founded on the primacy of the social, this presents a key challenge but also opens up a number of different anthropological starting points for exploring people's lives by beginning instead, for example, with the personal or a feeling of bodily unease (Al-Mohammad 2016); the idiosyncratic and eccentric (Rapport 2008); a sense of weightlessness or vertigo (Irving 2013); or finding oneself at the boundary of life and death (Jackson 2016), so as to refocus the epistemological presuppositions of anthropology on the particularity of the living and moving body in a world of action and change.

An ethnography of particular bodies in action—rather than presupposing normative capacities and abstract potentialities—focuses on the body as it makes its way in the world and draws attention to how bodily potentials are constituted within moments of health, well-being, disruption, decline, and inability. Too often, the literature on bodies, embodiment, and the environment is located at rarefied levels of theoretical abstraction or solipsism that has little relevance to the diversity of bodies on the ground where obstacles such as stairs, hills, stamina, coordination, and the differentiation of actual bodies in health and sickness are overlooked. Fortunately, queer theory, gender studies, and disability studies continue to destabilize the statistically normalized and socialized human body. Here, Eli Clare writes from a queer and disabled perspective:

> I want to write about the body, not as a metaphor, symbol or representation, but simply as the body. To write about my body, our bodies, in all their messy complicated realities. I want words shaped by my slurring tongue, shaky hands, almost steady breath; words shaped by the fact that I am a walkie—someone for whom a flight of stairs without an accompanying elevator poses no problem—and by the reality that many of the people I encounter in my daily life assume I am "mentally retarded." Words shaped by how my body—and I certainly mean to include the mind as part of the body—moves through the world. (Clare 2001: 359)

In these words a sense of impatience can be discerned about the way writings about the body often gloss over corporeal differences to reinscribe social norms and values to produce sterile theories about messy bodies. In talking about bodies in their specific, complicated, and untidy realities rather than through assumptions of habitual unity or presupposing every body can enact universal phylogenetic abilities, Clare avoids reifying and generalizing his own bodily experience or simply reversing the gaze by privileging the experience of one particular body over others. The fact that "no one is ever more than temporarily able-bodied" (Breckenridge and Vogler 2001: 349) cautions us against setting up "the abled-body" as the norm and thereby mistaking social and linguistic labels of difference for empirical or ontological differences, as highlighted by Clare's observation that "words" are more often shaped by his body as it extends out into the world rather than the other way around. By paying closer ethnographic attention to the variability of the body—including moments of bodily instability and the effect this has on personhood, gender roles, sexuality, identity, and status—it is possible to provide a better understanding of how the body creates the conditions for multiple modes of experience and expression. Indeed a more empirical, in-depth analysis "of bodily difference might open up new avenues of exploration, or stretch existing ones" (Staples 2003: 295), and allow us to understand how different bodily experiences facilitate different modes of being-in-the-world (Rapport 2000).

Significant levels of variation are found not just between persons but also within the individual, whose body changes over the life course, including during periods of health and sickness. There is as much diversity within an individual's bodily history as between different individuals, given that people grow and age and do not go through life with an invariable body, making it difficult to ascribe any single social or universal characteristic to the body. Or as Canguilhem states, it is not possible to "determine the normal by simple reference to a statistical mean but only comparing the individual to itself, either in identical successive situations or in varied situations" (2008: 113).

During periods of illness, many simple tasks and modes of embodied knowledge become compromised by an inability to carry them out to the same level, revealing facets previously naturalized through practice but now tarnished and degraded, as described by anthropologist Robert Murphy, whose ethnography of his descent into quadriplegia includes the following account of trying to brush his teeth:

> I brush my own teeth, using a toothbrush with a special thick handle, but Yolanda [Murphy's partner] first must squeeze the toothpaste tube—my grip is no longer strong enough. Since I cannot lean forward over the sink on my own, she has to push my head over it so that I can rinse my mouth afterwards. (Murphy 2001: 197)

> [Inability and impairment] is a precondition of my plans and projects, first premise of all my thoughts. Just as my former sense of embodiment remained taken-for-granted, positive and unconscious, my sense of disembodiment is problematic, negative and conscious. My identity has lost its stable moorings and has become contingent on physical flaw. (Murphy 2001: 105)

The mind and body of someone diagnosed with a life-threatening illness constitutes an entire anthropological field in itself, and Murphy brilliantly combines anthropological theory and personal reflection on learning to live with existential uncertainty, sickness, disruption, and a changing body, all of which form part of the apprenticeship to illness and a new social identity. Stoller similarly combines personal experience and anthropological theory to describe the state of "betweenness" that is common to both anthropology and illness (2005, 2009). Stoller draws upon anthropology's extensive use of spatial metaphors in its theoretical descriptions of social life to suggest an anthropologist's fate often involves being located between different social, cultural, and moral understandings of the world. Living between things, Stoller asserts, has several existential repercussions in that a person gets pulled in different directions at the same time and often experiences a sense of indeterminacy.

The figure of *the between* offered Stoller a more explicitly personal perspective following his diagnosis with cancer. By using anthropology to understand his illness journey and confrontation with death, Stoller developed an approach to living with cancer by resorting to the incantations and practices he learned while training as an apprentice sorcerer among the Songhay. For the Songhay, it is not possible to avoid illness, as it is constitutive of life and therefore a person must be willing to face it. At the same time, divination, spirit possession, and other mediating actions can help restore balance, which for Stoller encompassed a personal and professional quest for meaning and an affirmation of sorcery and storytelling.

Murphy's and Stoller's books stand alongside a number of other excellent first-person accounts by persons diagnosed with serious or long-term illnesses that provide intimate empirical insights into people's lifeworlds during illness or when engaging with mortality (e.g., Hull 1992; Toombs 1992; Stacey 1997; Bauby 2008; Marks 2016). Especially relevant to this book are first-person accounts of HIV/AIDS by persons all now departed (Collard 1993; Guibert 1995, 2015; Brodkey 1996; Moore 1996; Monette 1997; Conigrave 2010) that attempted to document and describe life with the disease, including the streams of inner thought and expression that are not necessarily externalized or made apparent to the wider world. The thoughts and ideas these writers left behind informed the writing of this book and its attempt to understand how lived experiences of illness are shaped by trajectories of inner expression, imagination, and reverie that exist beneath the surface of people's public interactions.

OUTLINE OF A SYNDROME

Drawing on over twenty years of research carried out among persons with HIV/AIDS in New York City, *The art of life and death* is based on a long-term

[handwritten marginal note:] SOCIAL DIVISIONS BASED ON RACE, ETHNICITY, GENDER, AND CLASS CAN INFLUENCE ACCESS TO HEALTH CARE AND SUSCEPTIBILITY TO DISEASE (THIS IS HOW TO USE MEDICAL ANTHROPOLOGY!) TO DEORIENT).

ethnographic collaboration with persons who consented to share their lives as they experienced illness, approached death, and eventually reclaimed life. By offering an ethnographic account of how the world appears to people close to death, it attempts to understand the diverse ways people engage with mortality and reestablish social existence amid conditions of liminality, betweenness, and uncertainty. Life with many illnesses, including HIV/AIDS, is not one of stasis or steady decline but consists of undulating cycles of illness and recovery that can persist for days, months, or even years. These cycles are closely linked to experiences of hope, elation, expectation, and self-reflection as well as sorrow, doubt, and despair, illustrating how illness is accompanied by ongoing shifts in perception, emotion, and understanding that are never fixed but emerge momentarily in relation to changing circumstances and existential concerns.

Today, over forty million people (forty million different minds, forty million different bodies) are living with HIV/AIDS. For every person living with the disease there are tens or even hundreds of others who are affected: friends, partners, parents, children, neighbors, relatives, work colleagues, medical staff, volunteers, counselors, et cetera. In many ways, these persons can also be said to be "living with HIV/AIDS" insofar as their lives and practices are deeply affected by this most complex and unpredictable of diseases. Thus, it is not just forty million infected persons whose lives have been touched by HIV/AIDS, but a substantial proportion of the entire human race.

HIV/AIDS is a relatively new disease. Over a few short decades, it has formed a diverse, global population of infected *and* affected persons that crosses oceans, continents, sexualities, and genders, and continues to cast an enormous shadow over the world as one of the leading causes of death. That HIV/AIDS has become a disease of global proportions in so short a period of time emphasizes how interconnected the world has become through cultural flow, mass-transportation, political and economic migration, wars, and tourism. In just a few decades HIV/AIDS has fundamentally transformed the minutiae of daily life and practice of millions of persons around the world from the workplace to the bedroom. But, as ever, these transformations are not equally distributed. Poverty, sexuality, gender, and ethnicity are some of the many factors that increase the likelihood of contracting HIV/AIDS and influence how people live and cope with the disease.

Living with HIV/AIDS is something that is experienced among others and is caught and passed on by others through a vast interconnected chain of body and being that stretches across time, history, and continents. At the global level, it is possible for people to identify certain commonalities in thinking and being that are potentially shared by millions of HIV+ people in which thoughts, dilemmas, and emotional responses cut across social categories and cultural boundaries to form a kind of global *communitas*. Meanwhile, at the local level, people's lives are grounded in specific social, political, and economic circumstances, and incorporate different religious and moral worldviews, meaning that even if certain experiences of AIDS are shared, they are not the same.

Importantly, HIV/AIDS is an *immune deficiency syndrome*; that is to say, a collection of different illnesses and symptoms brought together under a single umbrella category. The difference therefore concerns the ontology of the disease itself because people do not die from AIDS but from the different opportunistic illnesses and infections that remain unchecked by a compromised immune system. As common ailments and illnesses vary between locations, HIV/AIDS is a different disease in different parts of the world. Each region has its own prevalent infections and people live with different illnesses. For example, tuberculosis is the leading cause of AIDS-related death throughout Africa, whereas in the United States it is pneumonia. Each involves a distinctive illness trajectory · and is characterized by a range of different symptoms. However, even common AIDS-related conditions, such as diarrhea, are likely to be experienced differently because of access to health care. A person might die from HIV-related diarrhea in parts of Africa but a person in New York will survive and in turn be exposed to further opportunistic infections and illnesses over the course of a longer illness journey. Consequently, it is not just life but also the potential roads to death that are different in different locations.

Even untreated, HIV/AIDS can have quite a long gestation period and people often live with the disease for several years before noticing any adverse physical effects. In many cases it is *the world* that seems to change before the person notices or experiences their illness (see Good 1994). Hidden behind these transformations lies the virus, busily implementing changes in body and consciousness that might remain unknown to the person themselves but have already become apparent to other people: changes that are betrayed by the way someone walks and holds their body or in the themes and concerns their conversations return to. After the onset of the first few episodes of sickness, HIV/AIDS becomes more recognizable and its effects can be slow and gradual, liberating and cathartic, or sudden and earthshaking.

When AIDS becomes part of one's social network, it becomes ingrained into mind, memory, and the senses in ways that are hard to forget. All the men and women in this book possess a tangible understanding of what the end of life looks like—of dementia, forgetfulness, and diminished linguistic capacity—of what can happen to people's cognitive abilities and their bodies during illness. Most have been in close proximity to others who have died from AIDS and have witnessed their own body as it declines and loses control of basic functions. Historically, the burden of caring falls on women and knowledge of illness is largely gendered (Obbo 1998). However, HIV/AIDS has formed an intimacy with disease and decline among a generation of gay men that many other men do not possess. The experience of caring for and nursing someone dying from AIDS exists in all the senses. Heart-wrenching scenes of pain and suffering—alongside sounds and smells—become impressed into memory and body, including unforgettable images from the final weeks of care and witnessing someone deteriorate, often eliciting thoughts, emotions, and images in which people are confronted by a sense of their own future, as expressed in the words *am I to become that?* For, as Euripides wrote so long ago, "the plain sight of our destiny is the cruelest thing of all."

Persons living with HIV/AIDS do not just look toward other people's bodies but also to their own to obtain a sense of their well-being and assess how active the virus is inside them: changes in skin complexion, deterioration in muscle strength or lung capacity, common colds, weight loss, infections, and new body shapes are all scrutinized through the frame of illness. This is not so much a self-directed glance as an extended practice of becoming attuned to and learning about one's body through the modalities of seeing, listening, feeling, smelling, and tasting. It is an ongoing interrogation and questioning of the body that is partly phenomenological, partly imagined, partly mediated by technology, and is interpreted through specific epistemological and discursive frameworks.

In *Teratologies* (1997), Jackie Stacey writes about her diagnosis with cancer at a young age and how she imagined and experienced her body in terms of the often unavoidable images and cultural representations of disease that circulate in popular discourse and media, including images of horror, abnormality, betrayal, vulnerability, and a body in disharmony or at war with itself. These sit alongside dominant moral and gendered expectations of meeting certain social responsibilities, aesthetic standards, and modes of suffering. Such images do not solely exist "out there" in culture but are incorporated within mind, body, and being itself. Stacey describes how she came to embody a series of cultural expectations in which she was required to act and understand herself through specific narrative tropes, including the feminized victim who is subjected to outside forces and the masculine hero who transcends them and conquers disease. She recounts how words, actions, and silences, alongside bodily symptoms and surfaces, are read and decoded as part of a broader semiotic system of images and representations that often become internalized by the patient as something shameful, monstrous, or unspeakable and that underpins language itself:

> **teras** (med.), *n.* a monstrosity:
> **teratogeny**, *n.* the production of monsters:
> **teratology**, *n.* the study of malformations or abnormal growths, animal or vegetable: a tale of marvels:
> **teratoma**, a tumour containing tissue from all three germ layers:
> [Gr. *teras, -atos*, a monster.]
> (*Chambers dictionary*, 1973; in Stacey 1997: 61)

The interior bodies of people living with HIV are dependent upon technology to render the virus and its effects visible. Scientific instruments allow the human eye to observe infected or damaged cells that exist beyond the threshold of human vision (Haraway 1991; Sturken 1997). Originally confined to medical practitioners, the general public now sees images of organs, cells, and viruses on television, in magazines, and on the internet wherein images of HIV, infected blood, and skin cells are blown up and reproduced in high definition and vivid colors. The images themselves are often ambiguous and are rarely looked at without also imagining some intent or agency: a surplus of meaning and emotion animates the abstract shapes and representations of the virus, placing the imagination at the center of people's understanding of interior body space.

The virus is imagined through prevailing social-political frames: the virus invading, the virus attacking, the virus eating away the immune system, an unwelcome alien whose origins lie elsewhere and the body as temple infected by something impure (Haraway 1992). People experience their bodies as an intimate and familiar source of understanding that they have known all their lives but in listening, attending to, and reimagining the body with a new purpose it also becomes unknown, other, and strange. It is simultaneously a realm of felt, subjective experience and an object of ongoing attention that is part of the external world. The body thus becomes a medium of individuation through which persons each learn to see and understand themselves as a particular kind of social, moral, and phenomenological being or self.

THE ART OF LIFE AND DEATH

The art of life and death: Radical aesthetics and ethnographic practice is the second book in HAU's Malinowski Monograph Series. Alongside its precursor, João de Pina-Cabral's *World: An anthropological examination* (2017), the book is committed to an open-ended, moral, and political exploration of human experience through ethnography. A central question for Pina-Cabral is how ethnography, as a radical intellectual endeavor, can shed light on what it is to be human by considering the mutual constitution of personhood and world. What do we actually mean when we refer to a world, in all its material, animal, and personal dimensions, and how is it shaped by perception, sensation, thought, and action? This poses difficult, occasionally intractable, epistemological and practical problems for anthropologists and their attempts to understand the many different ways of being human. *THE STUDY OF THE NATURE AND GROUNDS OF KNOWLEDGE*

A principal aim for both books, and the series in general, is to build new ethnographic approaches to understanding social and cultural life. A further objective for the book at hand is to engage with recent debates in visual, sensory, and medical anthropology concerning phenomenological experiences and ways of knowing not just through theory—whose relationship to ethnography exists in a productive and unsettled alliance—but as signified by the book's title, through the development of new ethnographic practices that aim to open up areas of research concerning the radical shifts in inner expression and aesthetic perception that have hitherto been overlooked in anthropology.

In its narrow etymology, ethnography means the act of *writing about people* but can be more broadly understood as the many and varied modes of working with people in the field that generate knowledge about social life and activity *and* the theorization, analysis, and documentation of this knowledge through writing, alongside alternative, artistic, and nontextual forms of representation (Cox, Irving, and Wright 2016). Not all would agree with this description, given that ethnography is a changing and diverse field within and beyond anthropology. It is therefore instructive that ethnography has recently been the subject of extensive debate and critical discussion that has disclosed many different approaches and understandings (see da Col and Graeber 2011; Astuti 2017; da Col 2017; Ingold 2014, 2017; Miller 2017).

I find it reassuring that no overarching definition has yet emerged from these debates. This leaves room for experimentation and reinforces how ethnography, whether understood as a fieldwork practice, mode of inquiry, or means of representation, is a creative and often-disruptive process of knowledge-making that resists orderly definition. Indeed, whenever a term's inherent polysemy and mutability becomes too restricted or stabilized it is necessary to look at the powers at work and their reasons for attempting to narrow and systematize a particular meaning, be that social, political, or academic (see Volosinov 1973). "I mistrust all systematisers and I avoid them," declared Nietzsche, "The will to system is a lack of integrity" ([1888] 2003: 35), underlining how ethnography's lack of systematic definition, which some find troubling, can equally be read as an index of vitality and a consequence of the new and unanticipated forms of anthropological knowledge that arise out of face-to-face fieldwork encounters and various other forms of research, including working with archives, artifacts, and media, which in my case also involved performance, diaries, notebooks, artworks, and first-person accounts of terminal illness. Whether fieldwork and complementary forms of research are framed as ethnographic or not is of far less interest, importance, and relevance than the shared insights and new theoretical possibilities that emerge concerning the human condition. *HAVING MULTIPLE MEANINGS*

Beyond questions of polysemy and power, *The art of life and death* seeks to extend the kind of practical understanding of humanity that Kant described as a "knowledge of the world" (*Weltkenntnis*) that develops through active participation (*mitgespielt*) as opposed to scholastic or speculative knowledge, which Kant regarded as mere intellectual posturing unless grounded in practical action and experience. This not only highlights the partial and provisional grounds of knowledge but also how the comparative and generalizing claims of anthropology are constructed out of particular ethnographic encounters and interactions. The ways in which the resulting materials are assembled into broader theoretical concepts and understandings of the world is written into the anthropological project itself: reinforcing the inseparability of ethnography from theory (da Col 2017) and Bronisław Malinowski's point that "theory without material is sterile and material without theory is not illuminating" (quoted in da Col 2017: 1).

Although Malinowski was referring to language and magic, ethnography also encompasses the embodied, inchoate, and tacit dimensions of perception that are the subject of this book. The assembled chapters attempt to develop an exploratory ethnographic approach to understanding the emergent and ever-changing realms of inner expression and imagery that comprise lived experience. Given there is no objective access to the minds, bodies, and experiences of other people—not to mention the inherent problem of comprehending and rendering intelligible our own mind, motivations, and actions—this presents a substantial challenge to the social sciences, sciences, and humanities. For anthropology, as I argue in the following pages, understanding people's emergent and situated modes of thinking and being is first and foremost a practical and methodological problem to be worked on in the field rather than a conceptual one to be written about from afar. I also argue, and then seek to address, how existing social scientific methods and measures are often too static to research and represent the complex assemblages of internally represented speech, perception, and imagery that are expressed in consciousness. Although these are central to social life and the human condition, they are rarely, if ever, the ethnographic focus of journal articles and monographs, and as I argue in later chapters, this means anthropology is currently only telling half the story of human life.

Formulating a better and more complete understanding of human beings requires engaging with the entirety of subjectivity and activity. A key contribution of the book therefore concerns how theoretical, philosophical, and ethnographic approaches might be combined to reconceptualize a fuller, more realistic, and empirically viable understanding of the human subject. In doing so, *The art of life and death* develops and advocates for new, ethnographically grounded ways of researching how lived experience is constituted by complex trajectories of inner dialogue and ongoing shifts in perception, and then seeks to understand how these relate to extrinsic audible and observable action. The intention is not to claim privileged access to human consciousness nor to reinvent the wheel (see da Col and Graeber 2011) but to offer an empirical and experimental contribution and counterpoint to recent theories of embodied cognition and experience in visual, sensory, and medical anthropology by making links across the arts and sciences, including the performing arts and neurology.

The relationship between life and death is rarely predictable or straightforward. When I started my research on HIV/AIDS in London in the early 1990s, AIDS was seen as a death sentence. The later development of effective antiretroviral medications (ARVs) in 1996–97 radically transformed HIV/AIDS from an acute to chronic illness across many parts of the world. Hundreds of thousands of people, who without medication would have died, found themselves alive. A collective reorientation commonly known as the Lazarus Effect moved people away from death and back toward life and the future. Nevertheless, there still remains an uncertainty as to where HIV/AIDS may take humanity. Huge numbers of people across Africa and Asia continue to die, infection rates are rising once more in many Western countries, while those who resist infection or remain healthy without medical intervention are in a position to pass on their genes, immunity, or longevity to following generations. Science and human adaptation might not be able to outstrip the evolutionary potential of the HIV virus, and mutant strains have become immune to certain combinations of antiretroviral medication. However, at the time of writing, recent breakthroughs in cell biology promise new ways of tackling both HIV/AIDS and cancer.

Between 2010 and 2014, I received two research grants from the Wenner Gren Foundation in New York and the Economic and Social Research Council (UK) to try to reestablish contact with persons living with HIV/AIDS who I worked with during the 1990s. Many of the people I worked with were learning the art of how to "live again," having experienced intense, life-threatening episodes of illness, negotiated the likelihood of death, and having often made irreversible life decisions. Unsurprisingly, many found it impossible to return to previous ways of thinking and being, and have made substantial lifestyle changes and career choices that affect how they live today.

By working collaboratively with persons from different stages of my research, *The art of life and death* attempts to understand how people have learned to live a meaningful existence in the pre- and post-antiretroviral eras while negotiating a terminal illness. Collaborative approaches with persons have the capacity to displace the historical power relationship between researchers and researched by allowing persons to be the subjects of their own existential inquiry rather than objects of study. Recognizing the capacity for people to be their own theorists, while taking seriously their role in shaping anthropological theory and debate, has the potential to open up new fields of interest and new directions for anthropology to follow. This not only allows for ethical, evidence-based understandings of the day-to-day experience of living with illness and uncertainty in all its complexity and diversity but also helps identify mutually shared areas of interest and concern between anthropologist and informant. This provides a means of ensuring that the debate is not conducted at levels of theoretical abstraction remote from people's lives and concerns and generates relevant empirical and analytical data about the lifeworlds of illness.

On these grounds, it makes no sense to categorize or reduce life with HIV/AIDS to one of sorrow and suffering. Emotions are mutable and overlapping in that happiness can be ambivalent and touched with sadness, while suffering can be welcome and virtuous, meaning that what can be distinguished analytically cannot necessarily be separated at the level of experience (Throop 2015). As importantly, although sorrow and suffering can be found in almost all human biographies and are certainly present in this book, the individuals I worked with rarely describe and understand themselves or their experiences in these terms. Indeed, it is often a source of considerable concern and frustration to persons with HIV/AIDS that their lives are so routinely and casually theorized in terms of suffering and other associated tropes within academic and public discourses that fail to represent the complexity, diversity, and mutability of people's lived experience. Persons are frequently placed in a sick role, reduced to instantiations of suffering or else denied the opportunity to be full persons based on common misunderstandings of the disease. Persons living with HIV/AIDS around all parts of the world are living healthy productive lives and experience extended periods of well-being—especially since effective antiretroviral medications were made more globally available following concerted political action in Brazil, South Africa, and India—but still often encounter discrimination—for example, when seeking work, in their parental role, and so forth—while being perfectly capable to perform their various responsibilities. Consequently, a shared aim of the research is to challenge one-dimensional connotations of suffering, inability, and distress by humanizing people's lives and experiences.

As such, the book's most important guiding principle is that the individuals being represented must be able to recognize themselves, their lived experience, and moral worldview within its pages. This necessitated forming socially inclusive dialogues with interested persons and according them an active role in shaping the book's subject matter, not just in relation to human finitude and existential uncertainty but also the properties of everyday life such as laughter, shopping, silence, lying in bed, or listening to music. Being open to the opportunities ethnography affords involves taking ideas, whether they are found in academic discourse, personal conversations and diaries, modernist literature, or pop songs, and then placing them directly into the field so as to explore the continuities and discontinuities "between who we are and what we might become" (Jackson 2011: ix). Each of the chapters presents a shared journey of knowledge and involves various changes in perception related to the city and its environs. Each then goes in different directions, to consider the historical, the material, the political, the confessional, the phenomenological, the aesthetic, and the ironic as experienced through people's changing circumstances of being. The reader may or may not agree with my theoretical approach and analysis, but I hope to have provided sufficient ethnographic depth to people's life experiences and stories, corroborated by those I worked with, to open up different theoretical paths and allow for alternative explanations and modes of analysis that I encourage and welcome.

I reestablished contact with around fifteen people, and many of their life journeys can be found in this book. Among these, seven underwent major career changes, five developed but survived HIV-related cancers, one attempted suicide, two returned to college, one person became a mother, one became an ordained minister, and one was incarcerated in prison: virtually all would be dead if not for antiretroviral medication. As such, they are currently living in a future and forging a life in a world they never thought they would be alive to see. This recalls how "the art of living" (Nehamas 1998) is a creative act of *poesis*, that is, an ongoing set of activities through which life is shaped, made, and enacted and entails manifold ways of living a life rather than just one. However, the art of living takes on a second meaning in many of the pages of this book, given the close attention to the processes of artistic expression and the inclusion of artworks made by people while experiencing bodily instability and confronting existential uncertainty.

Many of the people I worked with found themselves asking similar questions about life and death—and were subject to the same limitations in understanding and responding to those questions as we all are—about how to carry on living in circumstances that were not of their choosing. Or put another way, what choices and actions do people make in order to have a good life? (Robbins 2013); to enable a good or bad death? (Desjarlais 2016); or when preparing for the personal, familial, and economic consequences of loss? (Irving 2017; Al-Mohammad forthcoming). Last but not least, although *The art of life and death* is about living with the uncertainty of illness, the intention is to offer a broader, collaborative exploration of existentiality and the human condition, including how human beings engage with questions of time and finitude, the phenomenology of the body, and what it means to be a mortal being in a world of perpetual change.

As such, *The art of life and death* is their story but also our own, for on some levels it is the story of all human beings

POESIS - THE ACTIVITY IN WHICH A PERSON BRINGS SOMETHING INTO BEING THAT DID NOT EXIST BEFORE.

CHAPTER ONE

Thrown out of the world
A city of flesh and stone

THREE VIEWS OF NEW YORK CITY FROM ABOVE

To see Manhattan from the 107th floor of the World Trade Center. Below the wind-stirred haze, the urban island, a sea upon the sea rises on the crested swell of Wall Street, falls into the trough of Greenwich Village, flows into the renewed crests of midtown and the calm of Central Park, before breaking into distant whitecaps up beyond Harlem. For a moment, the eye arrests the turbulence of this sea-swell of verticals: the vast mass freezes under our gaze. It is transformed into a texturology.

–Michel de Certeau, *On signs* (1986: 122)

From up high where I was, you could shout anything you liked at them. I tried. They made me sick, the whole lot of them. I hadn't the nerve to tell them so in the daytime, to their face, but up there it was safe. "Help! Help!" I shouted, just to see if it would have any effect on them. None whatsoever. Those people were pushing life and night and day in front of them. Life hides everything from people. Their own noise prevents them from hearing anything else. They couldn't care less. The bigger and taller the city, the less they care. Take it from me. I've tried. It's a waste of time.

–Louis-Ferdinand Céline, *Journey to the end of the night* ([1932] 1983: 180)

In so many travelogues the filmmaker looks down on and never up to his subject. He is always the big man from New York or from London.

–Robert Flaherty, Director of *Nanook of the north* (1950: 18).

***

This chapter tells two stories: that of New York City's obsession with capitalism, construction, and creative expression over the last two hundred years, and the story of how life was altered at the turn of a millennium that coincided with the arrival of HIV/AIDS. New York is a city founded on immigration, trade, and manufacturing, and its buildings and infrastructure bear witness to a long-standing relationship between people, commodities, and money. The city's elongated straight avenues allow for the circulation of citizens, merchandise, and dollars and are crammed with entrepreneurial activity and advertising. These come together to forge the content and character of the city we know today: diverse, contested, and always under construction, in the thrall of capital, often overly sentimental, riddled with inequality, and above all, a city full of commercial and artistic energy. It is a city whose buildings, architecture, and population, like the human body and nervous system, are in constant change and movement. A city whose brick, concrete, iron, steel, and glass structures still speak of the aesthetic, economic, moral, and material values that dominated successive eras as New York developed into a world capital and emboldened people's hopes and visions for the future.

The spectacular ascent of New York City as a political, cultural, and economic center has been the subject of countless novels, articles, and films that combine to tell a story of commercial enterprise, technological innovation, and rapid social change. Perhaps what is less well known is that New York's layout, infrastructure, and social character are also the outcome of the vulnerability of the human body to infection and disease. Accordingly, this chapter describes how the city's design and layout emerged from an attempt to impose order on the maladies and disorders of the body, and how many decades later disease once again shaped the lives of its citizens following the arrival of HIV/AIDS in the 1980s. The attempt to organize the lives, bodies, and desires of citizens through the design and construction of architectural space incudes within it a history not only of money, rationality, and labor but also of different medical epistemologies and the successive diseases that threatened the population. This history can still be found among the small details in the urban environment, which are picked up by the eye of the artist but sometimes go unnoticed by others, and are brought to our attention through photography, painting, and writing. The artist's eye opens up a window onto the city and becomes a particular way of understanding New York's history of social and economic change, including the undulating fortunes of its citizens.

The story begins with an overview of the changing cityscape of New York before offering a series of ethnographic portraits of persons, also artists, who found themselves thrown out of the world after being diagnosed with HIV/AIDS in their 20s and early 30s. No longer planning for a long-term future, career, children, or retirement, they were also thrown out of the conventional life narrative and no longer beholden to the rules of capitalism. By making a series of life choices, they illuminate what might not be immediately visible to their fellow citizens and provide a perspective on what the city looks like when the fragility and vulnerability of the human body is made explicit. The artists in this chapter, Frank Jump, Holly Rivers, and Benjamin Trimmier, introduce us to the streets of New York City to tell a story of lives lived through irregular lines of desire, (ad)venture capitalism, and the redemption of one's existence from life-threatening diseases.

SINS OF THE FATHERS

New York City, which until 1898 largely meant Manhattan, was founded in 1626: construction began at the southern tip of the island and thereafter expanded northward (MacKay 1987). By 1653, the city only extended a few hundred yards to modern day Wall Street, which marked the city's northernmost extension. Even by the first US census in 1790, building had barely reached the modern-day City Hall, the population was only 33,111, and the entire city measured less than a single square mile. New York's paths and roads meandered in accordance with the population's agricultural needs; Chelsea and Greenwich were outlying villages; Midtown was farmland; and the remainder of the island was covered in swamps, marshes, and thick woods. However, just ten years later, the population had almost doubled to 60,489 and by the 1810 census it would increase again to 96,373. As the city began to take shape, the governing administration predicted a massive tenfold increase in New York's population over the next hundred years and anticipated it could even reach as many as a million people.

Disease was rife, including regular outbreaks of yellow fever—caused by mosquitoes that thrived in the city's summer climate, stagnant swamps, and pools—whose symptoms included skin eruptions, black vomit, incontinence, jaundice, and eventual death. After the terrible yellow fever epidemics of 1794, 1795, 1798, and 1805 (Burrows and Wallace 2001), it was evident that bold steps were necessary to combat disease and ensure the future health of the city. Would it be possible—the city's commissioners speculated—to fight disease and enhance the body's vigor and defenses by radically altering the city's layout and by building health and well-being into the physical structure of the city itself?

Yellow fever increased the city's death rate by over 50 percent (Condran 1995). However, it was not known to medical science at the time that yellow fever was caused by mosquito bites and instead the epidemics were attributed to the foul-smelling air and odors of a population living in close proximity in narrow, filthy streets. Medical understanding was dominated by Miasma Theory, which proposed that diseases were caused by the presence of miasma in the city's air, a poisonous vapor consisting of particles of decaying matter characterized by its foul smell. Accordingly, the solution that was put forward was that a more orderly, controlled city—in which air was allowed to flow more freely and people were separated from each other—could prevent further outbreaks of disease, as the city grew inexorably northward. The task was to redesign the city in such a way that would help regulate physical space, odors, and the population so as to "unite regularity and order with the Public convenience and benefit, and in particular to promote the health of the city" and prevent disease and contagion by encouraging the "free and abundant circulation of air" (Morris, De Witt, and Rutherford 1811).

In 1807, the city commission engaged twenty-year-old surveyor John Randel to map the entire island, with the purpose of transforming its natural woods, swamps, and grasslands into a terrain "composed principally of the habitations of men" (Morris, De Witt, and Rutherford 1811). Randel and his team spent three years painstakingly mapping Manhattan, and were forced to develop innovative new technologies, including improving theodolite design, inventing a custom-made fifty-foot measuring instrument designed like a suspension bridge, and calculating the precise rate of expansion caused by different temperatures throughout the changing seasons on their metal rulers (Holloway 2014). Compasses and measuring rods also presented magnetic challenges: Manhattan was formed by volcanic activity that began over a billion years ago and contains different kinds of rock, ranging from 1.1 billion to 190 million years old, which have different magnetic strengths and signatures (Holloway 2014).

Three years later, the resulting ninety-two by twenty-five-inch (234 x 65 cm) map offered unprecedented levels of accuracy and detail about the island. Crucially, Randel did not simply map Manhattan's existing streets, farmlands, swamps, and wilderness but superimposed a grid over the landscape that determined the exact lines along which the city would be built over the forthcoming century. The grid proposed that all roads should be straight and numbered rather than named. Streets ran horizontally across the island and were numbered one to fifty-five, while avenues ran vertically and were numbered one to twelve, with an additional A, B, C, and D covering the swell of land on the Lower East Side. It was determined that no consideration was to be given to natural variations in the land, existing roads, or property divisions but that the grid would take priority over all (MacKay 1987). Avenues were specified to be precisely one-hundred feet wide and streets were to be sixty feet wide, while their exact lines and points of intersection were marked out by thousands of marble stones and iron stakes, some of which are still visible today. Streets were designed to run from river to river so as to serve the docks and "ensure cross breezes to rid the city of stagnant air" (Holloway 2014: 51).

As such, Randel's map (see fig. 1.1) is none other than Manhattan's *founding text*, whose official ratification on March 22, 1811, marks the point at which the city council confirmed they would attempt to build bodily health, reason, and rationality into the layout of the city itself. The repercussions of 1811 remain visible today in the change of landscape north of City Hall, whereby virtually every street and avenue testifies to this twin desire for health and efficiency. The most notable exception is Broadway, which by legend follows a pre-existing American Indian track and cuts a maverick path across the grid's straight lines and right angles.

The spectacular rise of New York City over the nineteenth century exceeded even the most extreme of the city commission's predictions. Construction expanded northward at a phenomenal rate in order to accommodate the rapidly increasing population. Nature was squeezed out as Manhattan's population swelled from 33,111 in 1790 to 96,373 in 1810, and to 2,331,542 in the 1910 census one hundred years later (and which following the incorporation of Brooklyn, Queens, Bronx, and Staten Island into the city in 1898 gave rise to a total city population of almost five million). Accordingly, by the 1910s, a new sense of scale, material infrastructure, and population density emerged. The

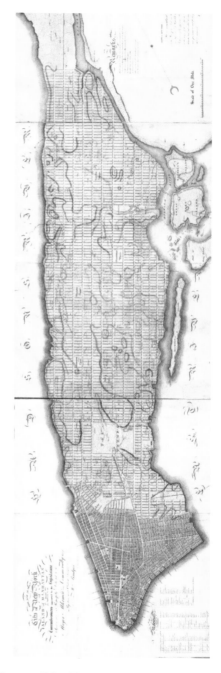

Figure 1.1 Randel's map of New York City, 1811. Reproduced with permission from the New York Public Library.

grid's long, wide, and straight avenues allowed the city's essential operations to be carried out and for businesses to transport their goods and services. The inventions of electricity, pressured water pipes, and the elevator made possible the building of taller and taller buildings against which individuals born when farmland still covered most of the island could compare their muddy agricultural practices and desires.

At the same time, the thousands of new buildings constructed along the grid's straight lines formed a succession of highly visible surfaces for advertisers to sell their promises and dreams. The dizzying height and volume of these buildings generated a massive surface area of bare brick and concrete, which allowed a whole new industry to develop that used size, scale, and attention-seeking color to convey messages to the people below. Enormous hand-painted advertisements, up to fifty feet tall and twenty feet wide, illustrated the sides of buildings and were designed to encourage New York's citizens to lift their eyes and noses from the grid and part with their wages. The majority of these advertisements have now disappeared: either when the host building was demolished or when covered by more recent constructions that testify to New York's desire to continuously remake itself on a grander scale. The destiny of other advertisements was more gradual for, regardless of the thickness of their paint or the vibrancy of their colors, their fate has been to slowly fade out of existence while exposed to the relentless cycles of New York's scorching summers, freezing winters, pollution, and humidity. The faded remnants of these gigantic advertisements—and the moral values, dreams, and anxieties they embodied—can still be seen around the city of today, nestled amid the buildings.

Throughout the first half of the 1800s, Miasma Theory continued to dominate medicine. The poorer neighborhoods mixed humans, animals, commerce, and residential housing: scavenging dogs and pigs roamed the streets, alongside mules, horses, and humans. Stinking outhouses located in the gaps between buildings were shared by up to twenty families, while slaughterhouses, tanneries, and factories fouled the air with noxious fumes. Although death rates were declining in towns, villages, and rural areas, they were still on the rise in New York. The rise of disease, especially during the sweltering and fetid summer months, was not only linked to miasma but also to social class, insofar as disease thrived most in overcrowded working-class areas and was seen as evidence of moral depravity, wanton uncleanliness, and debauchery. Cholera hit in 1832 and 1849, killing 3,513 and 5,071 people respectively (Condran 1995). In the 1840s, olfactory maps of New York City began to emerge that mapped the smells that were seen as detrimental to health (Kiechle 2015). Odors and stench were mapped both horizontally and vertically, together with air currents and the precise locations of buildings, such as slaughterhouses and other unclean establishments. Concern about stinking air and disease increased as the century wore on and led to the creation of the Metropolitan Board of Health in 1866: "The physicians cited certain businesses as infecting the atmosphere and, when located in populous areas, classed these with filth as nuisances "injurious to public health and to individual welfare." Inspectors thus focused on the proximity of slaughterhouses, hide and fat depots, bone-boiling and fat-melting establishments, gas manufacturers, and manure-yards to residential areas and crowded tenements" (Kiechle 2015: 10).

It was not until the Germ Theory of Disease emerged in the second half of the 1800s that Miasma Theory's influence began to decline, and a new episteme of medicine and bodily health developed that remains an important guiding principle of modern medicine. However, regardless of the shift in medical knowledge toward Germ Theory, contemporary New York remains tied to the logic of Miasma Theory and the layout of John Randel's map of 1811. The commission's attempt to impose order on the city and combat disease through the circulation of air is permanently embodied in the city's grid system, ensuring every New Yorker plays out their lives in a city built upon the idea that the most efficient way of organizing social life and human bodies is through straight lines.

The combination of verticality, nervous stimulation, and the grid produces a compressed theater for social life and phenomenological experience. A frame of mathematical ratios, receding perspectives, and diminishing angles guide the eye, and often the body, toward a vanishing point on the horizon: a destiny distant in time and space that is "mathematically known in advance" through modes of scientific reason embedded in trigonometry, military technology, and perspectival painting (Heidegger 1977; Pinney 1995). It is a rationality that comes to life every day through the vistas and horizons formed as one moves around the city's streets and avenues. The buildings constructed along the grid furnish mile upon mile of straight edges that allow New York's citizens to look far into the distance to create the effect of moving within a Euclidean drawing or one of Canaletto's paintings. The grid helps regulate how people get around the city while reinforcing how bodily movement is fundamental to defining scale and establishing visual vergence: a simple secret that Richard Sennett (1991) argues renaissance painters understood but many modern day planners have forgotten, or else lack the technique and resources to implement. There are only a few ways to exit the grid—by bridges, underground tunnels, ferry, or helicopter—leaving the remaining bodies to partake in a daily ritual encounter with straight lines and a future that can seemingly be seen, calculated, and offers an ever-present metaphor for the rewards and assurances of capitalism: *look to the future, work hard and save, your pension and golden retirement awaits.* The future becomes a way of justifying and giving purpose to the increasing costs of urban existence and a life tied to the grid: long working hours, exorbitant rents, dirty subways, traffic jams, and crowded streets.

The pace set by people on the street toward this double destiny is rapid; New York pedestrians often average three hundred feet per minute (Whyte 1992). Moreover, as an island bounded by the East, Hudson, and Harlem Rivers, the restricted land mass of Manhattan comprises only 22.96 square miles—or around 7 percent of New York City's total land area of 305 square miles— meaning that spaces for living, working, and making money do not just extend laterally along the lines of Randel's map but also vertically toward the heavens, the consequences of which were described by Rem Koolhaas in *Delirious New York*: "The grid's two-dimensional discipline also creates undreamt of freedom for three-dimensional anarchy. The Grid defines a new balance between control and de-control in which the city can be at the same time ordered and fluid, a metropolis of rigid chaos" (Koolhaas 1994: 20).

The grid offers well-worn lines of navigation and desire but also allows the possibility for wandering without purpose or weaving idiosyncratic trajectories (de Certeau 1986). As such, walking in New York elicits contradictory feelings of possibility and confinement as one walks along the long, straight avenues of capitalism while simultaneously glimpsing other possibilities, distractions, or escapes. The three-dimensional volume of vertical living space gives rise to a population density of more than 70,000 souls per square mile (as compared to London, for example, whose density is nearer 13,000 per square mile, or one person for every five in Manhattan) and whose collective pounding along Randel's grid slowly but steadily makes an impression on the sidewalks. However, for a more accurate understanding of Manhattan's density, it is necessary to calculate the city's dynamic—as opposed to residential—population by incorporating the thousands who flow in and out of the city for work, leisure, and according to the seasons (Moss and Qing 2012). Each day Manhattan's already crowded streets and buildings are swelled by workers, tourists, students attending schools and universities, people attending hospitals, and out-of-towners going to concerts, sports events, nightclubs, theaters, and restaurants, meaning that on a typical week-day, four million people cram into a mere 22.96 square miles (Moss and Qing 2012). By midday, up to 1.2 million people—a population three times greater than Iceland—pass through a single square mile of midtown Manhattan, with 132 people per minute walking past a given point on the 22.5 foot-wide sidewalks (Whyte 1992). This produces a highly condensed arena for social interaction, where people are mostly present to each other as strangers and engage in distinctively urban forms of social interaction, body movement, and eye contact as they walk the streets.

When Aristotle proclaimed "a city is composed of different men; similar people cannot bring a city into existence" (quoted in Sennett 1994), he envis-aged a city of ten or twenty thousand people—far less than the amount that pack into Yankee Stadium to watch a ball game. Today's scale is qualitative-ly, not just quantitatively, different and represents a foundational diversity that is responsible for bringing many different types of city into being: the ethnic city, divided city, gendered city, contested city, de-industrialized city, modernist city, postmodern city, fortress city, sacred city, and traditional city (Low 1996), to which we might add the soft city (Raban 1998), the mythi-cal city, the late-night city, the working city, the remembered city, and the diseased city.

Today's city of concrete, steel, glass, iron, brick, granite, chrome, plastic, and other durable materials, exists in combination with a varied and fluid population to create a diverse, contested cityscape in constant movement and transformation. It is apposite therefore that Richard Sennett (1994) describes the city as a constellation of *flesh and stone*—that is, a social, political, and phenomenological gathering place in which manifold sensory, organic bod-ily experiences combine with architectural materials to produce shared spaces of dwelling, diversity, and difference. In response, the following section jux-taposes the work of artists so as to extend Sennett's metaphor and explore how a city's flesh and stone is mediated by the passing of time and nature. The artworks are by Frank Jump (Stone), Holly Rivers (Flesh), and Benjamin Trimmier (Nature), each of whom I have worked with over many years. Each work marks a meeting point of self and world wherein idiosyncratic acts of perception and aesthetic appreciation combine with a wider history of HIV/AIDS and a possible escape from the social, political, and economic structures of the grid.

FLESH AND STONE

Frank Jump teaches at a school in Brooklyn. When school finishes he spends evenings and weekends walking around the city looking for evidence of time. He wears bright Hawaiian shirts and takes pictures of garbage, rotting fruit, and extreme close-ups of objects and materials using a homemade lens. However, his main obsession is photographing and archiving the fading advertisements painted on the sides of brick and concrete buildings. He documents these before they fade away or disappear and puts them on his website, www.frankjump.com.

Frank has photographed and archived somewhere in the region of five thousand fading advertisements across New York's boroughs, of which perhaps only one thousand can be seen today. Many of these advertisements are well over one hundred years old. They were painted in attention-grabbing colors up to fifty feet high and were considered eyesores at the time they were painted. Mostly they advertise products that can no longer be bought, made by companies that no longer exist, painted on buildings whose original occupants are forgotten, by men long since departed, to a public who no longer believes or is not interested. Instead, what remains are the faded traces of

Figure 1.2 *Omega Oil*, West 147th Street, Harlem, NYC © Frank Jump Originally painted circa 1910 for Omega Oil, an all-purpose miracle oil. The company was incorporated from February 3, 1870, through April 2, 1924.

the manual labor of these men, creatively marshaled into a form of advertising and rhetoric popular in its day, which used color to convey its message to the people walking on the grid below.

Frank was twenty-six when he was diagnosed with HIV/AIDS and told he had "a couple of good years left to live." Consequently, Frank decided to take himself out of college, given that there was little point in spending his remaining time studying for a career, and filled in all the offers for new credit cards, loans, advances, and bank accounts that came through his door in the junk mail, thinking, "I've never got to pay any of this back." For a time, Frank no longer had to play by the rules of capitalism. Stores, credit card companies, and banks kept giving him money. He bought a piano and other instruments, high-tech electronic equipment, and a home recording studio. He went on holidays and ate in renowned restaurants. Given that he only had a couple of years, he lived well and money no longer presented a problem as banks and loan companies kept asking if they could lend him more. He tried to condense as much life as possible into those years and borrowed and spent over $100,000.

Only Frank didn't die, and the same doctors who predicted his early demise were puzzled. At the same time, the banks, stores, and credit card companies wanted their money back. When I first met Frank he had been HIV+ for ten years, had recently been declared bankrupt, and was re-enrolled in college. Frank was acutely aware of the fragility of the human body in an urban landscape and of himself as a body that might disappear. His body, like the painted advertisements that surrounded him, was fading and not supposed to last as long as it had but nevertheless somehow remained part of the city. Accordingly, Frank still sees his reflection not in the mirror but in the fading colors of advertisements that line New York's streets. They continually provide him with evidence of his existence and provide to us a visual record of the on-going effects of time on the city and the body.

New York's surfaces offer an ideal medium for presenting goods and other promises of life. They continue to weather and betray the passing of the years on the sides of buildings all around the city, while the products that gave birth to them have become obsolete and reclaimed by time. As more time passes, the skin and epidermis of the city fades and eventually peels off, to be replaced by a new skin constructed by succeeding groups and generations. It is evocative of the difference between cutis and pellis—cutis being the living skin that breathes and renews itself, while pellis is the dead, discarded skin that has become scoured, loosened, or simply falls away from the body. It seems that like the skin, the city too has a complexion that weathers and betrays the passing of years.

Because Frank defied predictions and remained mostly healthy, HIV/AIDS was less of an illness and more of a psychological burden and brooding presence that overshadowed his existence and put his future into question. The doctors were amazed and said his body had responded to the disease in an extraordinary way. So much so that Frank Jump's body became an object of medical curiosity and doctors kept devising challenges for it. Some doctors got curious and wanted to know what would happen if they took him off antiretroviral medications. Ordinarily, when someone is taken off antiretrovirals the disease returns and becomes more virulent and takes an even stronger hold than before. This is one of the pitfalls of triple-combination medication: once you're on it, you tend to be on it for life or you risk a more potent infection. You learn to live with the side effects: the distended belly, the nausea, the diarrhea, the low testosterone, the nightmares, and the crixivan crystals forming in your kidneys.

Frank agreed to stop his medication so that his doctors could observe what would happen. They told him he would become sick and were curious as to whether conventional wisdom was right; namely, typically in chronic infection the body's ability to mount an immune response becomes diminished, but perhaps Frank's body would develop a stronger immune response. The idea was that after eight weeks Frank would resume his medication and then the process would be repeated three times. After each hiatus, the amount of virus in Frank's blood would be measured to see if his body had been able to fight back. Frank likes to throw himself into the fire and was ready to face three bouts of miserable, painful sickness. Frank emailed me thus:

> *My viral load has shot up from 0 to two million in less than 6 weeks. My T-cells have dropped to my lowest ever and I panicked. When I discovered these results I went back on antiretrovirals (but only after I visited my physician who didn't check my viral load until my normal appt). The study apologized to me for not keeping me abreast of the T-cell numbers and let me know that my viral load was tremendously high. I said I'd try this twice more. If after the second time, the viral load increases as high again, I won't try it a third time. If the numbers peak at a considerably lower number, indicating some kind of "intelligence" on behalf of my immune system, I will try a third time. If this doesn't work—tant pis—I'm ready for another theory.*

Field notes: July 2000. *Called Frank Jump today. He said he was thinking of becoming a high school teacher, which is a sign of his interest and commitment to the future. He even mentioned that although high school teachers don't get a lot of money, they do get (of all things given his initial prognosis), a pension! Later on, I met Frank at the Gay Dentists on West 21st and we headed down to the Indonesian restaurant for* roti canai *and to catch up. I asked what was happening in his life. I already knew that Frank had recently volunteered to come off the combination therapy so the doctors*

Figure 1.3 *Radway's Ready Relief,* Delancey Street, NYC © Frank Jump Originally painted circa 1890, for Radway's Ready Relief, a miracle cure for rheumatism, neuralgia, gout, sciatica, nervousness, fever and ague, small pox, measles, spasms, kidney and menstruation problems, and heart disease. The company was founded circa 1847.

Figure 1.4 Frank in front of a fading advertisement. *Photograph by the author.*

could see how his body responded. Up went the viral load, down went the T-cell count, and down went Mr. Jump.

However, now he's back on his feet. Things are good with Vincenzo, his HIV-negative partner who is a workman, street-corner anthropologist, and acute social observer, and they have just had their tenth anniversary. So that meant ten years of being a discordant couple and ten years since they were munching away in a little Cuban restaurant about to share their lives. "Home" is apparently looking more like a home. It has new windows, a new kitchen, and is currently inhabited by a 320lb workman who keeps bending over, working for a bit, bending over again, and turning round every fifteen minutes and saying to Frank: "Was that you touching my ass?"

With the idea of becoming a schoolteacher floating around, it seems that Frank has become increasingly weary of his job down at the Gay Dentist's and finds his position as a receptionist there unrewarding. What previously were positive aspects about his job, such as not being taxing, unchallenging, requiring little training, and no career structure or prospects are much more problematical now Frank has found out he has a future.

Field notes: Aug. 2000. *Frank H. Jump left a message on the answering machine. When I called back it turned out he'd been to see his doctor earlier that day, who told him he had cancer . . .*

UNDER THE COVERS, UNSAFELY

Holly was born in New York City in 1973. She grew up in Montreal and returned to New York, first as an apprentice photographer and then to study at the New York Fashion Institute. When Holly is out on the streets of New York she recognizes something in the way some people carry themselves and how they sit and look at the world. More often than not, Holly notices these people seem slightly removed from those around them and are marginally out of step with the rhythm on the street. She has become attuned to the people of New York City: the people in her neighborhood, people eating in diners, people waiting in post offices, and people riding on the subway. Holly often finds something in the faces and bodies she sees around her that can't always be put into words.

In the public spaces of cities, people mostly engage with each other as strangers and through established social roles: their biographies remain unknown, their concerns un-articulated, and their stories untold. Paradoxically, although all kinds of emotions are close by and witnessed on the streets of cities, they also seem more distant as the person, name, and life story behind their faces remain unknown to their fellow citizens. Holly says that she can often sense when people have been through something; she can see in their faces that somewhere in their history is an experience that changed them, perhaps something that was overcome or an accident or a misfortune or an episode of illness. Whatever the something is or was, it is also carried around in the body. Maybe it is present in their posture or is betrayed by their relationship to what's going on around them. Sometimes eyes meet and once in a while, something of another citizen's life can be glimpsed or sensed. Holly stops these people, an act that interrupts the every-day order and social manners of city. It is a simple act that creates an opening in the quotidian activities of the street, including its collective habits and established rules of movement and walking-by. By creating this opening, Holly establishes a new context for identification and opens up an exchange that normally would remain unseen and unarticulated.

And then Holly asks if she can take a picture of them.

Holly thinks she caught HIV at age eighteen in 1991, by a boy whose whereabouts or own fate is no longer known. Only her second-ever lover. However, it was not until 1994 that she found out her HIV status and that she had already been living with the virus for three years without knowing about it. Shortly after the revelation of her HIV status, Holly rapidly progressed to having full-blown AIDS. At the time it was thought that the average gestation period of HIV was usually around six to eight years and the life expectancy of someone with AIDS was perhaps ten years. However, Holly had only had the virus for three years and it had already developed into AIDS. Holly, who was still only twenty-one and was infected when she was eighteen, was confronted with only having five or so years to live. That meant twenty-six, twenty-seven, maybe twenty-eight. She lived with an established expectation of death.

Things progressed much more rapidly than expected and the following year, to-ward the end of November 1995, Holly began to quickly decline. Her T-cell count went down to four, she weighed seventy pounds, and continually had pneumonia. Her mother could not cope and Holly could not get out of bed herself. Holly described to me how something had eaten into her lung, how she couldn't lift a plate, and how she couldn't eat or keep anything down or breathe well. And so, at the age of twenty-two, Holly entered into palliative care and was moved into a New York hospice.

While Holly was in the hospice, her city was reduced to the hospice bed and her sensory world extended as far as the walls and the view outside. Every slight move-ment of the head or body brought about great pain. She continued to deteriorate and waste away. Spending extended periods in bed constitutes part of the apprenticeship to illness. Nevertheless, a bed-bound person is not a passive entity but continues to make their daily experience by way of their thoughts, movements, and actions: whether to spend the hours gazing out the window or with their eyes closed, trying to sleep or imagining oneself elsewhere. Illness is radically differentiated through action—for example, a person who turns away from social contact and spends their day looking at a wall is also closing down their sensory nervous system by reducing external stimulation, while another person may attempt to retain a sense of social and existential continuity amid the disruption of illness by listening to the radio, making conversation, and forming relationships. During extended periods of illness, people can often be found dwelling in times and places far beyond the confines of the bed, assembling life's materials into complex montages of memory and emotion that move from regret, to hope, to melancholy, by venturing back to childhood and forward in time to impending demise so as to construct stark contrasts between sickness and health, between life and death.

Holly survived just long enough to be one of the very first people to be put on antiretroviral medications. They were untested but given her bodily condition, lack of weight or immunity, and the speed of her rapid deterioration, there was little to lose. Slowly, she began to recover.

When Holly left the hospice, she was still too weak to walk any distance or hold her camera. Whenever she contemplated walking, each imaginary step was weighed down and wrapped up with the pain of her current situation. Space was no longer transparent, something that one passes through without fully being conscious of it. Instead, rather than something that enables a person to get from one place to another, space constrains and becomes an obstacle to movement. However, as Holly's health and resilience improved further, her perception and experience of space altered yet again. The city slowly opened up once more, different neighborhoods became accessible, which potentially allowed more possibilities, opened up more itineraries.

However, when Holly began to reengage with the city, she did so in a different way. Rather than seeing a city full of hope, potential, and a "land of opportunity" as she had when she first arrived, she started to become aware of the disconnection that is also present. When she returned to photography, the first image she took was of an imaginary mermaid, lying naked by the sea. Holly described her as an urban mermaid and then went on to do a whole series of mermaids. They were naked women draped against a backdrop of New York Harbor.

After she shot the mermaid series, she commenced on a series of photographs of strangers that she encountered in the street, which she entitled "Vagaries of the flesh." It was an activity that emerged out of my own struggle with my body. I became acutely aware of the changes of my body that occurred with having HIV. The way our emotions are expressed with the body and the way our expressions take shape in our body. Of the mysterious way in which we transfer our thoughts into movement. The correlation between posture and emotion, or the way someone moves and emotion, or the way someone holds themselves and emotion, suggested to me something based upon a commonality of experience. In fact, each movement condenses many different emotions, many of which I experienced when I was ill but I could not describe.

When Holly walked the streets, she began to see something in people's faces and postures that told her something had happened to them too. It was then she stopped for a moment and spoke to them and asked to photograph them. Holly says she doesn't know how she knows and can't tell precisely what had happened. Moreover, she doesn't want to know. It doesn't matter. She just says that she knows something has happened: the kind of "tacit knowledge" that is hard to codify, verbalize, or know how one knows it, which Michael Polanyi (1969) describes. Whatever this something was, it was rarely negotiable and never far from consciousness. Holly recognized and identified with this through her own experiences over the last few years and what she had gone through in the hospice. In asking to take a photograph, two life stories converge not through commercial exchange but via a shared sense of liminality and empathy and the knowledge that somewhere in their lives are events, including those that are unsightly.

"Vagaries of the flesh" portrays different moods where a certain movement, posture, or gesture denotes something that she also experienced and went through, such as isolation or losing understanding, and so forth. In Holly's portraits there is an identification between subject/object or photographer/photographed that is often absent in the relationship between hardened, commercial photography of trauma, whose perfectly framed images of victims and tragedy grace the press. The people in Holly's images are not objects of spectacle or curiosity but are of a shared, unarticulated, and tacit understanding that goes beyond the clichés of the genre. This is not just my opinion. I showed them to a war photographer—a long-term professional who had covered conflict in Afghanistan, Somalia, and Rwanda—who said they were unique, original, and illustrated how different types of intensity can be drawn out of everyday situations and encounters.

By the millennium—a landmark Holly never though she would reach—the city started to become more unsightly to her, and so she moved to a small town by the ocean in California where she now lives. Since the move, her work has undergone a subtle change from identification to contemplation, as has the artist herself. The ideas, *images, and subjects are now less concerned with experiences that Holly identifies with, and instead her camera focuses more on entities, such as the ocean. This time there are no urban mermaids, no rusting industrial towers, just the vast expanses of endless ocean. In some ways, to live where Holly does makes contemplation the most likely option. One cannot really identify with the ocean any more than a mountain. An ocean as a backdrop to life is too big, too permanent, and too impenetrable when compared with a person living beside it. It was there before you and will be there after you've gone and one's whole lifetime is encompassed in but a moment of the ocean's vast history. The ocean is constant but not static, and is open to contemplation because it can be repeatedly revisited and thought about at different times and in different moods. It is the ocean, rather than New York's streets, that now provide the backdrop to the routine of Holly's everyday life.*

Holly never imagined she would have a child. With the development of preventative mother-to-child transmission medications, she and her partner—a set-designer from Madrid whom she met at a social event for HIV+ persons—had a son in 2006. They called him Xenon, a Spanish name that means "receiver of life." Life has been passed on and Holly is living in a future she never imagined she would see. I visited her in her little house by the ocean in 2013 and met Xenon. I asked Holly to do a series of five-minute filmed portraits for me on anything she liked, using a film camera and a tripod. She did twelve, from which the screen grab below is taken: it shows Xenon playing by the ocean.

Figure 1.5 Xenon by the Pacific Ocean. Screen grab taken from a five-minute portrait of Xenon playing by the ocean, by Holly Rivers, 2013. *Reproduced by permission from the artist.*

I WANT TO SEE OBSESSION

Benjamin "Benjie" Trimmier hails from Mobile, Alabama, in the Deep South. Consequently, Benjie's social observations and stories about New York City—like those of Truman Capote and Tallulah Bankhead who likewise left Alabama for New York City—are delivered in a Southern accent and offer a distinctive perspective on the city and its social, cultural, and moral manners. When I first became friends with Benjie in the 1990s, he was working on a series of paintings that explored the relationship between organic matter, light, and the act of representation. When I last saw him, prior to finalizing the research for this book, Benjie was lying in a hospital bed on the 14th floor of St. Vincent's Hospital. This would have been around 2004. When I said "see you later" to Benjie on that day, I remember it being in the unspoken knowledge that this might be the last time I would see him.

Words and gestures sometimes possess little significance in their own time and place and are only retrospectively inscribed with importance and meaning. However, in the case of HIV/AIDS and other life threatening conditions, words, events, and relations are often already ascribed with a potential future significance. To say see you later is not always the same casual act of ordinary everyday speech but an unresolved statement or question that resonates in people's eyes, is heard in their voices, and felt in handshakes, reinforcing Schopenhauer's observation "that every parting gives a foretaste of death." Small talk and tiny gestures, such as a passing comment or smile, which may possess little import in and of themselves, become infused with meaning and emotion in the knowledge that this might be the last time a friend or family member is seen alive. This reminds us that meaning is never fully contained within an action, utterance, or moment but remains indeterminate and open to later re-signification. Happily, Benjie made a complete recovery and I got to see him again in 2011 and 2012. He even outlasted the hospital in which he was being treated in, as St. Vincent's Hospital, which began by caring for people caught up in the cholera epidemic of 1849, was torn down in 2013.

Benjie's ongoing series of still lifes of plants and flowers are positioned in between the realm of representational and abstract painting. Representational art typically depicts bodies, objects, and events as they exist in "the real world" to produce works where the subject can be recognized as truthful, natural, and realistic. Benjie purposefully works in the genre of representation because of the way that representational paintings are generally looked down on or seen as passé in the contemporary art world. That is to say, representation is routinely and ruthlessly stigmatized. For Benjie, this is an important, even vital, reason for continuing to work in the realm of representative art insofar as it provides him with an effective metaphor for how bodies with HIV/ AIDS are also routinely stigmatized and ignored. In Benjie's hands, painting plants and flowers can be political; bodies with AIDS can be beautiful; representative art can be radical, which is all "part of the challenge of making art while sick." It is a crucial point as it reminds us that expressions of artistic and aesthetic appreciation are not fixed properties but are generated within particular moments, encounters, and states of thinking and being.

Benjie often paints common organic materials, such as plants and flowers, which are on the verge of being transformed into something else though the passage of time. The subject matter ranges from plants that have just started wilting or losing their vibrancy to those that exist on the border of recognition as a plant. Benjie's attempt to show organic matter in the process of transformation brings to mind anthropology graduate Kurt Vonnegut's observations about painting. In his novel Bluebeard, *Vonnegut compares paintings that are truthful about material things but lie about the passage time vis-à-vis those that successfully incorporate a sense of time into their brushstrokes: "Life, by definition, is never still. Where is it going? From birth to death with no stops on the way. Even a picture of a bowl of pears on a checkered tablecloth is liquid, if laid on canvas by the brush of a master" (1987: 83).*

Anthropology often involves the sharing or comparison of people's social lives and understandings from different parts of the world. Art itself can be employed as a method to facilitate this. In 1999, I took a number of artworks made by people living with HIV/AIDS in New York with me to Kampala, Uganda, to show to other HIV+ persons I had been working with. The aim was to use art to create a cross-cultural dialogue. I would share some artworks and something of the artist's life story and then listen to people's responses and ideas. As such, art was used as a material basis to facilitate an exchange of experience between HIV+ persons living under very different social, cultural, and political conditions and likewise often possessed very different ideas about art, life, and death.

An HIV+ Ugandan artist, Daniel Kafeero, was particularly interested in the collective hopes, fears, and concerns being expressed and not only identified with people's embodied experiences and emotions but also with Benjie's interest in nature and the practical problem of how make art during times of illness. When Daniel was sick, feeling stressed or stigmatized, he would go to a spot overlooking the city, where he would spend the day sitting among the trees and flowers and draw them with a stick in the red earth, or else make batiks of the nature that surrounded him. This is how Daniel responded when we discussed Benjie's paintings on a hot and sunny day somewhere near the center the world:

Figure 1.6 *(Sepia) Dreams and false alarms*, by Benjamin Trimmier, 1994. Oil on wood. *Reproduced by permission from the artist.*

Figure 1.7 *The sun goes down on beauty*, by Benjamin Trimmier, 1995. Oil on linen.
Reproduced by permission from the artist.

This person is interested in nature but also what nature depicts. They are plants with thorns. This is a plant, which is a living thing, actually. The thorns mean this life has thorns but that we can still live with them. It is a sign of perseverance. He is interested in grouping things together. The cord means that it is something artificial that has joined these things or people together. And at one time the branches and thorns are upside down, and like life itself, it is not what is expected. If you spend a lot of time looking at something you begin to see the details. You can appreciate it. In this case, he is interested in representing loss. It is a very beautiful loss that shows us the loss of a flower over time.

Like Daniel, Benjie actively seeks out nature in the city as a means of negotiating life with illness. Benjie regularly goes to Washington Square Park to sit with a particular tree that he has been drawing and communing with for over two decades, especially during times of uncertainty or when life begins to lack direction. He named the tree "Yoda," and it has accompanied Benjie throughout most of his experience of HIV/ AIDS. So much so that when Washington Square was closed off to the public for the better part of a year as it underwent a major restoration around 2010, Benjie made friends with the park-keepers and landscapers so that he could still sneak into the park to visit and draw Yoda.

For those who live in New York, Yoda can be found on the east side of the square. On some days I would go to the park with Benjie when he went to draw Yoda. I became interested in capturing the emotional and artistic interaction between Benjie and Yoda in real time, including the inner dialogues and conversations that Benjie would have with himself and with Yoda while he was drawing. I attached a radio microphone to Benjamin's shirt and asked him to speak out loud the stream of his thoughts as they emerged in real time.

Here is a brief extract of Benjie's emergent thoughts and conversation as he addresses Yoda, in a short excerpt taken from a one-hour drawing session:

I want to see obsession in work, that's what I admire most. And at the time, and even now, I think it is that I became obsessed on some level with coming here to commune with you [Yoda]. I've always had a propensity to anthropomorphize, well, organic things especially, but you were so easy to take to that place, because you were such a person to me, and in a sense that you were a refuge, I took refuge in you then, and that was a different kind of refuge than the refuge that brought me back to you. I had not . . . I had pretty much become artless. And I was . . . I'd lost my faith in my ability to make things, or that things weren't, you know, to my satisfaction, which was a completely different experience for me.

Figure 1.8 Benjamin sitting opposite Yoda (2012). *Photograph by the author.*

Yoda the tree is an aging, gnarled, and weathered presence in the midst of the city and has long provided Benjie with a ready-to-hand source of aesthetic inspiration and existential continuity. As a symbol of patience, endurance, and understanding, Yoda offers a reassuring and nonjudgmental audience for the expression of feelings, stories, and dilemmas or for making important decisions, thinking through issues and gaining a better understanding of life. The use of inner speech and dialogue is an important, often crucial, mode of expression for establishing well-being and negotiating illness, and takes place in dialogue with a broad range if human and nonhuman forms including pets, trees, inanimate objects, and dead persons. As he sat and drew Yoda, Benjie's thoughts, ideas, and memories would emerge into consciousness, sometimes self-directed but as often unbidden. Likewise, Holly spends time watching the ocean as a meditative space to negotiate her life with HIV and Frank Jump has an extended relationship with four or five particular fading advertisements that he calls his "divas," which he visits and photographs on an ongoing basis.

People have internally represented conversations with particular buildings, significant objects, dead or distant others, and cats, all of which provide a readily available interlocutor, akin to a religious figure or close friend, for maintaining well-being, contemplating life decisions, negotiating disruption when feeling down, and as a means of therapeutic interaction in one's life. As such, simple actions—such as going to the park, looking up at an advert, or sitting by the ocean—generate specific modes of experience and expression that shape people's sense of being and understanding of the world, and reveal different existential and emotional qualities that mediate the experience of illness.

NEW YORK'S NIGHTTIME

No disease since the terrible yellow fever epidemics of 1794, 1795, 1798, and 1805 has overshadowed New York City to quite the same extent as HIV/AIDS. By the 1980s, the city was once more beholden to a deadly disease about which little was known and whose presence throughout the city reaffirmed the vulnerability of the human body. The virus charted the limits of medical understanding, changed sexual practices and moral attitudes, and soon became part of New York's social, cultural, and political fabric. Frank's, Holly's, and Benjamin's works bring new insights into the relationship between body and city, including the frailty and resilience of corporeal life, in a city that has itself survived radical shifts in health and fortune, from commercial boom to near bankruptcy and back again. It is a city that offers a dynamic, diverse, and rapidly changing environment for persons living with HIV/AIDS, who have faced life and death, depression, marginalization, and stigma—as well as love, care, empathy, and community support—and in doing so have been exposed to the social tensions and contradictions of contemporary America. Indeed, perhaps no other disease has condensed and symbolized the sexual, political, economic, and religious anxieties of a nation—or been so extensively documented by artists—as HIV/AIDS.

When *Radway's Ready Relief* (1890) and *Omega Oil* (1910) were first painted, tens of feet high in bright marine blue, they suggested to the aching bones and bodies of the citizens on the streets below that the remedy to their bodily discomfort could be found by purchasing their magic elixir. The advertisements' continued presence in the era of HIV/AIDS—long after the original products stopped being sold—attests to the capacity of color and paint to transcend social, political, and economic eras. When *Radway's Ready Relief* was painted, in an attempt to entice weary workers to soothe their bodies by purchasing relief in a bottle, the world was a very different place. Most people did not travel at more than the speed of a horse-drawn cart; electricity and running water were not yet established in homes; and the average life expectancy at birth was around forty-three. Medicine, as we know it, had not been developed, women were unable to vote, and colonialism was violently subjugating vast swathes of the world's population. The claims of *Radway's Ready Relief,* as broadcast in the *New York Times* on the December 4, 1863, were as bold as its advertisement's colors:

A New Method of Curing Certain Diseases, by the Use of Radway's Ready Relief

Has been recently discovered, and is calculated to supersede the use of all electro-magnetic machines, external applications, liniments, plasters, emenagogues, medicines for fever and ague, rheumatism, paralysis, numbness, neuralgia, &c. The application is simple, the effects pleasant, and the cure positive and infallible. It proves what we have for nearly a quarter of a century maintained, that Radway's Ready Relief is the best, quickest, and most important remedial agent ever discovered. It is, however, only recently that we have discovered its immense curative power in certain diseases by this new process.

The Secret of Its Application

was suggested to us by Professor Reid, Professor and Lecturer of Chemistry for many years in the New-York College of Physicians, the New-York Hospitals, Edinburgh University, &c., &c. We have tried it in a number of cases that had previously resisted all other treatments. Every case yielded with astonishing rapidity. The success of the Ready Relief, in its ordinary application, has been greater than all other remedies in use. This can be vouched for by thousands who have used it. Let those afflicted with the following complaints use it under the new method, and we guarantee an immediate cure: RHEUMATISM, NEURALGIA, Gout, Sciatica, Nervousness, Fever and Ague, INDIGESTION, SMALL POX, MEASLES.

Cramps, Spasms, Lumbago, Headache, Heart Disease,

FEMALE COMPLAINTS,

Retention, Suppressions, or Misplaced Menstruation,

URINAL ORGANS,

Diseases of the Kidneys, Bladder, Urethra, Weakness, Spermatorrhea, Pains, Aches, Spasms in the

Back, Thighs, Hips, &c.

THE APPLICATION

in these cases must be made

TO THE SPINE.

Rub the entire length of the spine and across the small of the back with RADWAY's READY RELIEF

for ten or fifteen minutes, night and morning, and a cure will follow. We do not recommend its application in this form as an experiment, but with a full knowledge that it will cure either of the above named complaints.

We are recommending no new or untried medicine—its merit and efficacy as a specific for many of the pains, aches and infirmities that afflict mankind, is acknowledged by thousands—but suggest to our readers and patients a new method of its application for certain complaints, which, if followed, will insure a more positive and rapid cure than any known treatment in vogue. In all cases ask for RADWAY's READY RELIEF.

Patients are invited to call at Dr. RADWAY's Medical Office, No. 87 Maiden-lane, New-York. RADWAY's RELIEF is sold by Druggists.

Radway's Ready Relief was manufactured and sold by Radway and Co. of New York City from the 1840s and ceased production shortly after the great depression began in 1929. The particular Radway's Ready Relief advertisement that Frank Jump documented was painted on the side of a building on Delancey Street in 1890 and was visible until 1998, when it was cemented over. Now it waits until the next time the building is remodeled and the advert is revealed underneath. It is no exaggeration to say that the lifespan of this single advertisement was not just a hugely significant period in New York's history but also in the history of the world.

Some of the advertisements Frank has documented were painted as far back as the 1850s and can still be seen today. In the time they have stood there, proudly advertising their goods and services to successive generations of New Yorkers, the world has undergone unprecedented social, cultural, and technological changes. A single advert may have witnessed the American Civil War and Lincoln's assassination, the first dollar bill, the invention of the film camera, the automobile, the first airplanes, the Wall Street bombings of 1920, the great depression, television, the Jazz Age, two World Wars, the rise and fall of Nazism and the Soviet Union, the jet engine, nuclear fusion, McCarthyism, the discovery of DNA, JFK, The Beatles, the civil rights movement, space travel, feminism, punk, hip-hop, portable computers, HIV/AIDS, the internet, 9/11, the gentrification of Times Square, and the first black President. Who would have thought a simple advertisement would see space exploration and endure the rise and fall of empires as the world changed beyond recognition? Certainly not the men who painted them and whose livelihoods depended upon their ability to make citizens look up to the goods and services on display and convince them that *their* lives would be better with *that* soap powder, *these* particular shoes, *those* garden shears.

The origins of HIV/AIDS remain unclear and may have been present in human populations for decades, if not centuries, without spreading beyond localized environments. By the late 1970s, HIV/AIDS was present in signifi-cant concentrations in the African Great Lake region around Lake Victoria and Lake Tanganyika, but the spread of the disease remained fairly limited. The seeds for change were sown during the last years of Idi Amin's dictatorship in Uganda. Amin's military incursions into Tanzania destabilized the already vola-tile political climate and enabled the spread of HIV/AIDS (see Hooper 2000 for a comprehensive overview). In 1978, Amin's army invaded and annexed the Kagera Salient in northwest Tanzania and blew up the bridge connecting the north with the rest of Tanzania. Losing patience with Amin's military activities in the area, the Tanzanian president Julius Nyerere ordered the country's forces to make preparations to invade Uganda and depose of Amin (Irving 2002). The Tanzanian army's 205th, 206th, and 207th brigades assembled for three months of training in Kagera, where HIV/AIDS had become established among the local population, before marching through the west of Uganda and taking the capital Kampala. It was still some years before the disease or its method of transmission were known to medical science. Furthermore, because of the dis-ease's long gestation period, infected people did not necessarily appear sick and significant numbers of soldiers became infected unknowingly.

War frequently spreads disease through troop movement, the mass mobili-zation of populations and consensual/nonconsensual sexual activity. The subse-quent spread of the disease around the western shore of Lake Victoria and into Uganda correlates with the troop movements of the three brigades (Hooper 2000). The local populations of strategic towns en route began presenting with symptoms that are now known to be the classic early signs of HIV/AIDS. By the early 1980s, "slim" had reached epidemic proportions in southwest Uganda, and the Rakai district was notoriously but mistakenly identified in the Western media as "the source of AIDS." Instead, Rakai was a key site of transmission, among others, during the unrest of 1979 that accelerated the spread of the dis-ease throughout the region (Irving 2002).

The world has long been interconnected through mass transportation, migration, money, wars, and tourism but perhaps never with quite the same intensity as over the last few decades. That HIV/AIDS has become a disease of global proportions in so short a period of time emphasizes how intercon-nected the world has become. By the mid-1980s, New York found itself in the throes of a citywide epidemic as death and disease entered via the city's social and sexual networks. The strange discrepancy of healthy, young, mostly gay men succumbing in large numbers to disease and death, in comparison to a general population steadily getting older, destabilized cultural expectations about what constitutes a natural life trajectory and reversed the established order of life.

In an uncanny and macabre coincidence, given the role of disease in establishing the city's grid system, the new disease was named GRID (Gay Related Immune Deficiency). GRID was later renamed HIV/AIDS and spread rapidly throughout the city; by 1990, exactly two hundred years after the city's first census, people with HIV/AIDS filled 8.5% of all New York hospital beds and by the turn of the millennium there had been 72,207 known deaths from AIDS in the city (including almost 10,000 infants) out of 116,316 people diagnosed up to that time. This is a figure that is almost four times the city's entire population in the first census and which did not include tens of thousands of persons unaware of their status. As of 2013, there were 104,690 people alive with HIV/AIDS in the city.

Moreover, and as previously stated, for every person diagnosed, there were tens, often hundreds of other persons who were affected, including friends, family, parents, children, neighbors, work colleagues, counselors, and medical-staff, whose lives became thoroughly intertwined with a highly unpredictable, life-threatening disease. HIV/AIDS soon formed a kind of "mental atmosphere"—a term George Orwell used in his radio broadcasts during World War II to describe the conditions under which people carried out their lives in wartime London—only in this case it was disease that spread far and wide across the city. Even those distant from "high-risk" groups made adjustments to their behaviors and lifestyle and adopted safe-sex practices.

Throughout much of New York's history, its surfaces have been used to sell medical products and cures, including the fading advertisements documented by Frank Jump; these present a highly visible public record of the diseases, health concerns, and bodily anxieties that defined successive eras. Some illnesses and conditions were associated with a particular community, social class, or generation. However, the demographic changes across New York City over the last hundred years mean the city's fading advertisements tell us little about the city's neighborhoods as they are today but instead illustrate how they once were, providing an index of the city's shifting fortunes and population. In a continuation of this tradition, for the last thirty years, extensive public health, political, and media campaigns by activist and support groups, such as ACTUP, GMHC, and Visual Aids has ensured that HIV/AIDS has become part of the visual surface and semiotics of the city. Advertisements and posters for

HIV clinics, antiretroviral medications, public health information, condoms, and AIDS-related magazines are found on trains, subways, buses, in cafes and libraries, and on the sides of shops and buildings. It almost goes without saying that HIV/AIDS does not extend equally across New York's neighborhoods and social networks, and its unequal distribution is reflected on the city's surfaces including the concentrations of HIV-related advertising and materials in Chelsea, Greenwich Village, SoHo, and the Lower East Side. However, the rapid pace of change and gentrification in New York means that many streets and neighborhoods that were once associated with HIV/AIDS are barely recognizable from the 1980s, when the disease first arrived in the city.

THROWN OUT OF THE WORLD

To paraphrase Karl Marx, people make history not according to conditions of their own choosing but under social, political, and economic circumstances that help shape the potentialities and possibilities of life. Persons are born into and raised in a specific social, cultural, and economic environment—be that of desert nomads or late capitalism—in which they develop and learn to understand themselves as particular kinds of moral and economic subjects. Frank, Holly, and Benjamin negotiated and adapted to illness in a city founded on a grid of straight-edged, commerce-lined streets and avenues that continuously enable citizens to look far into the future and work toward an economically productive life and retirement. After diagnosis those same commerce-lined avenues, brandishing their assorted messages of pensions, retirement plans, and medicines promising a long and healthy life, ceased to have much meaning for Frank, Holly, Benjamin, and many others. In New York alone, HIV/AIDS created the conditions for thousands upon thousands of young men and women to be thrown out of the grid of capitalism in order to confront a future of stigma, terminal illness, and death. Holly entered a hospice at the age of twenty-five, Frank took himself out of education and the workforce at age twenty-six, filling in every offer for a new bank account or credit card, while Benjamin—originally from America's Deep South, unlike Frank and Holly who were both born in the city—took out a $100,000 bank loan and decided to spend his last years taking a four-year degree in fine art, confident in the knowledge that he would be dead long before he needed to repay the bank: "*Only, dammit, I lived and now I've got a $100,000 debt hanging over me.*"

Such actions are representative of how living with HIV/AIDS involves continuously remaking one's life—including one's social, economic, and moral expectations—while simultaneously negotiating a changing body and the ever-present possibility of death. There is no single, authentic way of living under such circumstances. Nor is a person being toward death reducible to the condition of finitude as in Martin Heidegger's (1962) mistaken conflation of finitude with death. Instead as Jean-Paul Sartre ([1943] 1996) argues, finitude is a property of people's situational circumstances and the limits of the body rather than the human destiny of death per se. This situates the person in terms of class and history, and reinforces how, even if human beings were not mortal, we would nevertheless possess finite bodily capacities shaped by health, gender, and so forth.

"It is in this sense that our body is comparable to a work of art. It is a nexus of living meanings," suggests Maurice Merleau-Ponty (1992: 175). For many of the people I worked with, the awareness of bodily vulnerability and mortality created the conditions for rethinking existing social practices and the development of new perspectives on the world. Under such circumstances, many taken-for-granted activities that previously grounded and gave pattern to existence are disrupted through the effects of knowing one has an unpredictable, life-threatening disease. Previously unremarkable objects, events, and places are invested with new poignancy and significance, in the same way that a family member's death sheds new light onto the past and imbues their belongings or the time spent with them with different meanings. One's body, familiar routines, and everyday surroundings are "made strange," revealing an almost poetic movement, whereby the ordinary becomes extraordinary and the extraordinary becomes ordinary. There are numerous occasions when people look to their familiar surroundings and neighborhoods in the hope of rediscovering continuity and stability, and instead experience what has been described to me as the wonder of existence or a kind of astonishment in the face of being. Things take on different qualities: fading advertisements, people in the street, money, trees, the sun, or a pop song might reveal intense and profound meanings as an appreciation of time and existence are incorporated into them. This is an aesthetics of astonishment and surprise that comes close to Merleau-Ponty's *il-y-a* or "there is" (not to be confused with Levinas' *il-y-a*) that transforms perception and makes the temporality, contingency, and value of being explicit in one's body and the things that surround it. This sense of astonishment, alongside new ways of seeing and attuning oneself to life and the city, are among the many positive things people take from their experience of HIV/AIDS and reframes their perception and experience of their surroundings.

I initially got to know Frank, Holly, and Benjamin through the Visual AIDS collective in New York, which was set up in 1988 to document the impact of AIDS and raise awareness through events such as *Day Without Art*, which takes place each year on December 1st, and *Night Without Light*, where cities nationwide turn off their lights as a visual metaphor for the loss caused by AIDS. In 1994, Visual AIDS set up The Archive Project to document and ensure a life and legacy for the extraordinary body of work made by artists with AIDS, many of whom are dead. The archive has documented the works of over three hundred artists with the aim of providing a legacy for the future. Consider the words of one artist I worked with, Frank Moore, founder (together with David Hirsch) of The Archive Project, who died aged forty-eight in 2002: "Many artists with AIDS die twice: first, when illness forces them to discontinue the creative activity, which has defined their life and given it meaning; second, when their biological functions cease. The Archive Project is an attempt to provide professional services, which can help forestall that first death."

Nonetheless, the future—like all futures—remained unwritten, and by the turn of the millennium, AIDS had begun to transform from an acute chronic illness, following the development of effective triple combination antiretroviral medications (ARVs). Antiretroviral medications reduce the viral load in the blood, boost the immune system, and stave off opportunistic infections, so as to stabilize health and offer a greatly increased life span. In New York, antiretrovirals reopened time and space for tens of thousands of men and women living with HIV/AIDS, triggering a massive shift in mind, body, and emotion away from death and back toward life. Many persons who were facing and preparing for death are now living in a future they never imagined they would see, have resumed careers, are experiencing the world through stabilized bodies, and are learning to live again. There are currently over a million people living with HIV/AIDS in the United States, many of whom had to reorientate themselves away from the prospect of impending death in order to reengage with the future, only under different circumstances. Death may no longer pose the same threat or feel so immediate, but life is no longer what it was either; it is informed by the kind of knowledge that emerges out of extraordinary experiences. It is unsurprising therefore that many people find it impossible to return to their previous ways of being. Together with thousands of their fellow citizens, Frank, Holly and Benjamin had to create a new context of dwelling that not only involved contemplating how they wanted to live the remainder of their life; they also had to contend with being thrown back onto the grid of capitalism.

WHAT NEXT?

Shortly after the development of antiretroviral treatments, I attended a one-day forum about AIDS in Greenwich Village that included talks, performances, and roundtables, and an exhibition of works by HIV+ artists. The forum was held at Washington Square Church on West Fourth Street, whose radical history encompasses Vietnam War protests, supporting the Black Panthers, and the United States' first openly gay reverend, Paul Abels, who himself succumbed to AIDS in 1992. The forum's theme, *What next?*, reflected the air of optimism now that the future had opened up. However, I was also struck by the fact that no matter how hard the speakers and audience tried to talk about the future or where life would take them, the forum kept returning to the past and the shock of living through the pre-antiretroviral years, when many thousands of young men and women were gravely ill and dying across the city. The atmosphere was dense with emotion as life stories and collective histories were spoken over the main microphone to the room. Some of these voiced tragic and tearful descriptions of loss, life, and HIV/AIDS, some were delivered with a sense of casual abandon and some good jokes, while others were raw, angry, and wrung out. Together, the forum evoked and betrayed a mixture of anxiety, uncertainty, and hope about the future: *what next?*

As I walked around the exhibition, I overheard a man saying that because he was from the Deep South and his Mama had raised him to be polite, he was going to treat the disease as a personal guest. He said he was going to be the best host possible and make the disease comfortable in his body and was going to look after it right until it was time for his guest or himself to leave. The person he was speaking with replied that he couldn't understand his friend's attitude of hospitality and had "always hated AIDS from the depth of his guts to the top of his head." He hated talking about it and having to acknowledge it to himself, hated going for regular check ups and having his blood taken, hated the medication and its side effects, hated telling other people he had a disease. It made me think about Emily Martin's argument, that endowing cells with personhood is a key means of trying to grasp and understand the boundaries of self and world. Whereas in earlier times, before modern technology, "the skin might have been regarded as the border of the individual self, now these microscopic cells are seen as tiny individual selves" (1992: 415). As I continued to walk around the exhibition, the snippets of conversation that I overheard were as revealing as the conference itself and highlighted the diversity of responses, attitudes, and ideas about HIV/AIDS.

I had arranged to meet Frank Jump at the conference. Tall, handsome, healthy, he was wearing a set of pirate earrings and an orange Hawaiian shirt. As we shook hands, I caught sight of his Dick Tracey Special Edition Millennium watch that he had bought especially so that he could program it to beep throughout the day when he needed to take his medications. His early arrival caught me off guard and soon he was conspiratorially close and sharing his thoughts about deadly viruses and being granted a new lease of life. No time to waste on small talk here. We sat down to catch the last conference session and then went out into the bright sunlight of Greenwich Village. Once outside the church, immediately to our left, a man stared furiously at us. The man was surrounded by posters and declarations of hate and was wearing a sandwich board declaring, GODS CURE FOR FAGS (sans apostrophe), in big capitals. As we walked past, he shouted out with spite and venom he was "glad so many gays are dying of AIDS and would be going to hell."

Such sentiments were a routine form of right-wing, Evangelical currency that judged and denounced men and women with HIV/AIDS but ultimately turned out to be indolent and lacking in coherence or backbone, and were surpassed by a much more humanitarian energy. I remember being outraged that somebody could still be bothered to drag their raggedy ass and heavy sandwich boards down to shout venom at people all day long. I looked into the man's eyes and found them oddly docile with a smattering of self-righteousness. Frank, meanwhile, carried on the conversation without a hint of acknowledgement. I kept meaning to find out the level of self-conscious performance involved and to what extent the man's shouting and spiteful sandwich boards affected him, but I never did. The conversation had moved elsewhere . . .

CHAPTER TWO

Detours and puzzles in the land of the living
Toward an imperiled anthropology

Landscapes can be deceptive. Sometimes a landscape seems to be less a setting for the life of its inhabitants than a curtain behind which their struggles,
achievements, and accidents take place.
>   —John Berger, *A fortunate man* (1997: 13)

Men are often haunted by things that happened to them in life, especially in
war or other periods of great intensity. Sometimes you see these men walking
the streets or driving in a car. Their lives seem to be normal, but they are not.
>   —Werner Herzog, *Little Dieter needs to fly* (1997)

It is only shallow people who do not judge by appearances. The true mystery of
the world is the visible, not the invisible.
>   —Oscar Wilde, *The picture of Dorian Gray* (1992: 34)

PERILS OF THE INTERIOR

As Oscar Wilde observes, because there is so much to be gained by observing surfaces, their study should not be seen as shallow, superficial, or trivial.

However, a few pages after declaring allegiance to the realm of appearances, Wilde then cautioned: "those who go beneath the surface do so at their peril" (1992: 3). With this warning in mind, I argue it has become necessary for anthropology to put itself in greater *peril* by venturing beneath the observable and audible surfaces of social life in order to gain a better understanding of the interior dialogues and imaginative lifeworlds that constitute people's daily lives and activities. The capacity for a rich and imaginative inner life—that simultaneously encompasses streams of internally represented speech, reverie, imagery, and other modes of inner expression that exist beyond third-party observation—is a distinctive aspect of human experience. Without inner expression, social life would be severely compromised, including people's abilities to plan, reflect upon and understand their actions, or form interpretations about other persons and situations. It would mean social relations and many routine aspects of daily life, from parenting and playing games to personal and business negotiations, would be rendered impossible in their current form, as persons would be unable to simultaneously hold private intentions, opinions, information, and ideas in their mind that differ from those that are publicly expressed.

When living with long-term illness, internally expressed thoughts, fears, and hopes form part of an ongoing daily narrative and are not always shared with others. Internalized modes of expression are a key means through which people reflect on life events, make decisions, negotiate moral dilemmas, and understand their changing situation and circumstances. Whether in the form of structured narratives or less coherent and fragmented forms, people's inner dialogues and expressions are foundational to experience and action. Even when publicly engaging in routine social interactions, people might be inwardly negotiating complex social, emotional, and existential dilemmas they are unwilling or unable to express to friends or family, including suicidal intentions, religious doubts, and moral anxieties about illness, death, and dying (Irving 2014a). Not all thinking takes place in language; it also encompasses inchoate and non-linguistic forms that are opaque—even to the thinkers themselves—alongside more self-directed forms of internal expression, which combine together to play a critical role in establishing the character of lived experience.

The centrality of inner speech and expression to human experience—or what William James termed the mind's conversations with itself (James 1890: 239)—is widely recognized in neurology and studies of cognition (Ward 2011; Fernyhough 2016) and has been studied extensively in relation to linguistics, learning, and development (Vygotsky [1934] 1986; Alderson-Day and

Fernyhough 2015) as well as self-regulation, psychiatric disorders, and auditory hallucinations (Fernyhough 2008; Hurlburt 1993, 2009). As Peter Carruthers notes in the *Journal of Behavioural and Brain Sciences*: "Although proportions vary, many people seem to spend a good deal of their waking activity engaged in "inner-speech," with imaged natural language sentences occupying a significant proportion of the stream of their conscious mentality" (2002: 657).

The ability to formulate internalized narratives about other persons, our surroundings, and ourselves is an integral part of what makes us human and is central to the negotiation of social life. From an anthropological perspective, I argue that inner expression constitutes a broad spectrum of experiences, from routine practices to extraordinary moments of existential crisis. The empirical content of people's inner dialogues and expressions ranges from shared social concerns and interests to highly individualized and idiosyncratic thoughts. Without some form of inner expression there would be no self-understanding or social existence, at least not in a form we would recognize. And yet, anthropology finds itself without a generally accepted theory of how people's interior lifeworlds relate to their public expressions, nor an established methodology for accessing people's interior expressions as they emerge in social life, action, and practice. Often people's interior expressions are seen as irrelevant or extraneous, rather than fundamental to embodied life and experience, and are seldom the primary focus of anthropological research or monographs. As such, anthropology—the quintessential study of humanity—risks only being able to tell half the story of human life.

To tell a more complete and credible story of human subjectivity and activity, I argue it is necessary to place our disciplinary epistemologies and presuppositions in *peril* so as to research and represent those dimensions of inner experience and expression that are rarely explored in the field. The notion of *imperiled anthropology* is one closely connected to experimentation and involves testing and broadening our theoretical, ethnographic, and empirical horizons so as to critically extend and evaluate the potentials of anthropological knowledge. Tellingly, the etymological root of peril, *peira* meaning "attempt, trial, test" is the exact same as empiricism, experimentation, and experience, revealing a shared impetus toward a testing out and modification of the existing knowledge. Moreover, as Michael Jackson (1996) observes, experience, coming from *ex* (out of) and *peira* shares the same root *per* as the Germanic *fahr* (to travel), which is to recognize that experience is not simply a category of the past but also the present and the future and involves moving toward something not yet specified or understood. Traveling with and alongside people in the field requires conceptual and physical movement and allows both parties to establish a series of different perspectives on the world, including seeing one's life and surroundings in a new way. This is the idea of ethnography as a shared experience or journey in which informant and anthropologist work together toward a set of questions in an attempt to generate new understandings about life and the world.

The ethnographic content of this chapter offers an account of how inner expression is constitutive of significant life events, focusing on the internalized dialogues, imagery, and lifeworld of a person going for an HIV test. By exploring the complex streams of thinking and being that emerge before, during, and after diagnosis with a terminal illness, the aim is to open up a discussion and critical rethinking of the ethnographic, ontological, and evidential status accorded to people's experiential interior within anthropology. Although such an *imperiled anthropology* may not ultimately succeed in getting beneath the surface, as Oscar Wilde and his fellow writers and artists knew, failure is necessary to the creative process—to which anthropologists might add that embracing failure is equally necessary to fieldwork, entering into new social worlds and learning about people's inner lives.

THE PROBLEM OF INTERIORITY

From E. E. Evans-Pritchard's declaration that individual perceptions have "no wider collective validity" and that the "subject bristles with difficulties" (1969: 107), through Clifford Geertz's (1973) long-standing commitment to external, publicly observable symbols as the primary realm of anthropological study to Pierre Bourdieu's dismissal of interest in lived experience as a complacent form of "flabby humanism" (1990: 5), the problems and pitfalls encountered when making anthropological claims about people's inner expressions means that they are rarely the subject of anthropological monographs or ethnographic accounts.

Nigel Rapport has observed that interior realms of being remain a "terra incognita" for anthropology and that social science generally finds the study of interiority problematical or else irrelevant to its dominant interests (Rapport 2008). Citing essayist George Steiner's observation that "it is very likely that [internal speech-acts] represent the denser, statistically more extensive portion of the total distribution of discourse" (Steiner 1978: 65), Rapport argues for an anthropological focus on introspection, defined as "an individual's inner consciousness, the continual conversation one has with oneself" (2008: 331), including those that elude the person's conscious control or play against conventional social perspectives and norms and are ordinarily hidden from public view: "I argue for recognising interiority as a crucial focus of anthropological endeavour, and I outline a possible way in which interiority might be evidenced as irrupting onto the social scene. Interiority makes its paradoxical appearance in social settings in the form of a strangeness, an individual purity and integrity, for which the term gratuitousness is apposite" (Rapport 2008: 331).

Recall Edmund Leach's (1982) observation that anthropologists are basically "bad novelists"—and Rodney Needham's (1978) decree that to achieve something of the "humane significance" of art, anthropologists should try to write with the introspective insight and perspicacity associated with the modernist novel. Rapport suggests we need to look more systematically to writers, artists, and painters to offer insights into the inner lives and realms of being that anthropologists overlook, either because they are methodologically unprepared to engage with such phenomena or are unwilling to venture into realms of consciousness that artists attempt to engage with when trying to understand the complex streams of inner expression that mediate experience. It is instructive that because people's inner expressions and lifeworlds are rarely the primary focus of anthropological research, Rapport is required to use novelists, poets, and painters, such as George Eliot, Virginia Woolf, E. M. Forster, Philip Larkin, and Stanley Spencer, rather than ethnography to make his case.

In contrast to the social sciences, writers of many persuasions have actively striven to explore and represent the complex streams of inner dialogue, thought, and reverie that shape social life and help define us as individuals and as a species. For example, in Fyodor Dostoyevsky's *Crime and punishment* ([1886] 1995), murder is literally on the mind of its main character Raskolnikov as he roams around the alleys and arcades of St. Petersburg looking for opportunities to kill. Raskolnikov's thoughts and purpose remain unbeknownst to the strangers he passes in the street as he silently debates the social, ethical, and existential implications of taking someone else's life. His murderous urges and internal moral debates are rarely articulated aloud and even his friends, family, and landlady are unaware that he possesses murderous intent. Raskolnikov becomes more intense in his desire to kill and once he talks himself into action, murders a harmless old woman whom he sees as expendable and performing no real purpose or function. Afterward, Raskolnikov is haunted by the act he has committed. His entire being becomes overshadowed by a kind of paranoia and he can no more escape thinking about his murderous actions by hiding away in his room than by going out into the streets. In the end, his attentions turn to suicide as a practical means of escaping the thoughts that consume him day and night but in the last instance he cannot summon the resolve to go through with it.

Most famously of all, James Joyce's mock heroic epic *Ulysses* ([1922] 2000) is constructed around the streams of inner dialogue and reverie of its three main characters to tell a story of a single day in Dublin on June 16, 1904. We are introduced to Leopold Bloom as a man who eats with relish the inner organs of beasts and fowls for breakfast. His hunger satisfied, Bloom's inner dialogue turns away from food and becomes infused with a gambler's optimism that he might back a winning horse in the day's big race. As we follow Bloom's inner commentary it takes on different guises throughout the day, from political analysis to childhood memories to petty grievances with work colleagues to sexual urges to jealousy to horse racing to his troubled relationship with his wife, Molly. We learn how his daily life is couched in an existential tension that oscillates between feelings of possibility, pride and contentment, and those of yearning, frustration, and dislocation.

As we listen to Bloom's intimate thoughts and desires as he walks around Dublin, we hear how he feels at home in the city in certain moments but at other times experiences and articulates a sense of disenchantment. For despite being born and raised in Ireland, Bloom often feels himself to be an outsider in the land of his birth due to his Hungarian Jewish ancestry, and his thoughts are frequently interrupted and overwhelmed by a mood of unbelonging. When a belligerent one-eyed nationalist, a.k.a. "the citizen," hurls a biscuit tin at him for being Jewish, Bloom engages in an internal debate on the nature of home and citizenship. In one of literature's most famous scenes, Bloom sees a young girl, Gerty MacDowell, on a swing near the beach and starts masturbating while partly hidden behind a rock. We enter Bloom's thoughts but also the young girl's as she notices the foreign-looking man watching her and casts him as a romantic figure and mysterious exile. As day and night unfold, Bloom's interior dialogue defines who he is in the specificity of the moment: sometimes immersed in the task at hand—such as when sitting on the toilet and enjoying the smells that come up or deciding which horse to back—at other times his mind wandering between teenage memories, Irish politics, and his wife, Molly, who lies in bed thinking about lovers and loss and wondering how or if she will ever be able to love again after the death of her child.

The figures of Raskolnikov and Bloom are so compelling because we are allowed to enter their minds and learn of the social and existential concerns that preoccupy them. Their being emerges from moment to moment, rather than as persons accorded a static worldview and fixed moral perspective or whose minds are empty vessels awaiting anthropological explanation and explication. They are alive and in flow and they come across as fully human characters whose quotidian lives and actions are accompanied by ongoing streams of internalized hopes, desires, regrets, humor, hunger, and complexity. To the outside world it may seem that nothing much is happening as they walk down the street but once we enter their inner lifeworlds, we discover layers of expressive activity that range across time, space, and subject matter, from sexual desire and cooking to murder and exile. And while the specific content and concerns of each moment may or may not be something we have personally experienced or identify with, the process of thinking and engaging with the world through inner speech is instantly recognizable.

Like Rapport, Vincent Crapanzano's landmark volume *Imaginative horizons: An essay in literary-philosophical anthropology* (2004) draws on a broad range of literary and poetic examples, alongside insights gained from psychoanalysis and philosophy, to explore how social life and experience are mediated by streams of imagination and reverie, as well as the gaps, ellipses, and partially formed or inchoate realms of thinking and being that exist beyond conscious knowledge or language. For Crapanzano, our imaginative lifeworlds are not extraneous to social life and action but are central to our embodied experience and understanding of a world in which we are simultaneously the subject and object of our thoughts. Crapanzano offers a sustained critique of the empirical presuppositions of social science, including how the complex lifeworlds brought into being by the imagination are largely understood as intangible, immaterial, and irrelevant, rather than as empirical phenomena worthy of investigation. However, Crapanzano's argument is not with objective, social scientific inquiry or empiricism per se but rather with the narrow definitions and reductive accounts of what constitutes "reality" in conventional approaches. Following William James' plea to reinstate "the vague and inarticulate to its proper place in our mental life," Crapanzano suggests that if we are ever to understand human behavior, it is necessary to pay closer attention to "a dimension of experience that insofar as it resists articulation, indeed disappears with articulation, has in fact been ignored" (2004: 18). In this, we see a spectrum of inner expression from the incipient, vague, or inaccessible realms of thinking and being that elude conscious control or coherent expression, to the type of self-directed inner voice through which people self-consciously understand, negotiate, and reimagine their surroundings, themselves, and others.

There is, however, a crucial distinction between literary and anthropological approaches. First, unlike poetic, literary, or artistic attempts to understand and represent people's inner lifeworlds, an ethnographic approach has a duty to offer truthful and empirically justifiable accounts of people's social lives in which persons are also able to recognize themselves, their own experience, and worldview in the theories and texts that purport to represent and understand their lives (see Jackson 1996). Second, because interiority and interior dialogue are closely associated with the advent of Western selfhood and individualism and are often seen as the preserve of European life, self-reflection, and modernist writing (Taylor 1992), they need to be researched and understood as an aspect of broader human experience and daily life across the world.

Douglas Davies (2006) is one of the few anthropologists to engage with inner speech, primarily in relation to Sikh, Zen, and Christian religious practice and the particular lifeworlds this produces (also see Luhrmann 2012; Lende 2013; Irving 2014b, 2016). Robert Desjarlais considers how experiences of interiority are not pregiven but are made possible, emerge, and become specified within particular social, political, and sensory environments (1997) and in relation to particular activities (2012). As a shared human capacity, persons across societies and cultures have the capacity for a complex inner lifeworld but the form it takes is differentiated in terms of specific moral concerns, modes of action, and ways of being.

Consequently, a major challenge across the social sciences is how we might combine theoretical and methodological approaches so as to practically research the complex amalgamations of inner expression and imagery that exist beneath the surface of people's public activities in ways that accord with general processes of knowing, memory, and cognition (Whitehouse 2001; Lende and Downey 2012), empathy and narrative (Hollan and Throop 2008; Kirmayer 2008; Mattingly, Lutkehaus, and Throop 2008), hearing voices (Luhrmann 2012; Fernyhough 2016) and shifts in identity and self-expression (Ewing 1990). In other words, to strengthen anthropological understanding about the human condition, it is necessary not only to open up a debate about the role (or otherwise) of inner expression in social life but to develop new practical ways of researching how people's inner lifeworlds might relate to extrinsic, audible, and observable expressions across a range of lived experiences and social contexts.

This presents a number of significant epistemological and ethnographic problems for anthropology and other evidence-based disciplines insofar as there is no independent, objective access to another person's consciousness or experience—more colloquially put, there is no way to "look inside someone's head"—and because understanding the empirical content of inner expression is primarily a practical, ethnographic, and methodological problem, to be researched in the field, rather than one that can be reduced to theoretical speculation or conjecture. Often, we are not conscious of what we are actually thinking, and even when we are it can sometimes be difficult to understand or put into language. Last but not least, conventional social scientific approaches are often too static to understand or represent the transient, stream-like and ever-changing character of people's interior expressions and experiences as they emerge in situ from moment to moment.

FIRST STEPS: WALKING FIELDWORK

The following ethnographic section, *Detours and puzzles in the land of the living*, combines image, voice, and walking to uncover how a city's streets, buildings, and neighborhoods are mediated by ongoing, often highly idiosyncratic, interior dialogues and emotional lifeworlds that are rooted in people's current existential situations. This extends the idea of walking fieldwork (Irving 2002, 2005, 2007), a fieldwork method I originally devised to understand the phenomenology of the body in action during episodes of illness, whereby I accompanied people as they carried out their daily routines and practices and asked them to narrate out loud their thoughts, emotions, and experiences in real time. When engaged in *walking fieldwork*, I witnessed those moments when people's bodies—or the surrounding world—became present to consciousness as people narrated their awareness of their body in relation to their surroundings and would describe—for example, the component stages, exact distances, or physical and emotional costs and benefits written into particular practices, from domestic chores to shopping and gardening. It became noticeable that the environment was rarely simply there but was forever constraining or enabling certain types of action, with gradients, road surfaces, stairs, noise, crowds, weather conditions, and so forth possessing dynamic, transforming properties that outline the possibilities available to *this* body, in *this* time, and in *this* place.

The act of narrating one's actions produces a heightened awareness of self, body, and emotion in relation to one's surroundings and makes explicit or recasts habitual embodied understandings of space and place. My cowalkers were extremely aware, during different intensities of illness, as to how the particular qualities of objects—chairs, the design of toothpaste caps, the positioning of light switches, the weight of water—interacted with the human body and how crowds, lunchtimes, rush hours, and weekends changed the habitual character, social density, and latent possibilities of public spaces. By walking around familiar places while narrating the objects, places, and people they engaged with, my cowalkers also offered glimpses into the streams of thought, mood, and emotion that comprise a person's daily life but exist beneath the surface of the observable and audible. I subsequently realized *walking fieldwork* was not solely a means of understanding the immune compromised body in action but also offered more general insights into how people attempt to maintain social continuity, negotiate critical events, and ongoing existential dilemmas.

Walking itself is a form of continuity over time and space, involving embodied learning and repetitive body movements. It is an activity that changes in different contexts, landscapes, and historical periods, placing it in the realm of culture as much as biology. As such, walking is not a precultural activity (Ingold and Lee 2006) but a practical way of worldmaking that is differentiated by bodily variables across social and historical contexts. From unplanned and ambiguous modes of walking to more formalized and choreographed forms, walking offers numerous ways of coordinating nerves, lungs, and muscles with a person's inner voice, thoughts, and emotions. Walking is a shared activity that combines different phenomenological qualities and wide-ranging trajectories of thought, mood, and imagination whose character is not necessarily expressed publicly. Most of the time, we know little about the inner thoughts, existential concerns, and imaginative lives of the people who we see in the street. For even when a crowd of similar bodies stride down the street to the same beat, people's thoughts and imaginations are not necessarily in step with each other, and their public actions do not provide evidence of shared or collective experience.

By placing the walking body directly into the field in terms of a collaborative ethnography, my aim is to move from the observation of others to a dialogic research encounter in which my co-collaborators actively create the fieldwork site and shape the direction of anthropological knowledge. The walks in question took place during the summer of 2008, when my friend Albert Velsaco—whose intense and striking artwork graces the cover of this book—and I recreated the journey he made in August 1987 when he went for an HIV test. The walks follow the exact same route Albert walked that day, and takes us from his apartment on East First

Street to the local subway at Second Avenue, to West 23rd and over to the Baumgartner Health Center on Ninth Avenue and West 28th Street where he was due to collect his results. We then retraced the journey he made when returning home after diagnosis and attempt to show the processes whereby a person becomes detached from existing ways of being and begins to reimagine their life and future.

We made the walk three times: first, as a narrated walk and photo essay; second, as a single-take essay film; third, as a point-of-view film in real time. The following is from the photo essay, which can be seen as a collaborative attempt by Albert and myself to combine walking, narration, and photography to understand the interior lifeworld, dialogue, and imagery of someone confronting the radical uncertainty of their own existence in a public place. That is to say, a person who remains a social being and is required to act accordingly on the street but whose inner dialogues and lifeworlds reveal layers of ethnographic depth. *Detours and puzzles in the land of the living* attempts to bring to life through a "dramatization of being" the thoughts, dilemmas, and urges Albert experienced while walking to and from the clinic, as retrospectively understood and represented in relation to his subsequent life history. I took the images while Albert narrated into a voice recorder as we walked. Here, I try not to prefigure Albert's experience or overinterpret his narrative by providing too much information or explaining the exact relationship between the images and the text. Instead, we rely on Albert's own words and the reader's imagination to understand how other "people immediately experience space and time, and the world in which they live" (Jackson 1996: 12).

DETOURS AND PUZZLES IN THE LAND OF THE LIVING

Leaving Albert's apartment: *"I'm wearing a shirt with red stripes, like blood, like the blood in veins, which I did on purpose. It's something that you can't forget. I'm reminded every day in that, well, number one, I like theme parties, but the other thing is that even though I don't live my life as a person with AIDS, I'm actually just Albert, but I don't deny it either and I can't deny it because twice a day in the morning and at night I have to take a handful of pills that remind me that I'm a man living with illness. With the disease it's the same way as being Mexican or being gay are aspects of myself. Someone asked me the other day what did I do, and I could think of two things, I'm an artist and a caretaker. But a caretaker is really what I am in that I'm taking care of myself, which—especially during these last couple of months with all these*

Figures 2.1-2.4 Leaving Albert's apartment for the clinic.

physical challenges—is often a full time job. But I'm grateful for so many things and wearing a shirt like this just reminds me that, yes, there is something that is coursing through my veins that is insidious, that is deadly, that can take a turn at any time, but I'm healthy now and have survived where so many others haven't and are dying. As we speak, two thirds of the world doesn't have the support of doctors or medications, and even those people that live here that can't afford to pay for the medications are struggling. I told my roommate that I was going to get tested and he knew that I was enduring the long wait. I don't remember exactly how long the wait was. I know it felt interminable then. It felt like forever. I think it was at least a week, maybe even longer. Time just crawled. I actually recall going to bed early just to make the next day come faster so that I would be closer to finding out my status even though the biggest part of me really didn't want to know and the other part of me assumed the worst. They called to tell me the results were in and could I come to the center to collect them. It is policy not to give results, whether positive or negative, over the phone, which was another annoying factor, as I don't know why they couldn't just tell me over the phone. I was hoping I might be negative, I am sure my roommate was also hoping that I might be negative, although unfortunately I wasn't."

Figures 2.5-2.8 Journey to the clinic: Crossing East First Street; Second Avenue subway station; Arriving at West 23rd Street; Empire State Building as seen walking along West 23rd Street.

From Second Avenue to West 23rd Street: *"I remember walking there on that day with a feeling of anxiousness. Anxiousness and ambivalence and fear, especially after the wait one had to endure back then. During the wait I had kept the anxiousness to myself, the frustrations and impatience about the time crawling. As I left my apartment I was filled with trepidation and I remember being upset too about how long it had . . . at the system that forced people to wait for so long for this life-changing result. If I'd been negative, of course I'd be thrilled as anyone else would and you could move on from there but I assumed I would be positive, as Stephen had died in May. And I'd waited this long to get tested, which took all my courage and strength just to go there those days previously because I really didn't want to know. At that point I hadn't known anyone that had died, except for Stephen, hadn't really read the newspapers or medical things, and had actually been consciously indifferent. Stephen died a horrible death from AIDS in Sydney, Australia, two weeks before he was due to visit here one last time before he died. We were going to meet him at the airport in his wheelchair but he ended up in coma. I spent the next few months assuming that I had it too but not wanting to do anything about it or confirming the obvious. But I finally did go for the test and then* *had to endure the wait. There was also hope as I walked. I was hoping I wouldn't be. I knew that whatever . . . . I'm sure I even bargained with the gods. God please make me not. Even though I'm a lapsed Catholic, I was a good altar boy at one time. I'm sure there's times when I have sought solace in that. The Virgin Mary, the Guadalupe, is such an icon in Mexican culture. I chose to go on my own, as I didn't want to burden anyone. One of the reasons I came by myself is that it took so much to get tested. I'd put it off for months and felt I needed to muster enough courage in that if the diagnosis was positive, from that moment I would have to find the strength, and so wanted to find the strength right from as soon as she said, "your result is positive." To carry on, to go on. I was twenty-six, soon to be twenty-seven. And so I took the subway to 23rd Street like I did today and then walked these blocks like I did today. Of course, the first time when I got the blood drawn I'd never been here but the second time I was familiar. And it's funny right now I'm seeing that soldier statue—which I don't recall from back then— which is perfect for this place as we recall fighting things in our life, and this is what I'm fighting with and that soldier with the gun in his hand is a pretty good symbol."*

Figures 2.9-2.12 Approaching the clinic: Approaching the Baumgartner District Health Center; Main entrance; Reception area; Chairs in the waiting room outside the HIV/AIDS clinic.

Approaching the clinic: *"Finally, just getting here and seeing this building—which looks like a bunker—and at the time, as now, there was a war going on against this pandemic but especially back then, there wasn't hope. To test positive was a death sentence and it was just a matter of time . . . of how much time you had. Right now I can tell you just seeing this building again really brought tears to my eyes in a way that surprised me again. Every time those feelings well up that I carry so much, I don't know . . . grief or loss . . . loss of a normal life . . . loss of maybe a long life. I really had to fight back the tears when I was looking, because this is where it all started for me. I don't want to go in closer, it's like a portal to a nightmare and I don't want to go there. It's like when you wake up from a nightmare and you don't want to go back to sleep because you're afraid of having it again: that's how I see that entrance. And I can tell you what it's like in there, I can tell you it's that off-green color and I can see the glassed-in reception booth. I feel that I am filled now with the same fear like I was that day . . . and it's like walking into that same sort of "should I or shouldn't I?" when you walk into a mausoleum or . . . . There's just memories there that are uncomfortable. Because it's here where it all changed. This was the place that was the beginning of a new chapter in my life that was at the time the beginning of the end because there wasn't . . . because when I tested positive there was no hope then . . . you could pray but then it was just a matter of luck of the draw of how long you'd have before that wasting-Kaposi's-sarcoma-covered death. I'm feeling stronger now. I feel like I've overcome my fear. I think that like any strong emotion, you need to go through it, and pass through it, and I think I did that by talking about it just now, by articulating it. This is the room. That's where I sat. I remember I sat right there by the wall. Just there. They took me into one of those little side rooms: that first room and that's where they drew the blood the first time and that's also where I was called back to collect the results, and I remember I was by myself and there wasn't anyone else in the waiting room when I got the results. The woman was very nice but matter-of-fact and she gave me more information than I needed, although I know she was just being thorough and doing her job. Information about condoms and safe sex. But when she told me the results, I couldn't hear anything else, just the scream in my head: And now what?"*

Leaving the clinic: *"All of a sudden I was part . . . . I was a person with AIDS. Back then it didn't matter, you were going to die, and so when she was telling me all these safe sex precautions I was reeling and thinking, what now? And how long? Get me out of here! I've got a lot of living to do and I actually sort of blanked out. She told me about a support group that was meeting for people with HIV/AIDS over in my neighborhood, but I remember not hearing much and just wanted to get out of the*

Figures 2.13-2.16 Returning from the clinic: Walking from the clinic; Passing liquor store on 9th Avenue; Crossing road on the way to West 23rd Street; Junction of West 23rd Street and Ninth Avenue.

room. I was drinking regularly at the time and my main thought was that I just need-ed to escape from what was reeling in my head, and back then alcohol was the easiest way. I walked in a daze and I remember I was holding back tears. And I wasn't sure what I was going to do. I was lost. I didn't know where to turn, what to do. I thought of Stephen but I also thought of the death, the wasting, the incontinence, the Kaposi's sarcoma, the purple lesions. Telling my parents. Who to tell? How to tell? When to tell? Who should know? Who needs to know? Who would want to know? I thought, even though I'm in this metropolis with hundreds of thousands of people it was just me and how I was feeling—nothing else mattered at that moment except what was going on inside my head, my heart. And of course that was all to do with what was going on in my body and that diagnosis. Did you notice that there wasn't a sign on the room? The other ones had natal clinic, immunization, but that one didn't have a sign. If I had any plans that day to do anything, they were canceled. I was wondering what to do next? Where to go? What to do? What to do at the moment? What to do with the rest of my life? Why do bad things happen on nice days? 9/11 happened on a most beautiful, clear blue sky and this happened to me on such a beautiful day too.

It was the first few days of August and this coincided with when I was hit by a car back on August 1, 1981, which was another life-changing moment. It's interesting that both these things happened in August. I don't recall much more because I really was walking in a daze. There's Night of the Living Dead. *Well, this was "Day of* the Living Dead," *because back then once you got that diagnosis, it was a terminal diagnosis—you were going to die—and by that time it was across the board: young, old, rich, poor, famous, and everyone else. Rock Hudson. I was like a horse with blinders on; the people I was passing were like cardboard cutouts. Nothing mattered to me. How they looked. Where they were going. I was just overwhelmed."*

Figures 2.17-2.20 Sushi bar: The sushi restaurant; Albert sitting at table; The counter where Albert drank sake; Arriving at West 23rd Street subway station.

Sushi bar at West 23rd Street: *"I was just walking and looking for some distraction and a way of numbing the emotions of the moment. That's pretty much how I operate now in times of stress, and back then drinking was my favorite distraction, a way of numbing and medicating emotions. I would drink to celebrate good news and to deal with bad, stressful news. Alcohol was a catalyst to bring out deeper feelings that me and my drinking buddies would share as a necessary part of my life. My heart went out to the people in the waiting room. Did you notice that they were all people of color?*

They could only have been there for one reason, the same reason I was. Though things have changed, no one wants to go there in the first place; they are as anxious, and hopeful, and scared, and fearful as I was. As I was walking to the train, I saw a sushi place and they were advertising sake and so I went in and sat at the bar, on the second chair at the end on the left. I ordered at least two of the big sake bottles and I didn't stop until I was drunk enough so that I was sure I could go on with the rest of my life. It was bizarre, the TV was going on as it is now but wasn't a flat screen. The world was going on as normal, people were eating, and I was looking out of the window at the people going by. People walking by blissfully unaware of death. I wanted to go out and tell everyone but at the same time I didn't because of the stigma. I sat and felt sorry for myself, was devising plans for how to deal with this new path. I remember the bartender asked if I was okay, if I wanted something to eat. He was probably concerned as I was just drinking, not eating. I'm sure I said I was okay, watching TV and looking distractedly out of the window. I want to say I was here for a couple of hours but it was probably not, although it was at least an hour. I was only twenty-six, and then all of a sudden I was sitting here with this diagnosis thinking I don't want to die now, I'm not ready. Life is too short to begin with, and I am given a diagnosis that might shorten my life to a matter of weeks, months. Years if I was lucky. The concept of time: plans, holidays, seasons. Our lives are sort of differentiated by these man-made markers of time. I had a birthday coming up; I was going to be twenty-seven. It reminded me how young I was. I knew I would be going back to see my parents over the Christmas holidays, but I didn't actually tell them for a couple of years."

Second Avenue and St. Mark's Place: *"I was wondering if I would see thirty and thought my goal was to see forty, which coincided with the millennium. I knew that I'd have to live each day one day at a time but I wasn't sure how, when, or if I was ready to. I waited until three years later until I actually saw a doctor. There was nothing really they could say or do at the time other than advise on diet and prescribe that poisonous drug, AZT. I wondered if there was someone I could put a face on that I thought could have infected me, wondered whether I had given it to Stephen. I sat there thinking I was too young to die, thinking about what I hadn't done, hadn't experienced, realized I needed to make decisions, to find a strategy for going on; in fact, even the getting drunk was strategic. A lot of these choices, or rather the rationale behind these choices only come in hindsight, you act first and then afterward think what brought me to that point: why did I make that choice? There's one thing I know but it's something I sometimes wish wasn't true and that is, we are what we are because of where we've been and that will always be the case. After I'd sat and drank three of those big sake bottles, I was very*

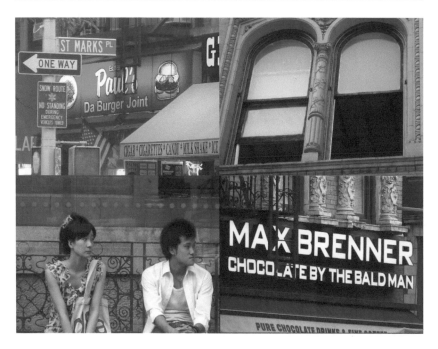

Figures 2.21-2.24 Second Avenue and St. Mark's Place: Street view; The support group; Car outside the support group; Second Avenue.

drunk but that gave me the courage to go to the support group they told me about at the clinic. One of my biggest fears was talking and speaking in groups, but the alcohol got me down there. Drinking always brought things to the surface that otherwise would have stayed repressed, that I wouldn't have the words for or time to talk about. If there was a day that I needed to share what I was feeling it was that day because I had been alone since I left my house, in the waiting room, leaving, sitting in the restaurant. I'd spent the last three hours dealing with it alone—which showed that I could—but I knew that this thing was bigger than me and that I couldn't cope with it alone. I felt that the alcohol might help me find a voice in the way that it did in other friendly, casual situations. To cross boundaries. Somehow I got myself there. I staggered up, and the meeting was already in progress, a circle of men, probably about a dozen, and a moderator. If I recall, everyone had just found out recently and so we were all in the same circumstance and sitting there, it immediately became clear that there was fear on every level: fear of living, fear of dying, fear of medication, fear of telling family, friends, fear of today, of tomorrow, and everyone had something to illustrate that. The fear permeating the room was the common denominator, which even then I understood that it was a natural reaction to a life without hope. What else could we expect from each other?"

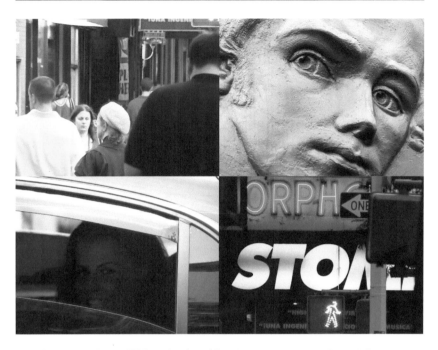

Figures 2.25-2.28 Walking back to Albert's apartment along Second Avenue.

Getting back home: *"I sat there listening, considering that I was dying, that I was going to die from this, but part of me was saying I wasn't ready to die. There were people sitting there of various ages, colors, sizes. And what my intoxicated ears heard clearly was that they were scared. They had seen the pictures, heard the stories, and were resigned to their death. Sitting amid all that caused a reaction. I reacted against it and I think I developed the fortitude and will to live there because I was so afraid of the kind of death that is shrouded in fear that I willed myself to try to find the strength or luck. Being surrounded by all of that fear, surrender to the disease, instilled a kind of defiance, a kind of resolve. I just wanted to live but I didn't want to live in fear and so I sat there for about twenty minutes. The fear people spoke about gave me a real strength and sobriety. I even began to get upset they were giving up, and realized that I didn't want to be resigned to my death. I wanted to tell everyone to stop, that they were going to kill themselves because of the fear. Someone else was about to speak and that is when I actually got up out of my seat and stood up. The moderator asked where I was going and I said I was leaving and said thank you for everything but this isn't helping me and I don't want to live my life in fear and I didn't want to die waiting to die. I said that I was going to live and walked out with a sobriety and clarity that I didn't have when I entered and held back the tears until I got back home . . ."*

GOD, ABSOLUTE TRUTH, THE COURT OF DISPASSIONATE HUMAN CONSCIENCE, AND THE PEOPLE

An HIV test is quite simple. Blood is drawn and tested for antibodies that indicate the presence or otherwise of HIV. Although it is technically possible for the results to be returned in thirty minutes, it more commonly takes up to fourteen days for the blood to be processed. Accordingly, the time between taking the test and receiving the results is a complex period of strangeness, liminality, and uncertainty whereby a person encounters the world as someone who may or may not have a terminal illness and confronts two radically different futures, which in the 1980s and 1990s, when Albert and most people in this book were tested, was seen as one of life and one of death.

A person is already a certain kind of person before taking the test, and their responses to diagnosis are informed by their individual character and temperament, together with their particular social, religious, and moral worldviews. However, it is almost impossible to sustain all values, relations, and practices following an HIV diagnosis, which marks a new social identity and existential territory whereby one's very being-in-the-world and conditions of existence are called into question. Knowledge of living with a life-threatening virus inside one's body exposes the contingency of life and undermines the possibility of engaging with the world in exactly the same way as before. Consequently, the period immediately after the test is typically one of disruption and destabilization in which the habitual world is unmade and a person not only reimagines their future but also the potentials, capacities, and contents of their body. Expectations of extended periods of ill health, social stigma, and the possibility of mortality appear to bring about substantial alterations in the aesthetic appreciation of time, body, and existence, often leading to a reappraisal of seemingly fundamental—and at times incompatible—values, dreams, and aspirations.

Diagnosis creates the circumstances for radically reevaluating one's entire mode of existence, including work, one's closest relations, and long-standing modes of being and belief, in what Jean-Paul Sartre described as a surpassing of the world, whereby a person "manages to realise the contingency of the world: that is, to raise the question, 'How does it happen that there is something rather than nothing?'" (Sartre [1943] 1996: 18). In becoming intensely conscious of the extraordinary fact of being alive and realizing life and society does not have to be the way it is, being diagnosed with HIV/AIDS also resembles what Veena Das terms a critical event (1996), that is, a rupture in life whereby people question the existing order of things and that often leads to new perspectives and forms of personal, social, and political action. Here *critical* possesses a double meaning, first in sense of being significant or important, and second in terms of engendering new critiques of established social forces and discourses of power. As a critical and collective rupture in social life, whereby people's social standing, bodily integrity, and ability to fulfill everyday tasks and responsibilities are called into question, an HIV diagnosis generates shared experiences, forms of knowledge, and new understandings concerning life's contingency and uncertainty.

In New York, this helped create the conditions whereby seemingly entrenched and established social, historical, and political structures and conventions of power were recognized as malleable and became the focal point for coordinated action whereby people affected by HIV/AIDS combined to effect social and political change through organizations such as ACT UP. Veena Das and Clara Han (2016) consider how the rights to a social and biological life among persons with AIDS, at the time Albert was diagnosed, involved a complex entanglement of identity, sexuality, and discrimination whereby the right to life and a continued social and bodily existence were not given as a human right but something that individuals and communities had to fight for. On this reading, neither life nor the social can be taken for granted; periods of social dislocation—especially when the relationship between life and ethics has broken down—provide an opportunity for new collective values to be established. Consequently, the advent of HIV/AIDS not only transformed people's individual and collective ways of being—right down to the minutiae of everyday thought and practice—but the social, biomedical, legal, and political landscape was reshaped through direct protest, the deployment of images, and by reframing popular discourse in terms of the ethics of life and death (Das and Han 2016).

At an individual level, people's responses to diagnosis, as with many other critical life events, are complex and varied socially, politically, and personally, and cannot be reduced to a single model or explanation of how people react to and negotiate life as a person with a terminal condition. In the moments immediately after diagnosis it may seem near impossible to proceed or make decisions, and yet, as Albert demonstrated, on leaving the clinic, persons are confronted by pressing concerns and dilemmas that are often privately debated while in a public social space, including the decision of whether to tell family, friends, and neighbors. By rewalking and narrating the route to and from the clinic, Albert offers us a glimpse into the shifting streams of thought, mood, and memory as they emerge into consciousness in moments of existential uncertainty and crisis.

His narrative ranges across many subjects, times, and places—from Australia to California to Mexico; from religion to art to global inequality; from his childhood to the 1980s to the millennium to an anticipated future—and poignantly captures a process whereby intense experiences, emotions, and events are remembered and reinterpreted in the process of walking. As he walks to the clinic, Albert is thinking in one instant about the inevitability of his impending demise and the wasting effects of disease on the body but just a few steps later is conjuring up images of his childhood, sees himself as an altar boy, and then attempts to bargain with the Virgin Mary to intervene and deliver salvation, indicating both the associative and dissociative character of thinking and how people continually switch between first-, second-, and third-person perspectives. The Virgin Mary becomes a key interlocutor, highlighting how inner speech often takes the form of a dialogue with others, including specific friends, family members, or individuals but is also directed toward historical figures, religious or metaphysical entities, and unknown or imagined persons. For Mikhail Bakhtin, such an audience is the *superaddressee* to whom inner expression is directed, ranging from oneself in the past, present, or future to friends, divinities, institutions, nonhuman agents, and even abstract concepts such as moral justice, emphasizing how inner speech and consciousness utilizes shared symbolic forms to work through, negotiate, and understand events and certain kinds of experience:

> Any utterance always has an addressee (of various sorts, with varying degrees of proximity, concreteness, awareness, and so forth), whose responsive understanding the author of the speech work seeks and surpasses. This is the second party (again not in the arithmetical sense). But in addition to this addressee (the second party), the author of the utterance, with a greater or lesser awareness, presupposes a higher superaddressee (third), whose understanding is presumed, either in some metaphysical distance or in distant historical time. In various ages and with various understandings of the world, this superaddressee and his ideally true responsive understanding assume various ideological expressions (God, absolute truth, the court of dispassionate human conscience, the people, the court of history, science, and so forth). . . . Each dialogue takes place as if against the background of the responsive understanding of an invisibly present third party who stands above all the participants in the dialogue (partners). (Cf. the understanding of the Fascist torture chamber or hell in Thomas Mann as absolute lack of being heard, as the absolute absence of a third party). The aforementioned

third party is not any mystical or metaphysical being (although, given a certain understanding of the world, he can be expressed as such)—he is a constitutive aspect of the whole utterance. (Bakhtin 1986: 126)

Albert constructed his narrative around certain thoughts, emotions, and dilemmas pertaining to his taking of the HIV test. It is simultaneously addressed to multiple audiences, including his past and future self, religious figures, and, as importantly, to the academic audience to which this research is directed. We are not hearing Albert's thoughts, nor a faithful representation of his inner dialogue and imagery—which as Lev Vygotsky ([1936] 1986) suggests would be liable to take an abbreviated and compressed form largely incomprehensible to others—but a performative and expressive representation that is couched in narrative and utilizes shared symbolic forms with the aim of communicating to a broad audience and shared realm of human understanding. This is not a claim for a universal subjectivity but a description of an active process through which intersubjective meanings are created between persons, in this case through the articulation of thoughts, memories, and emotions as they emerge in action while walking in the midst of significant places and buildings. This is illustrative of how thought, subjectivity, and what a person "is saying to himself" (Peirce 1998: 338) comes to life in the flow of time and combines various modalities of the self (the critical self, the persuasive self, etc.) alongside actual and imagined persons and the broader social and moral perspectives they represent.

Albert's narrative indicates how developing an anthropological approach to people's inner lifeworlds does not imply a bounded person or static dichotomy of inner-outer. In Andy Clark's model of the extended mind, he describes how the "brain-meat" of the body incorporates flows of information and feedback that continuously moves back and forth across the boundaries of brain, body, and world (Clark 2008). At all times the body is interacting with the surrounding world as smells, sights, sounds, tastes, and textures impress themselves onto the nervous system as part of a continuous dialectic with an environment—which is also modifying and transforming itself from one thing into another—emphasizing how both the perceiving organism and the world are in constant process. In this model, people's thinking and being are not contained by the boundaries of the physical body but are an emergent property of the interaction between body and world. This reinforces Karl Marx's ([1844] 1988) discussion of the effects of labor and capitalism upon the sensory body in his *Economic and philosophical manuscripts of 1844*, and also recalls Gregory

Bateson's ecological anthropology (1972), wherein persons are seen as constituted via a complex set of interactions with the environment, highlighting how inner expression is neither bounded nor fixed but continuously generated within the interaction between persons and their surroundings. This challenges any assumed opposition of inner-outer in which interiority is seen as directed "inward" and sociality "outward" and allows us to take the inner lifeworlds that writers and brain scientists show are fundamental to human life—but do not ascribe ethnographic content to—and attempt to show the process at work within a practical fieldwork context whereby the life story and emotional content emerge in situ in the very places that witnessed both the original events and their retelling.

In Albert's case, his words simultaneously combine two different experiences of walking along the same streets, separated by twenty years. The first was bathed in the intense emotions of having just been diagnosed with AIDS, followed by thoughts of suicide and a drunken public declaration about how he intended to live with the disease. The second, while retrospectively narrating the same route during a piece of performative ethnography, was shaped by the intervening events and the fieldwork encounter with myself. The resulting testimony includes various detours and shifts in time and space and describes different dangerous substances such as blood, alcohol, tears, and pills, which are intertwined with emotions such as hope, fear, defiance, and empathy.

Needham (1981) observes that there is no reliable social scientific method for distinguishing between the physiological and cultural constitution of inner states. We might extend this to argue that once people's activities are understood as whole-body experiences—which combine inner speech, mood, emotion, heart rate, lungs, muscles, and so forth—irreducible and unobservable discrepancies appear between people's expressive inner lifeworlds. This means that seemingly congruent practices and activities (e.g., working, exercising, commuting) and shared social environments (e.g., a street, forest, gym) might be radically differentiated by an inner territory that is largely uncharted by social science and remains unrepresented within ethnographic accounts. Such is the complexity and diversity of people's inner lives that two people walking down the same street might be engaged in radically different forms of inner dialogue and imagery with one person thinking about sports or what to buy for dinner, while the other is communing with God and dealing with a major life change such as having lost their job or spouse or having been diagnosed with a serious illness. The extent to which these people are engaged in the same practice remains an open question given the constitution of their internally expressed lifeworlds.

This has important epistemological implications for disciplines based on empirical evidence and reminds us how the etymology of evidence derives from *videre*, "to see," and frequently involves the construction of evidence based on visible correspondences between actions that appear superficially similar. In Geertz's (1973) reworking of Ryle's problematization of reading people's actions, he describes how a (i) blink, (ii) conspiratorial wink, and (iii) involuntary twitch of the eye that look alike, may lead the observer to the erroneous conclusion that they are witnessing the same action unless they are aware of the relationship between intentionality, action, and cultural meaning. While Geertz advocates for thick description, attention to semiotic detail, and better guesses to understand people's moral intentions and worldview, Crapanzano (1992) critiques Geertz's approach for offering little or "no understanding of the native from the native's point of view" and providing "no specifiable evidence for his attributions of intention, his assertions of subjectivity, his declarations of experience" (1992: 67). As Albert walked down the street—both at the time of the original diagnosis and during the performative recreation—external observers had no means of knowing or guessing that the person walking alongside them was pleading with the Virgin Mary to save him. *We* are made aware of his emotional lifeworld and the specific debates and dilemmas that Albert was negotiating, but these were unbeknownst to the people around him, illustrating how seemingly common collective actions, such as walking, are accompanied by diverse realms of internally represented speech and imagery that cannot be discerned through observation.

From Leonardo da Vinci, Charles Darwin, and Jean-Martin Charcot to the first anthropometric impulses of anthropologists, the attempt to classify the emotions, temperament, and character of persons based on the observation of external appearances has been of equal interest to art and science. Albert's journey makes us aware that it is not just paintings, images, and photographs that are emotionally and existentially ambiguous, but also the multiple scenes of routine everyday life—a person waiting for a train, walking along the street, or sitting in a sushi restaurant—which in our case were rendered meaningful by Albert's public and purposeful exteriorization of his interior dialogue. The articulation of his thoughts while walking to and from the clinic provides a particular declaration of experience and evidence as *voiced in action*, which adds layers of vital depth. Otherwise, such scenes of everyday life would possess certain informational and aesthetic content but would largely remain untethered from the ethnographic reality of Albert's lived experience and situated understanding of the world.

Although human beings are skilled at looking at, reading, and interpreting other persons in social life, it is by no means straightforward to discern the thoughts, intentions, and existential state of the people we encounter or work with by their external appearances alone. Nowhere is this made more explicit than in Eric Steel's documentary *The bridge* (2006). The bridge in question is the Golden Gate Bridge, where Steel and his twelve-person crew filmed the bridge for 365 days to document a year in the life of the bridge. The film captures twenty-three of the twenty-four known suicides that took place on the bridge that year, alongside numerous others who were talked down or otherwise dissuaded. The film crew managed to intervene on six occasions to prevent people jumping, but often there was little warning or indication about who was contemplating ending their life. The very first suicide captured by one of the film crew's telephoto lenses was not acting in the manner that any of the camera operators expected. He was not crying, looking agitated, or anguished or showing any extraneous signs of distress but rather was jogging and talking and laughing on his cell phone. Then all of a sudden he climbed the barrier, made the sign of the cross and leaped to his death.

Among the thousands upon thousands of inner dialogues being simultaneously articulated inside people's heads in the streets, cafes, shops, subways, offices, work-places, and domestic spaces of New York, it is reasonable to assume that a substantial proportion are rooted in people's current life situation and existential concerns. As Albert's narrative unfolds during his walk to and from the HIV test, we get to understand him as a person engaging in specific social, cultural, and religious modes of thought as they emerge in action. By publicly articulating and externalizing his stream of consciousness to an imagined readership, Albert's narrative combines both the private and public realms of experience and evokes the way that narrative often merges spontaneous thoughts, memories, and urges with ongoing and familiar forms of expression. Moreover, because fieldwork depends on people's expressive activities, data and evidence generated in the field needs to be understood in relation to the specific action being performed. For example, Albert's recollection of walking from the clinic after diagnosis was experienced and expressed in a very different way through the act of walking through places of personal significance than if we talked about the test while sitting in a café or his living room. Expression-in-action encompasses both walking in the street and sitting in the living room. Both generate valid modes of thought and recollection but also reveal how different places and types of action are responsible for producing different kinds of empirical and ethnographic data.

Because people's experiences, expressions, and understandings of the world are not fixed but emerge in the field in relation to different places and activities, then no act of recollection or description (of an event, object, situation) is anything other than a momentary expression related to a specific mode of action. We are simultaneously the subject and object of our self-directed expressions (Peirce 1998), and at times we are distant observers of our own thoughts and experiences or else find it hard to understand and make sense of our emotions, actions, and responses. This raises further questions about what counts as evidence and what ontological status we should ascribe to people's ever-changing inner lifeworlds and expressions without reducing them to static or reified dimensions of being. Researching the role of inner expression in illness and social life more generally requires a critical rethinking of the epistemological basis of anthropological knowledge and evidence not only at the level of theory but through the development of appropriate fieldwork methods and techniques that can explicitly engage with the complexity and mutability of people's thinking and being. In employing such approaches, the theoretical and documentary imperative found in anthropological analysis might productively be transformed into fieldwork techniques and ethnographically grounded modes of representation to communicate people's streams of thinking and being as emergent in action.

LAST STEPS

There is no objective, independent access to other people's thoughts and experiences. Moreover, although a person's internal expressions and lifeworlds are continuous with—and indivisible from—their public actions and expressions, they are not necessarily identical to them. Consequently, while thought and experience can be publicly expressed and externalized in linguistic, narrative form (Carr 1986; G. Becker 1997; Mattingly, Lutkehaus, and Throop 2008), it is not possible to understand people's utterances and narratives as simple representations of experience unless one adopts a misplaced commitment to referential models of language and correspondence theories of truth (Quine 1960; Berger 1982). This implies some degree of disjuncture between people's internal expressions and their outward manifestations, which may be exacerbated when considering realms of experience and action that exist beyond language. In other words, inferences and evidence derived from outward appearances and publicly available forms are not necessarily justifiable in their own terms, raising critical questions about the epistemological and evidential basis for making ethnographic claims about persons without attempting to account for their interior modes of expression.

The means through which anthropologists read and interpret other people's intentions and actions is a long-standing, often contentious, aspect of ethnographic research (Leavitt 1996; Rosen 1996; Throop 2008). The epistemological privilege frequently granted to the exterior within philosophy and social science (Johnson 1999) has allowed social theorists to claim knowledge about people by theorizing people's worldviews as being formed through the internalization and embodiment of abstract social and cultural structures, rather than providing necessary empirical evidence about the actual—and quite possibly discrepant and oppositional—content and character of people's interior expressions and practices.

For anthropology, this might be as much a question of disciplinary authority and ventriloquism (Appadurai 1988) as the erroneous—but epistemologically convenient—practice of inferring people's experiences and worldviews on the basis that they share the same social and cultural environment, say, a particular practical daily habitus, categorical identity, or social context. However, it is an act of bad faith to confuse the metaphorical abstractions used to theorize and explain people's lives and actions with the reality of their lived experiences. As Michael Jackson (1996) argues, these are metaphors of theoretical analysis and explanation, rather than determining agents, and their ontological status is not that of an empirical but explanatory kind. Indeed, following Jackson's (2013) observation that a human life cannot be reduced to the conceptual language that renders it intelligible, I would maintain it is virtually impossible to offer an empirically reliable and grounded account of the diverse combinations of inner speech, intentionality, and emotion that accompany people's public actions from theoretical or contextual analysis alone. Therefore, in attempting to bring a practical, empirical research focus to the HIV test—and more broadly to the lived quality of social life—my aim has been to engage with people's inner expressions as situated, tangible dimensions of thinking and being that emerge in action rather than regarding them as completely unknowable or subjecting them to ethnographically unsubstantiated claims.

From thinking about sex, sport, or suicide to silently commenting on other people's fashion choices, New York's streets, cafes, and public squares contain everything that life has to offer, from the trivial to the tragic. It is a *thoughtscape* that consists of the continuous streams of inner dialogue, memory, and imagination that course through the city and mediate people's engagement with their social and material surroundings. Although we ourselves are part of the surrounding thoughtscape, we are mostly unaware of the thoughts of other persons that unfold around us, insofar as "no one but ourselves can dwell in our body directly and know fully all its conscious operations but our consciousness can be experienced also by others to the extent to which they can dwell in the external workings of our mind from outside" (Polanyi 1969: 220).

It is possible, according to Michael Polanyi, to dwell in another person's expressive actions, including their linguistic and physical expressions, but not in the specificity of their embodied experience. As such, the act of codwelling with and alongside persons, whether in the field or elsewhere, does not provide access to the *Lebenswelt* or lifeworld of others but allows for modes of interaction in which shared intersubjective experience, empathy, and understanding emerge and are made possible (Throop 2010). The sharing of experience or people's proximity in time and space does not mean both parties are experiencing similar things, inhabit the same emotional or moral register, or possess commonalities in thinking and being. There are always irreducible asymmetries and differences in personal experience even among those who we are most closely attuned to such as intimate friends and family (Desjarlais and Throop 2011), including those who have gone through the shared experience of being diagnosed with a terminal illness, indicating the presence of substantial hermeneutic borders and limits between persons (Irving 2011).

It is important here to delineate a critical difference between a border and a limit (Casey 1993). Whereas a limit is an absolute that cannot be surpassed, borders (alongside thresholds, frontiers, and boundaries) have the potential to be crossed, seen across, thought beyond, or else acted upon in ways that transform and recast them. In other words, borders, be they moral, empathetic, epistemological, or phenomenological, are subject to personal action and negotiation in ways that limits are not. Persons are continually shifting perspectives and attitudes toward themselves and others, and have the capacity to change their emotional, empathetic, and intersubjective orientations (Throop 2015). The very act of attempting to reach across a hermeneutic divide during fieldwork, even if it results in failure, opens up the possibility for those small movements in perception, personhood, and understanding in which someone comes to the realization that life can be seen, felt, and known from another perspective (Sartre [1943] 1996).

Consequently, epistemological and empathetic borders, rather than simply being fixed impediments to understanding other people's embodied experiences of the world, can also open processes of critical reflection, moral questioning, and intersubjective transformation that do not presuppose a commonality of experience but produce an embodied recognition of the irreducible alterity and differences between people (Throop 2010). For example, when witnessing the graphic pain and distress of a bone-setting operation following a young girl's accident that was conducted without anesthetic by a local Micronesian healer, Jason Throop not only found himself in tears alongside the girl, her father, and the healer but questioned what right he had to be present at and document such moments of extreme suffering and pain for the purposes of anthropological knowledge. In a culture that has established moral expectations of emotional calmness and comportment, Throop's tears and his witnessing of the father and healer's emotions could have been highly problematical and embarrassing. But rather than causing social division and estrangement, the sharing of tears facilitated a shift in people's respective moral relationships and intersubjective understandings. The alterity of the girl's suffering resolutely remained beyond the limits of perception and experience, and as such was not assumable to Throop's own experience, but instead elicited its own embodied and empathetic response. In doing so, Throop's participation in an exchange of sentiment and breakdown in social and emotional conduct that is normally only shared by family members elicited a transition in personhood in which Throop was no longer purely an outsider or anthropological researcher but was incorporated into family and community.

In my case, when Albert's voice and body started welling up with emotion and tears, it was not only that I was seeing my friend suffer and relive the moment of his HIV diagnosis but that I had actively created the situation myself under the rhetoric of collaborative anthropology and a supposedly ethical, empowering approach to the coproduction of knowledge. Feeling guilty and racked with unease at the sight of Albert's emotions and tears, I called an end to our collaborative walk, but after a brief hesitation Albert insisted in continuing and recounted his personal history of how he purposefully went for his HIV test alone rather than take someone along for support as recommended. Albert explained that if his blood revealed he had HIV/AIDS he would have to face many of the consequences alone and unaccompanied. As such the test, Albert suggested, is both a medical test and a test of fortitude and oneself in the face of adversity, and thus always possesses an excess of meaning. In this it is possible to discern Albert's gentle strength of character, which is that of the grass, rather than steel, that always grows back regardless of how life treats it.

The sharing of time and space that occurred when walking alongside Albert to and from the clinic is grounded in physical, emotional, and cognitive movement, which facilitated different modes of experience, expression, and moral understanding that were not pregiven in our existing relationship but materialized and were articulated in the moment. The moving body, as the basis of perception and expression, continually establishes and transforms people's sense of the world. No two bodies embody the exact same perspective or path through time and space, and generate different personal, moral, and existential standpoints that are continually transformed by interacting with and incorporating the ideas and experiences of others.

Ideas of empathy and its relationship to the moving body are often traced back to the work of Thomas Lipps and his influential concept of *Einfühlung*: a term that was later translated and introduced into the English language as *empathy* in the early 1900s. Lipps demarked a form of empathetic and aesthetic appreciation whereby an individual is able to gain access, no matter how limited, into the subjective experience of another through a process of what he described as "inner mimesis" or *Nachahmung*, whereby we feel as though we are acting in or through a person (Reynolds 2012). In describing his experience of watching an acrobat on a trapeze wire, Lipps recounted, "I am therefore up there. I have been moved up there. Not beside the acrobat, but right there where he is" (quoted in Reynolds 2012: 127). Lipps was later criticized by Edmund Husserl's doctoral student Edith Stein—whose ideas about empathy were informed by her experience of nursing soldiers as a Red Cross volunteer in World War I—and who herself was to die in the gas chambers of Auschwitz and was later canonized as a saint. In her thesis, *On the problem of empathy* ([1917] 1989), Stein argued that there is no direct access to the subjectivity or lived experience of other persons. In the case of the acrobat, she maintains that Lipps confuses his feeling of being drawn into the other's experience with the actual experience itself. Instead of feeling what another feels, we continually fill in other people's streams of bodily experience and consciousness and project ourselves into their lives from the positionality of our own embodied—if imaginatively decentered—perspective and experience of the world (Stein [1917] 1989). Importantly, Stein observes, we are not just presented with bodies that are animated or tearful or in motion but as *persons* who appear to us as overjoyed or disconsolate or in a rush, including children, intimate friends, and family or the strangers we pass in the street.

My bodily mimesis of walking to the clinic in Albert's company rarely, if ever, accorded with Albert's own experience but nevertheless offered numerous opportunities for dialogue, reflection, and empathy in which differences between our embodied experience were articulated. Experience and action often exceed the bounds of language: nevertheless, every act is left open for comparison and interpretation. Maybe the walking body—this enacted mime—does not intentionally convey meaning, and its constitution as a source of empathy and knowledge is erroneous. Nevertheless, it has the quality of a good error that reveals the body's mimetic potential to build a comparative and empathetic—although never fully intersubjective or hermeneutic—understanding of other people's experiences where the differences between persons are not obstacles to understanding but the grounds that bring it into being.

To conclude, when I walked alongside Albert, listening to his narrative and engaging in a type of step-by-step bodily mimesis of his actions, I did not gain privileged access to his interior lifeworld, as this was beyond the limits of my intersubjective horizons. Consequently, my aim has been less to explain or analyze Albert's experience of diagnosis but instead has been an exercise akin to Trinh Minh-ha's experimental 16mm *Reassemblage* (1982) of *speaking nearby*. There were a number of occasions where I also felt deep emotions welling up and dwelled in an emotional context generated by Albert's external expressions. This suggests that although partaking in a shared activity in the field does not offer sufficient grounds to form a shared, embodied understanding of action (for example, as often argued in terms of theories of apprenticeship or mimesis), it nevertheless opens up the possibility for other types of knowledge and appreciation that do not presuppose commonality but are just as valid.

The ethnography and methodology presented here do not give direct access to Albert's lifeworld. We are not hearing Albert's thoughts in and of themselves but their verbal articulation in an explicitly performative, ethnographic context. Therefore, the ethnography and methodology do not claim to provide a comprehensive approach to the issue of interiority, and highlight the limits and irreducible alterity of other people's experiences (Levinas 1996). Instead, Albert's words offer to us a partial and fragmented understanding of how being diagnosed with AIDS is mediated by complex streams of interior dialogue, mood, and emotion—as articulated to a range of figures including himself, parents, friends, dead lovers, religious figures, and an imagined anthropological readership—and provide an empirically grounded, rather than speculative, starting point from which to explore a set of epistemological and ontological issues concerning the relationship between inner and outer expression. Although the resulting account cannot necessarily be accorded the status of objective truth or evidence, it can be regarded as a tangible, if imperiled, anthropological basis for engaging with and learning about other people's inner lives as they emerge and are lived.

Such as when traversing the ground on foot . . .

CHAPTER THREE

To live that life

Painting raises a series of questions that are unique, specific to its own history and materials. Like each of the arts, painting addresses problems about the relations between the body and the earth, between corporeal and terrestrial forces, but each does so in its own way, with its own materials, its own techniques, forms, and qualities.

—Elizabeth Grosz, *Chaos, territory, art* (2008: 70)

I am astonished that while we have such refined issues about other subjects, we are so deprived about the subject of death. We do not know how to speak of death or of colours either.

—Albert Camus, in *Albert Camus: A life* (Todd 1998: 36)

The more horrifying this world becomes (as it is these days) the more art becomes abstract, while a world at peace produces realistic art.

—Paul Klee (1915) in *The ethnographer's eye* (Grimshaw 2001: 32)

To what extent—we must ask—is it possible to grasp experiences and understandings of the body through the artworks someone makes or leaves behind? Does art offer reliable evidence about the phenomenology of time and space? How might a work of art be used to go beyond the artist's own embodied experience to think about collective modes of perception, experience, and understanding? What forms of empathy might be generated, and does this count as ethnographic knowledge? In response to such questions, my aim is to use painting, photography, and other artistic productions made by persons confronting their own mortality—including Vincent van Gogh, Dennis Potter, and artists Juan Arellano, Rebecca Guberman-Bloom, and Ricardo Morin—as a basis from which to understand people's changing perceptions and experiences of time, space, and the body. The intention is to examine the necessary conditions and limiting factors that make possible an imagined or empathetic *mutuality of the world*, that is, the sense of living and dwelling with others who experience and understand the world in a similar fashion as well as the critical differences between persons.

For Maurice Merleau-Ponty, mutuality is not pregiven by virtue of mind and body but is formed through an active process of negotiation between self and other insofar as within "the experience of dialogue, there is constituted between the other person and myself a common ground [where] my thought and his are interwoven into a single fabric" ([1945] 1992: 354). This suggests that diversity, difference, and otherness are *not* the opposite of mutuality or empathy but the conditions that bring shared understanding into being as people attempt to understand one another through language, dialogue, and interaction. The body, as the ground of perception, continuously establishes and locates the person in time and space and provides a unique point of view. As no two bodies occupy the exact same space and time or follow the same path through life, each individual person sees the world from a succession of different embodied perspectives and in relation to different life events and moral understandings. This brings mutuality into the realm of ethnography and anthropology, including how people experience and encounter the world from a range of social, moral, and political positions, that are continually being generated, tested out, and reworked through their interactions with others.

Mutualities of perception tend to be based on two prevailing epistemological approaches: those that assert commonality on the grounds of species-wide phylogenetic capacities, shared biology, and cognitive mechanisms (so, for example, the idea that we perceive color in a similar way because we have the same cognitive equipment, physiological makeup, and nervous system); and those that presuppose a common worldview by virtue of people being raised in or sharing the same social and cultural environment (say, a specific daily habitus, categorical identity, or social context whereby persons embody culturally similar ways of thinking and being or share certain moral values and worldviews). These approaches are not incommensurable and are often combined to explain how diverse cultural forms and practices can emerge from universal, phylogenetic capacities—for example, when radically different forms of being and expression are seen as deriving from the same basic needs or desires.

However, even in combination, our disciplinary and epistemological foundations are challenged by the specificity of persons with their individual biographies and idiosyncratic bodily experiences of the world. Consequently, if we are to better understand the indeterminacy and diversity of human experience, it is less a case of asserting the precedence of biological unity over cultural difference—or vice versa—than of opening a space to discuss the specificity and contingency of people's embodied being in the world. This is not to minimize the impact of social, political, and economic forces on persons, for these are often the main source of contingency, contradiction, and uncertainty in social life, and are generative of remedial and anticipatory action (Crapanzano and Jackson 2014). However, to begin speaking about lived qualities of perception and experience, we need to move beyond the universality of *anthropos* and diversity of *ethnos* (see Stocking 1992) and reinstate people into their own life histories, bodies, and imaginations—if only because the figure of the person overcomes the epistemological divide between biology and culture (or to put it another way, a person incorporates both) and offers a way of understanding human action beyond entrenched epistemological frameworks.

Mutuality, defined for present purposes in relation to material productions and artifacts, offers a framework for understanding the intersubjective basis of perception and action, as well as the critical differences between persons. Beginning with Van Gogh's iconic painting *Wheatfield with crows* (1890) and the words of playwright Dennis Potter, this chapter then considers the work of three artists I worked with: Juan Arellano, Rebecca Guberman-Bloom, and Ricardo Morin. By focusing on the relationship between the processes of artistic production and the material forms that subsequently come into being, I argue we can investigate experiences of time, space, and the body in ways that recognize their specificity and empathetic potential but do not marginalize people's embodied experiences in favor of the broader disciplinary truth claims of science and social science.

Painting uses impressionism, exaggeration, embellishment, caricature, abstraction, irony, and other distortions to convey different perceptions and understandings of the world. At the same time, it is a bodily activity that is rooted in life, limbs, hands, and eyes. Understanding the body's role in art was one of Merleau-Ponty's major concerns in his writings about Paul Cézanne. He noted how Cézanne would take 150 sittings to paint a single portrait. "Nine days out of ten all he saw around him was the wretchedness of his empirical life and of his unsuccessful attempts, the debris of an unknown celebration" (Merleau-Ponty 1994: 75). What others would call a *work* was for Cézanne an attempt, an approach toward representing the world, which like a life-story or human being is complete at every stage of its unfolding but never quite finished. Merleau-Ponty observed how evidence for Cézanne's "trouble with his eyes" could be found in the landscapes he painted and that indicated an intertwining of a specific bodily experience and the resulting painting: "The painter 'takes his body with him,' says Valéry. Indeed we cannot imagine how a mind could paint. It is by lending his body to the world that the artist changes the world into paintings. To understand these transubstantiations we must go back to the working, actual body—not the body as a chunk of space or bundle of functions but that body which is an intertwining of vision and movement" (1994: 123–24).

Vincent Crapanzano (2004) likewise considers the role of the body and movement in Chinese scroll painting, including how a painting creates a sense of temporality between artist and audience. The viewer's perception of a painting incorporates into it an understanding of process and movement—for example, in the sweep of the artist's brush strokes or the time it takes to draw something carefully or messily—so as to obtain a sense of temporality that is more readily associated with literature and music. By thinking about works of art as an outcome of the intertwining of body, vision, and movement, a key aim is to extend Merleau-Ponty's model of mutuality from an ethnographic perspective by exploring how people's embodied experiences of time and space are incorporated into artistic production and material representation.

A SERIES OF QUESTIONS

Wheatfield with crows is one the world's most instantly recognizable paintings, whose forceful, swirling brushstrokes have become synonymous with creative passion and artistic intensity. Copies circulate on book covers, t-shirts, posters, postcards, and websites. John Berger discussed the painting in his groundbreaking BBC television series and accompanying book, *Ways of seeing*, asking the reader to *look at it for a moment*.

Figure 3.1 *Wheatfield with crows,* by Vincent van Gogh, 1890. Oil on canvas.
Reproduced by permission from the Van Gogh Museum, Amsterdam.

Berger then informs the reader on the next page, "This is the last picture that Van Gogh painted before he killed himself. It is hard to define exactly how the words have changed the image but undoubtedly they have. The image now illustrates the sentence" (1972: 28). In Berger's hands, the painting not only highlights the complex intertwining of language, knowledge, and perception, but also provides a material basis for understanding the relationship between an artwork and the life circumstances of the person who produced it.

Although the exact circumstances are not known, shortly after Van Gogh painted *Wheatfield with crows,* he walked into a wheat field with a gun and shot himself in the chest. It is impossible to determine from the painting itself if there is any correlation between its subject matter and Van Gogh's suicide, or to measure what passes between the painting and the viewer's body on learning about its circumstances of production. It is the same sky and wheat fields, painted in the same colors that are sensed by the same retinal cells, and processed via the brain's same V4 visual pathway. However, it becomes almost impossible to see the painting as before because its colors and textures have become animated by the act of taking one's life and a surrounding discourse that draws heavily on the romantic correlation of suicide and the tortured genius. Once *Wheatfield's* circumstances are known, they cease to be external to its content and become part of our experience of the artwork itself. The painting takes on a deathly aura that changes our perception and imagination in ways that cannot be dismissed as irrelevant or immaterial, if only because of the complex electro-chemical and physical effects in our brains and bodies.

The perception and sensation of an image or object resides in the interaction between body and world. Research in art and neurology carried out by my colleague Dee Reynolds at the University of Manchester, as part of the *Watching dance: Kinaesthetic empathy* project, shows how the interaction between dance and its audience has a material basis by measuring the responses in audience members' nervous systems as they watch dancers on the stage (Reason and Reynolds 2010; Reynolds 2012). Building on Thomas Lipps' theory of *Einfühlung* (esthetic sympathy, feeling into, empathy), Matthew Reason, Dee Reynolds, and assembled artists and neurologists sought to understand the connection between an artwork or performance and the viewer. How do different forms of visual expression project meaning and emotion in ways that affect and transform the viewer's nervous system through a process of what Lipps called "inner-mimesis," or what might be thought of as a material basis for empathy? A dancer's movements incorporate turns, leaps, falls, a sense of balance, and much else besides. However, it is not only their body and nervous system that registers these movements but also the audience whose neural activity anticipates and mirrors what is seen on stage, much as the reader's own nervous system might wince when imagining someone running their tongue along the edge of a razor or when seeing an eye cut with a blade in Luis Buñuel and Salvador Dali's *Un chien andalou* (1929).

How curious it is then that the imagination has for so long been seen as the faculty of fancy, immateriality, and a disengaged mind rather than a fundamental part of bodily experience. And yet, if we trace back the etymology of imagination, we find that *imaginem* derives from *imato* (to copy) and *mimos* (to mime), thus evoking body and movement (Casey 1991). This suggests that the relationship between image and imagination is in part a physical, embodied phenomenon that involves the body's moving and being moved through exchanges of meaning. Just as a dance or mime possesses a "volume" that extends out from the body into the world (Irving 2007), a painting or photograph can transcend its frame by acting through the imagination and out into the world.

Viewing or being in the presence of an object closely associated with death plays on the imagination in multifarious and unexpected ways. And although people's responses to such artifacts reveal shared moral perspectives about death and dying, they also evoke diverse—and sometimes contradictory—feelings and sensations. The complex range of emotions experienced when contemplating mortality means that responses to death or dying are not reducible to generalizable social or universal factors. Instead, responses to Van Gogh's painting are best understood as partial, situational, empathetic responses to death and dying based on the existential particularity of the moment, rather than as reflections of a specific cultural anxiety or universal dread.

The painting's aura is not restricted to the original but extends out into the world through its many reproductions. However, knowing where, when, or how one first encounters widely circulating works such as *Wheatfield with crows* is difficult. Fredric Jameson (1979) draws attention to the frequent impossibility of hearing pop songs or seeing mass-produced images for the first time insofar as they are often already known and internalized prior to our conscious awareness. I have never seen *Wheatfield with crows* in its original form and cannot say, for example, when I first saw it, heard a Beatles song, saw roses on a birthday card, or encountered a photograph of the Eiffel Tower, because each had already been embodied through a thousand fragments encountered in cafés and waiting rooms, on magazine covers, and television sets, and constituted part of my being long before I consciously became aware of them. As such, my own response to the painting is formed by the way Van Gogh's works and life story circulate in popular forms and discourse, by the angst written on Kirk Douglas' face in *Lust for life* (1956), and by my own moral perspective on suicide, alongside the emotional distress I imagine Van Gogh felt on that day in July 1890.

Although the physiology of Van Gogh's body and the movement of his wrist, elbow, and arm can be clearly seen in the painting's brushstrokes, can we say the same about his psychological condition and suicidal consciousness? Can we discern Van Gogh's suicidal intentions within the artwork itself? This question is further complicated by the fact that later studies suggest the far less portentous *Daubigny's garden* and *Cottages with thatched roofs* are likely to have been his final two paintings, while *Wheatfield* may have been painted as much as ten days before Van Gogh's suicide (Hulsker 1996). However, despite this knowledge, the painting still troubles and plays upon the viewer's mind and body, leaving us to wonder to what extent the imagination is actively constructing the portent of the picture. The painting penetrates into the viewer's nervous system and elicits complex material changes in electrical and chemical activity that are not only responses to color, shape, and form but an imaginative and empathetic reconstruction of Van Gogh's lifeworld that is not so easily reversed in light of new knowledge and information.

Because we can never be certain that the imagined life and attributed meaning actually inheres in the artwork itself—i.e., the extent to which Van Gogh's suicidal consciousness is inscribed into his painting alongside the movements of his hand, wrist, and elbow—doubt and skepticism emerge about the interpretation of Van Gogh's intentions. For while the viewer's responses can be accorded an emotional, embodied, and material reality, the painting raises yet more questions about the uncertain relationship between knowledge, perception, and language rather than providing access to and evidence of Van Gogh's mental state or grounds for establishing mutual understanding.

THE TROUBLE WITH WORDS

"The trouble with words," as the playwright Dennis Potter once remarked, "is that you never know whose mouths they have been in" (1993). In doing so, Potter describes the difficulty of finding modes of expression that are not overwhelmed by cultural history and foreshadows his own struggle to articulate the relationship between perception, experience, and expression. When Melvyn Bragg interviewed Potter on live television in the spring of 1994, Potter was dying of cancer:

> Below my window, the blossom is out in full now. It's a plum tree, it looks like apple blossom but it's white, and looking at it, instead of saying, "Oh that's a nice blossom," last week looking at it through the window when I'm writing, I see it is the whitest, frothiest, blossomest blossom that there ever could be, and I can see it. Things are both more trivial than they ever were, and more important than they ever were, and the difference between the trivial and the important doesn't seem to matter. But the nowness of everything is absolutely wondrous, and if people could see that . . . . There's no way of telling you; you have to experience it, but the glory of it, if you like, the comfort of it, the reassurance. The fact is, if you see the present tense, boy do you see it! And boy can you celebrate it. (Potter 1994)

Potter's characters forged new ways of speaking. In his plays, old words yielded new meanings and provided unsurpassed insights into illness and human frailty based on his life-long experience of illness and chronic pain. In *The singing detective* (1986), the main character, Philip Marlow, is rendered immobile with skin disease—much like Potter himself was—and lies barely able to move for weeks on end in a hospital bed. Marlow's thoughts about his condition merge with memory and vivid, lifelike hallucinations, caused by his infected skin's inability to regulate body temperature. As he lies there, a succession of significant people, including childhood friends, former teachers, his parents, and ex-wife, merge with fictional characters from the detective stories he writes for a living, to produce an elaborate plot in Marlow's head. Immobile, overheated, and unable to sleep, Marlow's inner commentary and intense imagery takes the form of an existential and paranoid detective story in which life and fiction are confused and intertwine as he tries to work out who he is, who he has been, and what has happened to him and his body. The integrity of space and the linear flow of time are troubled as past, present, and future continuously weave into one another. Marlow finds himself cast adrift in a story that is only partially of his own making and endures the sense of helplessness experienced in some dream states. In one moment he is witnessing his wife's betrayal with someone he suspects is one of his own fictional characters, and in the next instance he is back at school reliving the complex emotions of having taken a shit on the teacher's desk and blaming another boy, which results in the boy being harshly beaten. Art, life, and illness—as well as time—are distorted on the screen to create a complex reality in which events held in memory may or may not have happened and different selves emerge, all or none of which Marlow thinks might be true, so as to blur the distinctions between fact and fiction—as was very much the case in Potter's own life. It is not so easy to express, let alone understand or empathize with one's own self or experience if you cannot say with any certainty who one is or what is being experienced.

In this we see another route to thinking about both the contingency and unreliability of memory, self-knowledge, and linguistic expression, including how these are transformed through instability of the body and attempts to render the flows and disjunctures of experience into comprehensible speech and language. Even Potter, whose struggle with illness familiarized him with the challenge of reclaiming meaning from bodily disorder, recognizes the impossibility of articulating and externalizing his perception of time and sense of wonder toward the end of life. Seduced by "the nowness of everything" in the days before death and knowledge of the last spring he would see, Potter finds himself near the limits of expression and declares, "There's no way of telling you; you have to experience it." Potter's forlorn attempt to describe his perception of "nowness" during his final days recalls Thomas Mann's observations on failing health, time, and illness: "Can one tell—that is to say, narrate—time, time itself, as such for its own sake? That would surely be an absurd undertaking. A story which read: Time passed, it ran on, the time flowed onward and so forth—no one in his senses could consider that a narrative. It would be as though one held a single note or chord for a whole hour, and called it music" (1999: 451).

The problem of how the linguistic self often becomes diminished when experiencing illness and pain has been well documented (Scarry 1987; Parkin 1999). Once language's capacity as a means for mediating between subjective first-person experience and objective third-person reality becomes compromised, intersubjective borders emerge between persons. To a certain extent, the person may even become distanced and alienated from their own self, body, and experience, given that intense episodes of illness or pain can undermine language and produce an unbridgeable gap between signified and signifier. As such, it is problematic to assume that people can vocalize—let alone understand or fully access—their internal states, especially during periods of illness, uncertainty, and emotional intensity.

When the expressive capacity of words is compromised, there is, on occasion, the possibility of other forms of action, including that of making art. The following artworks by persons living with HIV/AIDS do not allow us to experience the world, its colors, or material forms as their creators do. Nor do they provide answers to the questions raised so far. However, attending to the circumstances under which these artworks were produced moves us away from more general models of perception and experience toward those of situated bodily action and aesthetic appreciation. For although these artworks cannot tell us about the truths of perception, they offer an opportunity to see how time, space, and color are embedded in personal biography, bodily discrepancy, and people's material productions in the face of mortality.

COLORS ON CARDBOARD

For Juan Arellano, the days merged into one another. Too weak to sit or stand, he lay in a hospital bed for weeks, waiting, even longing, for death. Unable to eat or hold a conversation, he witnessed the overshadowing of the surrounding world and its colors by the unceasing presence and intensity of pain that had become his own world. Juan's reality was untied from reason and language, and neither medicine nor his severely weakened body formed a basis on which to build hope, meaning, or action. His existence became unstructured by pain, and the only things that unified his consciousness or held his world together were his ever-present desire for the pain to cease and his futile attempts to fight it.

In her poem "Pain has an element of blank," Emily Dickinson—trying to describe the unceasing continuity and presence of pain—wrote that pain "cannot recollect when it began" and "has no future but itself," while Drew Leder (1990) asserts that pain possesses a distinct episodic temporality. These are less epistemological contradictions than reflections of the difficulty of depicting how one experiences time while in pain, and an acknowledgment that severe pain is based not on duration but on endurance. For Juan, pain revealed the hidden viscosity of time. The awful paradox was that since his diagnosis, time had unrelentingly passed and brought him closer to death, but now time was static and no longer flowed. He willed for time to pass, willed for oblivion and the annihilation of death to bring his pain to an end. Accordingly, what Juan desired most intensely was the negation of consciousness and through it the absence of pain. For one in severe pain, it is difficult to imagine what it feels like not to be in pain, confirming that the imagination is a bodily property rather than an aspect of a disembodied mind. Here, desire and imagination become radically discontinuous insofar as "pain-consciousness is a project toward a further consciousness which would be empty of all pain; that is, to a consciousness whose contexture, whose being-there would not be painful" (Sartre [1943] 1996: 333).

After Juan had spent nearly six months in the hospital, his pain gave way to weakness and exhaustion, and the world slowly came back into view. He ventured out, picked up a piece of cardboard, and smothered it in color. Thus, the first painting he created after the months of extreme pain had abated was of simple, broad brushstrokes of various colors on rough cardboard, the first surface at hand.

Figure 3.2 *Colours on cardboard*, by Juan Arellano, circa 1997. Oil on cardboard.
Reproduced by permission from the artist.

Figure 3.3 *Tricolor man*, by Juan Arellano, circa 1997. Acrylic on canvas. *Reproduced by permission of the artist.*

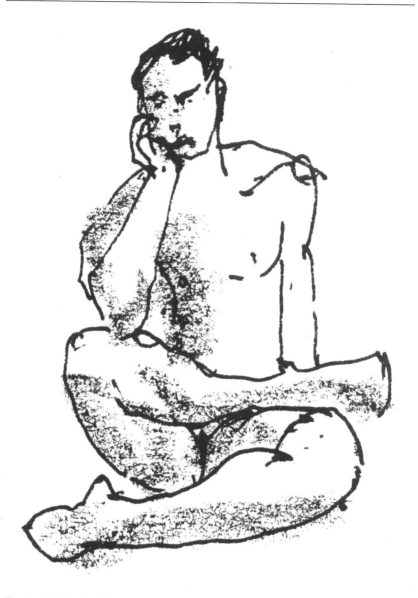

Figure 3.4 Untitled charcoal drawing by Juan Arellano, circa 1999. Charcoal on paper.
Reproduced by permission of the artist.

*From all the colors he could find, he painted the reddest of red and the yellowest of
yellow, going through whole tubes of paint. He was filled with the simple joy of there
being such a thing as color in the world—the blueness of blue, the redness of red, and*

the yellowness of yellow—for while these colors already existed, they were now no longer overshadowed by pain.

Juan remained too weak to return to work. He had trained as an architect in his native Colombia, but now he decided to fill his world with color and die as a painter. Painting consumed all his energy. He worked intensely, each painting taking him three or four hours. His illness returned, and Juan found himself back in the hospital, preparing for death once more, too weak to paint, and having to have his diapers changed by his sister. He was able only to hold a piece of charcoal and make small sketches, his world reduced to white paper, black charcoal, and grey smudge.

One's perception of color is, before all else, a way of being-in-the-world. Over the course of the 2000s, Juan's health had stabilized through medications, and he began painting again. He put on weight and regained his bodily integrity and his future. Thus, he now spends a whole month on each painting, rather than just three hours. Through Juan's drawings and paintings we can trace not only an undulating trajectory and experience of time and space but also the waxing and waning horizons of his world as encountered through his changing body.

BLOODLINES AND OTHER THINGS

Three days of blood, *an extraordinary piece by Rebecca Guberman-Bloom, uses color and its transformation to speak about things such as life, death, and the passage of time. It shows the double indeterminacy of blood, in that while blood is a substance that gives Rebecca life, it also carries a virus that threatens her existence. The piece shows how blood changes in color, consistency, and texture over time and reveals how her blood possesses a language-like quality that structures time, creates a narrative, and refers to events in the world. Like language, blood is fluid and carries irreconcilable ambiguities that tend to solidify and otherwise change in status when they leave the body to speak about things the artist never intended.* Three days of blood *not only physically inscribes HIV into the canvas (and thereby renders it harmless, as it cannot live long outside the body) but also makes aspects of Rebecca's personal biography and circumstances publicly visible.*

Rebecca was infected with HIV a few days before her eighteenth birthday by a boy who knew that he was HIV-positive but did not tell her (and who chose not to use a condom). For her, the purpose of her art is "a lot about the process of living and dying and the intensity that comes with it, much of it focuses on myself—that is, my pain and my vision." Rebecca had to see the HIV in her own blood to break down the denial she experienced after her diagnosis. Her art also uses skin and (found) dead animals;

Figure 3.5 *Three days of blood*, by Rebecca Guberman-Bloom, 1996. Copper, blood, plastic. *Reproduced by permission from the artist.*

Figure 3.6 *Blood work* (detail), by Rebecca Guberman-Bloom, 1997. Photograph. *Reproduced by permission from the artist.*

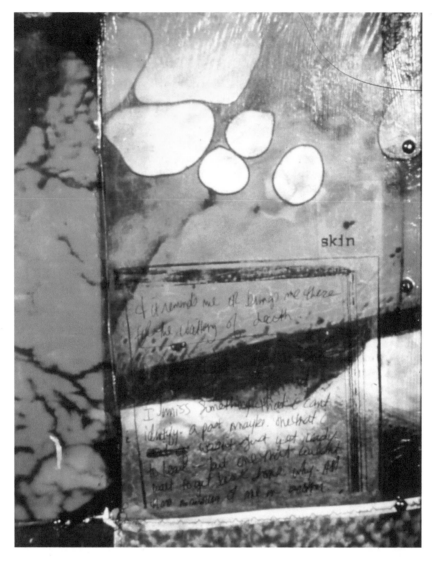

Figure 3.7 *Skin* (detail), by Rebecca Guberman-Bloom, 1997. Gel medium transfer.
Reproduced by permission from the artist.

*in many ways it is not really about AIDS but reflects the wider existential and aes-
thetic dilemmas of being an organism aware of its own mortality and continuing to
live in a world of infinite objects, possibilities, and variety.*

    *Rebecca's art reminds us that skin, like persons and social life, can be broken to
reveal blood and other things that are not immediately visible. The skin covers depths*

that are not often publicly accessible. But Rebecca uses her own skin and blood to allow us to witness both the surface and the interiority of her existence and to show just how close to the skin the ambiguity and complexity of her life is. The close link between complexity and complexion, from the Latin com, *denoting "with" or "together," and* plectare, *"to plait or twine," suggests how the complexion of a person's skin combines many stories. Although in modern usage, complexion refers to the surfaces of the body, if we trace its history beyond the past few hundred years, we find that complexion once was used to describe not only the skin but also the character and constitution of the body (Connor 2004).*

The changing colors and textures of Rebecca's blood and skin do not expose a greater truth, for probing further into the matter of her art only reveals more surfaces. We glimpse the inner surfaces of Rebecca's life through an event that she experienced as a teenager but whose formative effects remain not just in her art but in her life. When I first wrote to Rebecca in 1998, she had been living with the virus for almost ten years, and she replied by sending not words but a feather from a dead bird and the skeleton of a leaf that had had its life juice taken away but had somehow remained intact. When I asked Rebecca what her art would look like without HIV, she could not say; having lived under the shadow of the virus all her adult life, she found it difficult not only to conceive of art apart from disease and death but to imagine what life itself might consist of or be like. For Rebecca, art, death, and disease are inseparable, as in Georges Bataille's idea of water dissolved in water. For her, sex is never normal, bodies are never stable, and different shades of blood tell all sorts of stories.

OBSERVATIONS ON THE NATURE OF PERCEPTION

Ricardo Morin is originally from Venezuela. Ricardo began painting as a young child and has been a painter most of his adult life. After working as a set designer, he began teaching painting and perspective at the Manhattan Pratt Institute. Ricardo was diagnosed with HIV/AIDS in 1984 at the age of 30, and with no effective medical treatment in sight at the time, he abandoned his commercial work in set design and painting and returned to Venezuela to be with his family. His return home was based on an intense yearning to work and express himself in his "own environment" near the equator. As the virus ravaged his body, art came to be the main stabilizing factor in his life: "As my health declined and my body withered, I began a series of contemplative paintings entitled, Aposentos (Blankets). *The resulting works were exhibited to critical acclaim in Venezuela.*

Figure 3.8 *Aposentos* (Blanket 2), by Ricardo Morin, 2000. Oil on canvas. *Reproduced by permission from the artist.*

When antiretroviral medications came out, they were not freely available in Venezuela. Given an opportunity to extend his life, Ricardo returned to New York and continued to paint, although he was no longer interested in being part of the city's commercial art world. Ricardo realized that the true measure of a painter is the making of art despite the obstacles and challenges one has to endure. Ricardo was particularly motivated by the fact that there have been innumerable artists whose accomplishments did not depend on engaging with the marketplace. He was drawn to "all the great works by anonymous artists from Greek and Roman Antiquity, that were plundered, destroyed, and stigmatized during the Dark Ages," as well as Cézanne, who endured forty years of obscure labor before landing a first one-man-show, and Van Gogh, whose sublimely "outsider" creations were only recognized after his death.

For Ricardo, the term "outsider art" often denotes a prejudice toward individuals perceived to be riddled by some sort of physical or psychological health impairment. As such, both academia and the art establishment tend to divide art on the basis of its cultural import or through an underlying bias that Ricardo suggests evolves according to market demands. Another term is folkloric art, deemed to refer to the art of the colonies or the cultural heritage of a nation, which is associated with ideas of shared roots and lived experiences. "Are these terms in someway similar or different from the issues involved in art produced during the struggle over chronic or terminal disease?" Ricardo asked after reading this chapter, "and while the notion of mutuality is essential to understanding the shared human condition, can it also help to expand sensibilities about understanding human expression in an interdisciplinary scientific context, bound by the myriad circumstances that may engulf human pathos besides biology, be it in the sociological survival to fit in or as an effort to therapeutically survive a chronic or terminal disease?" Ricardo's response and analysis continued:

> *There is great intelligence in the creative efforts made by the human mind to survive any circumstance. Besides, it is undeniable that bodily pain and mental pain are ubiquitous in life, be it one of privilege or alienation. The logical concepts of cognitive science with averages, classifications, and algorithms will serve no other purpose than to provide a mere approximation to understanding the complexity of human expression, its diversity, heterogeneity, and inenarrable nature. Can we really come to understand the ways in which different modes of inner expression—such as people's ongoing interior dialogues, unarticulated moods, imaginative lifeworlds, and emotional reveries—if they remain hidden beneath the surface of public activities, hence hidden from research? Ultimately, that which is mystical about the cycle of life and death may not be elucidated by a tactical approach, but through a profound introspection that is very difficult to articulate.*

In 2008, Ricardo was diagnosed with Non-Hodgkin Lymphoma, a cancer associated with AIDS that affects white blood cells and can emerge when the immune system is weakened for prolonged periods. Throughout his illness, chemotherapy treatment,

Figure 3.9 *Self-portrait in a chair*, by Ricardo Morin, 1998. Oil on canvas. *Reproduced by permission from the artist.*

and convalescence, Ricardo spent many months sitting in silence in his chair. Beds and chairs are often dynamic sites of thought, expression, and memory for people living with an extended periods of illness, whose thinking ranges freely across the past, present, and future. People remain thinking and speaking beings even when lying or seated in silence for long periods and may be negotiating critical issues, dilemmas, and decisions regarding treatment, work, or faith and be engaged in emergent streams of interior dialogue, thought, and emotion.

It was during this state, which Ricardo describes as one of "high inertia" that he came to recognize the simplicity, power, and aesthetics of silence, especially "when compared with all the noise and visual cacophony of the tangible world at large." Of course, a silence is never simply a silence. Different days are mediated by different silences; an uncertain silence, a good silence, a heroic silence, a surreal silence, a painful silence. A silence can contain the faces of the people closest to you, thoughts of suicide, images of the world outside, daydreams, and future-orientated life projects. After months of dwelling in silence, Ricardo wrote a "Manifesto of silence" to help him think through and articulate his thoughts. It begins as follows:

> *The verbalization of an aesthetic reality implies its own death; no matter how precise, the very accuracy of words resists the magnitude of that reality. It is found in the open space of silence, in the virtuous stillness of a meditative contemplation, in the freedom itself of the known, free to observe with a heightened attention, where questions are unnecessary and responses trivialize the very observation.*

Figure 3.10 – 3.12 *Silence 6; Silence 8; Silence 9,* by Ricardo Morin, 2012. Oil on linen. *Reproduced by permission from the artist.*

After finishing the chemotherapy, Ricardo came down with severe tendonitis, which meant he no longer had the requisite strength to stretch canvases in order to paint. Consequently, when he started painting again he did so on hanging scrolls. Ricardo came to understand the scroll material and how it behaved in its simplest of terms and in relation to his own physical limitations. Between 2009 and 2010, Ricardo started to work on a scroll series called Metaphors of silence, *in which "it was this incidental simplicity of the medium of scrolls and my empathy for the nature of silence that produced the subject matter."*

SPEAKING OF LIFE

It remains an open question whether these artworks would exist without the artists' HIV diagnoses or the subsequent effects of the disease on their lives and social relations. Would Juan have abandoned his career as an architect and painted colors on cardboard had it not been for those weeks lying on what he thought was his deathbed? Would Rebecca have used her own blood in her paintings or been curious enough to magnify her skin and make art out of the viruses inside her body? Would Ricardo have painted his scrolls of silence had he not spent weeks sitting in a state of inertia and then come down with tendonitis? At the very minimum we can say there is an experiential affinity between Juan's, Rebecca's, and Ricardo's lives with HIV/AIDS and their art. The very existence of the paintings and photographs offers a route to the uncertainties of living with an unstable and immune-compromised body, even if the path remains fraught with epistemological obstacles. Just as important are the discursive and aesthetic influences on Juan's, Rebecca's, and Ricardo's works, although it is difficult to establish with any precision how these are realized within each artwork. This leaves the existence of the artwork itself and its bodily production at a specific point in the person's life history and illness trajectory, so as offer a material basis from which to discuss how the world is transformed by contingent life events, bodily instability, and existential uncertainty.

This shift in emphasis, from understanding an artwork through discourse and signification to understanding it through the constant transformations of the body, opens up a space for us to speak about the empathetic and aesthetic appreciation of phenomena—such as time and space, the color of blood, language, and also silence—and gain a brief insight into the lifeworlds of people who have been diagnosed with a terminal condition. For example, Rebecca's work speaks about the ambivalence of a young woman whose red blood contains traces of both life and death. Juan's colors, painted on the first surface he could lay his hands on—followed by his black and white sketches—reveal how the world continually expands and contracts with an unstable body. Ricardo's precise attention to the qualities of silence emerged out of an enforced stillness and extended convalescence in his chair.

Although each artwork's aesthetic and material qualities are explicable in terms of how the brain's pathways respond to certain frequencies of color and light, or in relation to cultural theory, art history, and symbolism, these remain fairly lifeless explanations unless the person's embodied experiences and existential circumstances are incorporated into them. Images do not exist independently of a perceiving body and accompanying lifeworld constituted through experience, emotion, and aesthetic sensibility. At this point, computational models that attempt to map perception onto the brain's cognitive processes begin to lose their empirical and explanatory hold, as highlighted by Paul Churchland's claim to have found "an effective means of expressing the allegedly inexpressible":

> The "ineffable" pink of one's current visual sensation may be richly and precisely expressed as a 95Hz/80Hz/80Hz "chord" in the relevant triune cortical system. The "unconveyable" taste sensation produced by the fabled Australian health tonic Vegemite might be poignantly conveyed as a 85/80/90/15 "chord" in one's four-channelled gustatory system. . . . And the "indescribable" olfactory sensation produced by a newly opened rose might be quite accurately described as a 95/35/10/80/60/55 "chord" in some six-dimensional space within one's olfactory bulb. (Churchland 1989: 106)

It is not that such descriptions are necessarily wrong but by reducing perception—and by implication the person—to the physiological mechanisms involved in producing sensations, they largely reinscribe the long-standing division between the theoretical explanation of a phenomenon and its realization in sensate experience. Such descriptions of experience do not traverse the divide between descriptive and inductive meaning or link the certain to the probable, which is necessary for understanding the relationship between the brain's physical processes and the phenomenological experiences they produce. Nor do they account for how meaning is generated between persons (Hollan and Throop

2008) or artist and audience (Sartre [1940] 2004). Thus, rather than being the "rich" or "precise" expressions of sensory experience that are claimed, we learn little about how the world is seen, sensed, and experienced by living, sensory beings, especially as there is little recourse to shared experience when the bodies and circumstances compared are so radically unstable or in pain.

The inherent problem of reducing perception and knowledge to the mechanisms of cognitive processes has been extensively critiqued, most famously in Thomas Nagel's "What it is like to be a bat" (1974). Consider also Frank Jackson's classic article, "What Mary didn't know" (1986), in which an imagined scientist called Mary knows "all there is to know" about the neurology and physics of visual perception but was raised in a black-and-white room. Although Mary has complete scientific knowledge at her fingertips, when she leaves the room she is unable to tell the difference between red and blue because it turns out, "Mary does not know all there is to know. For when she is let out of the black-and-white room or given a colour television, she will learn what it is like to see something red" (F. Jackson, 1986: 291).

If Jackson is right (although see Churchland's 2004 response), then Mary will learn and experience something new when she encounters the red of "ripe tomatoes" and the "blue of the sky" for the first time. In other words, there remains an unbridgeable gap between subjective first-person experience and independent third-person knowledge—at least in terms of current technology—and access to experience can only be achieved via public signs and representations, such as language, self-reporting, and brain imaging, which are necessarily subject to interpretation and are thus neither neutral nor objective. Recent technological developments mean the scenario of "looking inside someone's head" has progressed from MRI (magnetic resonance imaging), which takes static images of the brain's gross anatomy, to seeing the brain at work through fMRI (functional magnetic resonance imaging), where changes in neural activity can be measured while a person is engaged in an activity. Although this shift in focus from *brain anatomy* to *brain activity* offers astonishing images and unparalleled insights into the brain's functioning, it still does not give us access to perceptual states or experience; instead, it offers representations of neural activity that need to be decoded and interpreted.

Models of cognitive functioning are a vital part of the story of perception—as are social and cultural theory—but if we are to tell the story of Juan, Rebecca, and Ricardo, we need to recognize their theoretical, explanatory, and hermeneutic limits and direct ethnographic attention toward the phenomenology of lived experience, including how people's perceptions of the world are differentiated through specific bodily biographies and existential circumstances. We can use the artworks in this chapter to discuss how time, space, objects, and colors are perceived and experienced in different ways in relation to people's specific life histories and circumstances, which can be no more reduced to the mechanics of perception than those of social identity and cultural habitus. The red of Rebecca's blood, the silence of Ricardo's paintings, and the lines of Juan's charcoal sketches each have a material presence but were made and arise out of a particular set of bodily experiences and understandings that cannot be easily elided or averaged out.

The idiosyncratic—as opposed to normative—character of perception is described in John Berger's collaborative exercise in storytelling *A fortunate man*, which was carried out in 1967 with an English country doctor, Doctor John Sassall, and the photographer Jean Mohr. The project documents Dr. Sassall on his daily rounds in rural England. At one point, Berger describes how there is a particular "bend in the river which often reminds the doctor of his failure" whenever he drives past it (1997: 23). The bend in the river possesses no shared, fixed, or social meaning that equates bend with failure, thereby opening up the possibility of a type of free play of signification and association that liberates perception and experience from overdeterminations of commonality based on shared social context or biological heritage.

Depending on the person, it might be a certain quality of light, turn in the weather, shade of green, or shape of a building that calls to mind his or her regret over a particular word spoken out of turn, a failed dream, or an unfinished conversation. As such, substance, shape, and color enter into a world of imaginative possibility and variety generated by the free play of imaginative signification that is not reducible to shared perceptual mechanics or cultural symbolism. No act of perception (of red) or interpretation (of a red painting) is anything other than momentary; further, they remain time-bound. The redness of blood is collectively perceived, and certain interpretations may be shared, but its redness is also inhabited and experienced in particular moments of being and imagination, as in Rebecca's many conceptions of what it means to live with infected blood for all of one's adult life. The lack of color in Juan's charcoal drawings testifies to a world in which time, space, and the movement of the body are called into question. Ricardo's chair is inhabited in the form of bodily feelings and associations rooted in Ricardo's lived experience and personal philosophy whose validity is equal to canonized interpretations of stillness and silence.

The colors, silences, and subjects of these artworks can never be pure, for they are too contaminated by disease, emotion, and imagination for the purposes of cognitive science and are too intertwined with specific personal biography and situation to represent shared cultural meanings. Different shades of red tell a thousand different stories of blood, death, and disease but when painted next to yellow and blue on a piece of cardboard, can convey a day without pain. Objects, colors, and textures are not always what they appear to be and often contain secret shades found in people's biographies, situations, and imaginations: "We must invent the heart of things if we wish one day to discover it," Audiberti informs us of milk, in speaking of its secret blackness. But for Jules Renard, milk is hopelessly white, since it is only what it seems to be" (Sartre, quoted in Bachelard 1971: 8). The perception and resonance of things is located as much in the conditions under which substances, objects, and colors are imagined, made, and unmade—including the challenge of producing art while sick—as in the finished artifacts and artworks themselves. This is the idea of meaning as embedded in life, purpose, invention, and imagination, and although it reveals little about scientific or social scientific truths, it says much about being a person whose existence is compromised and who finds purpose in creating art in the face of pain, silence, or mortality.

ENDING: TO SEE THE SKY

Fieldwork—like art and painting—is something made: a sensory-aesthetic activity of the body that involves perception, imagination, and communication. Art can also be used in fieldwork to create dialogues between people. When I showed copies of artworks made by Juan, Rebecca, and Ricardo to other HIV+ persons I had been working with in Kampala, Uganda, my aim was to create a cross-cultural discussion about living with HIV/AIDS. In April 2001, when I visited Harriet Nabesse—a twenty-three-year-old HIV+ Ugandan artist—with a new set of artworks, her health had radically deteriorated since the last time I saw her. She was clinging to life and was too weak to look at art. Her appearance suggested that nothing but pain and suffering lay beneath her sunken eyes and her diseased and blemished skin. The room was small and dark as I sat there with her. From her bed and my chair, we both looked through a small window at the fading yellow paint of a colonial bungalow—the same one where she and her grandfather had lived when she was a child—whose walls were set against a blue equatorial sky. Although she could barely move her body, lift her head from the pillow, or form coherent sentences, she still wanted to talk about what the world meant to her and make sense of the things around her. She wanted to talk but she was too weak, and so I said I would come to see her the next day. When I arrived the following day, I found a fire burning outside her home, a sign that she had died in the night.

I do not know what Harriet saw as I sat with her in those final hours—as she looked at her childhood home and the sky—any more than I know what was going on inside Van Gogh's head when he painted the swirling skies filled with crows above the wheat fields. I cannot name or imagine the things Harriet felt as she gazed at her grandfather's yellow house and the blue that stretched above. But as an act of looking, it reminded me of Dennis Potter staring out of his window at inexpressibly white blossoms while dying as well as the last days of a personal friend of mine, Will F. Willis, who died of HIV/AIDS the same spring of 1994 that Potter succumbed to cancer. Will was an enthusiastic amateur painter and the paintings he created shortly before he died resonated with a life and intensity that was absent from his earlier work. His last and best painting was of yellow daffodils outlined against a blue and purple sky, painted in the explicit knowledge that this was the last time he would see spring.

Figure 3.13 Wall of Harriet Nabesse's grandfather's house. *Photographs by the author.*

Figure 3.14 *Untitled*, by Will F. Willis, 1994. Oil on canvas.

Will, Harriet, and Dennis Potter each had access to the sky, which became central to their experience of dying during their last days. In some ways it was the same sky, but it was also a sky mediated by different life stories, emotions, and aspirations, and moral worldviews about illness and whatever is imagined to exist after death, which is something that resonates with accounts of soldiers looking skyward during World War I:

> The Western front's interminable trench warfare created a bewildering landscape of indistinguishable, shadowy shapes, illuminated by lightning flashes of blinding intensity, and then obscured by phantasmagoric, often gas-induced haze. The effect was even more visually disorienting than those produced by such nineteenth-century technical innovations as the railroad, the camera or the cinema. When all that the soldier could see was the sky above and the mud below, the traditional reliance on visual evidence for survival could no longer be easily maintained. . . . Escape was provided by focussing on the one thing that remained visible from the trenches, at least when the gas or smoke was not interfering: the boundless sky, whose dreamy beauty could be ironically juxtaposed to the brutal reality of earthly combat. (Jay 1991: 15–16)

The common act of looking at the sky in the face of mortality (Leed 1979) brings people together in mutual appreciation while simultaneously emphasizing the empathetic and hermeneutic borders that exist between them, thereby challenging Merleau-Ponty's assertion that a common ground is constituted through dialogue, where thought is "interwoven into a single fabric." Instead of a common ground of meaning, we must recognize the experiential and biographical diversity of persons and their idiosyncratic, bodily constructions of the world. Such differences mean that although blossom, skies, and colors possess mutually defined cultural meanings and are processed by shared cognitive mechanisms, our theories and measures are sometimes too static to capture the ways that people experience and encounter the world; they are not grounds on which to assert the unity of perception, given the extent to which people's subjective experiences are differentiated by individual excess and radical otherness.

I would argue that such borders and limits are not barriers to understanding but are instead a rich source of knowledge about people's experiences of illness, insofar as they mark the beginning of other forms of aesthetic appreciation, empathy, and tacit understanding. The limits of intersubjectivity and objectivity demand a recognition of the radical alterity and excess of other people's experiences (Levinas 1996). By allowing certain experiences to remain theoretically and scientifically underdetermined, a type of knowledge and appreciation is created that cannot be fully defined in terms of mutuality, intersubjective understanding, or objective truth, but nevertheless offers a basis for engaging with the experiences of other people. And it is perhaps the sharing of life and the recognition of alterity in these moments that allow the colors of art to resonate most vibrantly.

It is important to resist the temptation to make this existential alterity known by reducing it to theories of perception, cognition, and context. Instead, the colors and textures of art demand to be aligned to personal biography, the creativity of the imagination, and the struggle to produce art and reclaim meaning in the face of disease, decline, and death. This elicits a recognition of both our shared humanity and the radical differences between persons. We may not be able to prove or deny the theories of perception, but by attending to the circumstances under which color and art are made, we can recognize people's aesthetic appreciation of the world as mediated by their situated circumstances. For while these artworks do not tell us about the truths of different disciplines, they present to us an opportunity to begin speaking about lived relations of the body to perception, including that of color, pain, and silence.

CHAPTER FOUR

Rethinking anthropology from a pragmatic point of view

When I enter most intimately into what I call myself, I always stumble on some particular perception or other, of heat or cold, light or shade, love or hatred, pain or pleasure. I never catch myself at any time without a perception, and never can observe anything but the perception. . . . The mind is a kind of theatre, where several perceptions successively make their appearance; pass, re-pass, glide away, and mingle in an infinite variety of postures and situations. There is properly no simplicity in it at one time, nor identity in difference; whatever natural propension we may have to imagine that simplicity and identity.

—David Hume, *A treatise of human nature* (1739: 252–53)

One thing is sure—human consciousness is seldom stable. At one extreme, our thoughts are idle, arbitrary, distracted, and diffuse; at the other extreme, we become conceptually fixated, obsessed, abstracted, and single-minded. We can be lost to the world one moment, and the next wholly engaged in a task at hand.

—Michael Jackson, "Afterword" (2015: 294)

I'm mapping myself or attempting to show you how my "self" is mapped on the streets of San Francisco. But mapping my life with its never-ending string of melodrama is, at best, an impossible task. . . . So let's just look through one window and see where it takes us.

—Kim Nicolini, "The streets of San Francisco: A personal geography" (1998: 79)

"Anthropology is philosophy with the people in" (Ingold 1992: 696), in that it addresses fundamental questions about human existence—such as those relating to knowledge, language, religion, art, ethics, life, and death—but does so by grounding these in the lived experiences and practical activities of people living in different societies and cultures across the world. Anthropology can also be understood as a *fieldwork science/documentary art* (Davis 2000) insofar as it employs practical research methods in the field to generate new knowledge about social and cultural life, and then uses written texts—and to a lesser extent images, objects, and recordings—to communicate its theories and findings.

One of the earliest considerations of anthropology, both as a philosophical and practical discipline, was Immanuel Kant's course on anthropology, which he taught for twenty-three continuous years from 1772 until 1796. Anthropology was a new field at the time and Kant's course and subsequent book, *Anthropology: From a pragmatic point of view* ([1798] 2006) was one of the first attempts at developing a systematic, anthropological approach to the study of human beings. Kant, who was famously awoken from his "dogmatic slumber" by the radical empiricism of David Hume, saw anthropology as a means for understanding the basis of people's thoughts and actions, given our status as unfinished, mortal beings with incomplete knowledge about ourselves, other people, and the world. Although Kant's anthropology mostly remained a way of observing and theorizing people's actions—as opposed to a fieldwork science in the modern sense—Keith Hart (2008–9, 2010) and Michael Fischer (2009) have forcefully argued it has much to offer today's discipline, insofar as Kant not only attempted to devise a practical and empirical approach to understanding humanity at a time of rapid social change but also sought a method for integrating individual subjectivity with the moral construction of the world.

For Kant, the sense of self or "I" is part perception and part constructed representation: a synthesis that comes into being through speech, language, and action. A person's self-consciousness and subjectivity therefore do not have preexisting form or given content but emerge and are defined in the moment through their practical activities, social relations, and surroundings. Although consciousness is divided in its operations, it is unitary at the level of the person insofar as "the fact that the human being can have the 'I' in his representations" makes him a person who "through all changes that happen to him, [is] one and the same person" (Kant [1798] 2006: 15). By drawing on Kant's conceptualization of the self and rethinking his anthropological project in terms of its ethnographic implications, my aim is to develop a practical means to explore and understand the immediacy of HIV/AIDS as it is lived by considering how subjectivity, experience, and memory emerge as part of people's ongoing engagement with familiar surroundings.

A NEW KIND OF QUESTION: AN ONTOLOGY OF THE PRESENT

Kant's interest in devising a systematic, scientific, and humanistic anthropology grew out of a "fundamental concern of the European Enlightenment, being conceived as an alternative to the theological understanding of the nature of man, and born of the belief that the proper study of mankind is man, not God" (Kuehn 2006: vii). Anthropology, while closely related to Kant's philosophical project, was its own discipline that studied how humans act in their everyday lives and used empirical observations of social life and practice—alongside knowledge about human beings derived from sources such as literature, biographies, world history, plays, poetry, and travel accounts of other cultures—all of which Kant saw as valid—in order to define anthropology:

> A doctrine of knowledge of the human being, systematically formulated
> (anthropology), can exist either in a physiological or in a pragmatic point of
> view.—Physiological knowledge of the human being concerns the investigation
> of what *nature* makes of the human being; pragmatic, the investigation of what
> *he* as a free-acting being makes of himself, or can and should make of himself.
> (Kant [1798] 2006: xx)

Kant's commitment to a practical and empirical understanding of humanity meant avoiding "futile inquiries as to the manner in which bodily organs are connected with thought" (Kant, quoted in Wood 1999: 197) and other deterministic or physiological explanations of human nature, which he regarded as simplistic and untenable. Instead, Kant intended for his anthropology to be "knowledge of the world" (*Weltkenntnis*), grounded in participation (*mitgespielt*) that stood apart from scholastic or speculative knowledge, which he saw as mere intellectual play unless grounded in practical experience and action.

For Kant, a fundamental obstacle to the development of a new anthropological science of humanity was how to account for the relationship between the subjective and moral constitution of the person—or following Augustine, what he ascribed to the *sensus interior*—and the public realm of people's observable routines and actions that comprise collective social life, namely the *sensus communis*. Accordingly, Kant's *Anthropology: From a pragmatic point of view* is organized into two parts:

> Part one: "Anthropological didactic: On the way of cognising the interior as well as the exterior of the human being."
> Part two: "Anthropological characteristic: On the way of cognising the interior of the human being from the exterior."

By organizing the anthropological project along the lines of interiority and exteriority, Kant highlighted the epistemological and practical difficulties of how to read, observe, and understand people's social actions, including how to relate people's subjective perceptions and experiences to their public and communal activities. It is telling that today—over two hundred years since Kant attempted to devise a means of observing and theorizing the human subject in action—a major problem persists for anthropologists carrying out fieldwork: how to understand and theorize other people's intentions, actions, and practices. The existence of a subjective, interior lifeworld beyond third-party observation and knowledge is a tangible but ultimately unobservable presence in the field. At times, people's internally represented thoughts and expressions might be diametrically opposed to their observable public expressions—an experience no doubt familiar to many anthropologists in the field and their own social lives—recalling Jane Austen's high-spirited heroine Emma, who "denied none of it aloud, and agreed to none of it in private" (1833: 315), undermining the evidential grounds for making truth claims based on the observation and interpretation of extrinsic forms, including language and action.

Kant's own approach considered the five senses of sight, sound, touch, taste, and smell; the cognitive faculties of imagination, fantasy, and memory; as well as the differences between ethnicities, the sexes, and different nations. This required him to establish epistemological and evidential grounds for making claims about people's perceptions and moral understandings—including how these might be deduced from the detailed observation of one's own and other people's daily practices—leaving him with the thorny and ultimately unresolved problem of how to relate "the interior of the human being" to those forms of extrinsic expression that are apparent to the eye and ear and that make social life open to anthropological observation and theorization.

Kant freely acknowledged that his own attempt at developing a reliable method of anthropological observation was limited, noting how self-consciousness and awareness, as potential accompaniments of action, mean people behave differently and are influenced by the act of observation—making analysis and interpretation problematic—and how the observer can never fully participate in any social situation if they are simultaneously observing and analyzing it. For Kant, the problem is exacerbated because, he argues, there is no objective understanding of, or unmediated access to, one's own consciousness insofar as when someone observes "his inner self [he] can only recognise himself as he appears to himself, not as he absolutely is" (Kant [1798] 2006: 30). Kant regards the modes of self-knowledge and understanding that derive from introspection and the *sensus interior* as unreliable and subject to self-deception and lies and an insufficient basis for establishing knowledge about oneself, other people, and the world. Not only are we subject to what Kant terms "internal illusions" and are "psychologically opaque" to ourselves (Wood 2003) but also we are inherently untrustworthy narrators who are constrained by the limits of perception and self-understanding. As such, Kant outlines the partial and provisional grounds of knowledge and offers a critique of naive empiricism while reinforcing how knowledge and understanding are formed through our practical and moral interactions among others or "acting in or having a world" (*Welt haben*).

In his *Introduction to logic*, Kant summarizes his approach in the form of four questions:

What can I know?
What should I do?
What can I hope for?
What is a Human Being?

In response, Kant suggests:

What can I know? is answered in the realm of metaphysics.
What should I do? is answered in the realm of ethics.
What can I hope for? is answered in the realm of religion.
What is a Human Being? is answered in the realm of anthropology.

Kant then went on to argue that, in fact, *all four questions* pertain to anthropology because "in reality . . . all these might be reckoned under anthropology, since the first three questions refer to the last" (Kant [1800] 1963: 15). Such is Kant's interest in trying to understand what "nature makes of the human being," and how persons, as free-acting beings, act in society, that it is "difficult to find a text [of his] completely free of anthropological observation" (Jacobs and Kain 2003: 1). Rather than seeing human nature as something fixed and predetermined, Kant saw it as "an evolving and emergent combination of technical, pragmatic and moral predispositions" (Fischer 2009: 220).

It is telling that Michel Foucault wrote and successfully defended his secondary doctoral thesis on Kant's *Anthropology: From a pragmatic point of view* in 1961, and translated the text into French for publication in 1964. Foucault argues that Kant is formulating a new model of human nature that is not fixed or determined by immutable essences but something enacted and produced in practice and thus part of historical process in which humankind retains a capacity to change itself. For Kant, human nature is not a state but an *activity* that is emergent, in process, and bound up with the use of language and practical and moral action. By suggesting that human nature is emergent and open to intervention, action, and agency, Foucault argues that Kant was developing a radical new inquiry into an "ontology of the present, and ontology of ourselves" (Foucault 1994: 148) and was asking a completely different kind of question from anything that had been asked before, namely: "The question of the present, the question of what is happening now; What is happening today? What is happening now? And what is this 'now' within which all of us find ourselves; and who defines the moment at which I am writing" (Foucault 1994: 139)?

This is not the kind of question that could be found in Descartes, for example—who Kant criticized because his model implies an observer who stands outside of nature, rather than an actor situated within it (Kant [1798] 2006)—but instead directly relates to how (i) perception and understanding of the world is constituted in the moment through process and action, and (ii) how elements of the present are recognized, distinguished, and deciphered (among others) in order to form our lived experience of the present and make it open to action, intervention, and reflection, which led Foucault to suggest that Kant's inquiry revolves around the question, "What precisely, then, is this present to which I belong?" (Foucault 1994: 140).

ADVENTURES IN NEW YORK CITY

The following section attempts to bring to life the experience and immediacy of living with HIV/AIDS, and uses collaborative ethnography to explore and understand the complex layers of thought, experience, and memory that constitute one's local neighborhood and surroundings: in this case, New York's Lower East Side. The intention is to create an ethnographic context for understanding the sense of self and subjective realms of emotion and memory that emerge in the moment when passing personal landmarks, familiar buildings, and shared public spaces. In particular, I am interested in understanding the relationship between the materiality of the city and the layers of "deep" memory that can be found in the minds and bodies of New York's citizens.

The method combines movement, performance, and photography and draws on the work of artist Jean Cocteau, anthropologist Jean Rouch, and sociologist Edgar Morin in order to investigate how experiences of urban space are mediated by complex trajectories of thought, memory, and expression that emerge in response to material surroundings. The use of performance and photography to document the social life of urban space stretches at least as far back as Pablo Picasso's walking tour of Paris, as staged and photographed by Jean Cocteau during World War I, on August 12, 1916. Since then, the combination of performance, imagery, and the psychological life of the city has found expression in numerous documentary, academic, and artistic forms, from the films of Guy Debord to those of Chantal Akerman and Patrick Keiller. Particularly relevant is Kim Nicolini's attempt to "map" herself onto the streets of her native San Francisco in order to identify and explore certain fractures and moments of transformation in her personal history where her life was subject to disruption, defamiliarization, or reflection, only to find that "mapping my life with its never-ending string of melodrama is, at best, an impossible task" (1998: 79).

Arguably, the most complete anthropological realization is Rouch and Morin's film, *Chronicle of a summer* (1960). The newly developed technology of synchronous sound together with Michel Brault's transformation of film praxis through the "walking camera method" opened up a series of new creative possibilities for experimenting with movement and narration (Henley 2009). Rouch and Morin combined participatory film techniques, performance, and improvisation in order to reveal but also generate truths about their subjects that would otherwise remain unarticulated. Such truths often emerged through the *rencontre*—the random, unexpected encounter between persons, places, and objects— which Rouch actively employed to bring out and make observable and filmable the realms of thought, emotion, memory, and imaginative possibility that are inherent within people's life situation and circumstances (Henley 2009). Rouch's extensive use of improvisation, spontaneity, and happenstance throughout his film practice recalls Susanne Langer's idea that "most new discoveries are suddenly seen things that were always there" ([1941] 1979: 8). Or as Paul Henley argues, Rouch's use of *rencontre* is not predicated on chance alone but also on hope, desire, and an existential openness whereby persons, sometimes unknown to themselves, might already be searching for something and respond positively to opportunities made possible by encounters with new persons and places.

In a famous scene in *Chronicle of a summer*, Rouch and Morin filmed a young Jewish woman, Marceline Rosenberg, as she walked around Paris some fifteen years after the city's occupation by the Nazis. The scene begins as Marceline is walking alone across the Place de la Concord while talking into a tape recorder hidden in her raincoat. The scene was filmed from a camera mounted on a Citroen 2CV, which was pushed rather than driven so as to minimize noise and to create a mobile dolly (see Henley 2009). As Marceline walks, she speaks the stream of her thoughts out loud until she decides to enter a deserted market building, Les Halles, where she looks up toward the roof and begins describing how she was arrested as a fifteen-year-old girl by the Gestapo and deported to the concentration camp at Birkenau. In the same way that Camus once described a man on his way to the guillotine, noticing the laces on his executioner's shoes amid the intensity of a moment overshadowed by death, Marceline notices the heavy iron girders in the roof of Les Halles, which remind her of the iron girders that hung overhead in the train station on the day she was deported to Birkenau. Marceline begins to talk about the moment that she and her father saw each other for the last time. In looking at the deserted marketplace of Les Halles, perception and experience of her surroundings are not constituted by what is perceived by her senses but by loss, grief, the memory of her dead father, and a future that was tragically denied. As Marceline was speaking into the tape recorder, neither Rouch nor Morin could hear what she was saying; it was only when they played the recording that they heard her calling out for her Papa and speaking about her experiences in Birkenau, reducing the film crew to tears (Henley 2009).

Fieldwork, like filmmaking, is a type of performative activity that can be used to craft contexts of perception, experience, and memory, which are lived in daily life but are not usually externalized or made public. Combining ideas of free association with ideas and techniques used by filmmakers and creative artists (Pink 2009; Radley 2009; Hogan and Pink 2010; Cox, Irving, and Wright 2016; Elliott and Culhane 2016) allows for the development of new, practical approaches to theorizing, knowing, and representing people's experiences and understandings. Accordingly, my aim is to create an ethnographic context for the generation of speech, memory, and imagery by establishing a different kind of relationship between people, their bodies, and their familiar surroundings. A person is asked to walk around their local neighborhood while narrating their stream of thought, consciousness, and memory as they emerge in the present-tense into a voice-recorder, while a second person (who is previously unknown to the first) interjects, asks questions, and takes photographs, thereby creating a moving, performative dialogue in which transient thoughts and memories emerge, are articulated, and then reflected upon in the public domain. The externalization of the person's thoughts and memories is carried out in the actual locations in which the original events and experiences occurred. As such, the method plays upon the capacity of familiar places to elicit interior lifeworlds and create a context for verbal testimonies and storytelling, including the emergent and associative properties of thought and expression.

For this project, I asked Neil Greenberg, an HIV+ dancer and choreographer to walk around his local neighborhood while narrating events from his life into a tape recorder, and I invited another informant, Frank Jump (whom Neil did not know and who is also HIV+), to be the interlocutor/photographer who accompanied Neil. As I was interested in capturing the historical nuances and collective deep memory of HIV/AIDS, it was important for this particular fieldwork encounter that the two persons were strangers to each other and thus were required to articulate themselves without relying on shared, often unspoken understandings that exist between persons who are familiar with each other's lives and history.

Although I knew both Frank and Neil well and had worked with them independently, they were meeting each other for the first time. This meant not only that they had to establish a sense of each other during the course of their journey around the neighborhood but also that the ethnographic content and direction of the research depended upon Frank and Neil's sharing of life experiences and their interactive reflections as they emerged in the ethnographic moment. Most image production in the field is to some extent collaborative (Banks 2001: 119), but for Neil and Frank, the choices of what to represent extends the collaborative aspect by actively creating and shaping the ethnographic, thematic, and aesthetic content. Frank (b. 1960) is in the same age group as Neil (b. 1959) and both were among the generation of gay men that came of age during the brief window of social and sexual liberation after Stonewall but before the arrival of HIV/AIDS, and both men were diagnosed in their twenties. This meant Frank could ask questions of Neil's life experience and memories that I could not even conceive of as a straight European without HIV. This not only created a fieldwork dialogue that emerged out of Frank's and Neil's embodied experiences of living with HIV but also allowed for the ethnographic site to be defined from moment to moment through the dialogue that emerged between Neil and Frank as they discussed issues that were relevant and important in their lives. The process was designed to be as straightforward as possible so as to facilitate rather than impede, and encompassed the following stages:

1) Outlining the nature of the project, separately, to both participants and identifying a set of ideas and themes.
2) Taking Neil's life history (that is, separately, without Frank).
3) Drawing a map of the neighborhood with Neil, whereby I asked Neil to locate a number of key locations and events taken both from his routine, everyday life in the neighborhood and his longer history of living there.
4) Walking the shape of Neil's life biography with Frank as the key interlocutor and myself accompanying, while being open to the various new routes, detours, and trajectories that emerged in response to Frank's questions, comments, and conversation.

I met Frank at the subway station and we proceeded to Neil's place on East Second Street. When Neil invited us in, Frank began to look at the photographs on display around the apartment to see if he recognized anyone. Frank did not know any of the faces, but after Neil mentioned their names, Frank realized some of those pictured were mutual acquaintances and he was familiar with their life stories. Neil said that out of the fifteen photographs in the room, fourteen were dead but added that the photographs were not intended to be memorials; they were simply snaps of his friends he put up when he first moved into the apartment. Neil explained that they were the type of friends he made in his late-teens and early-twenties that often go on to become the close, intimate friends that someone carries throughout adult life, to which Frank, identifying with the experience of having lost many friends, observed "but not since AIDS." One by one the young faces in the photographs had died and the images thereafter became memorials, illustrating the extent to which HIV/AIDS decimated a generation of significant relationships.

The manner in which a shared realm of experience and memory had already begun to open up—before the journey around the neighborhood even commenced—reminded me of how the first lines of a play, film, or novel already presuppose a series of events that have taken place before it has started. When the Countess of Roussillon opens Shakespeare's *All's well that ends well* with the lines, "In delivering my son from me, I bury a second husband," it gestures toward events, emotions that have already happened, and are set in motion. In our case, what existed "beforehand" was a particular experience and understanding of New York that was common to both Neil's and Frank's lives. At this point, I took a passive role, only occasionally interrupting to ask a questions or to obtain some background information.

The excerpt begins at the point where Neil, Frank, and I were trying to track down the very building where Neil caught HIV.

EVERYDAY ADVENTURES IN FAMILIAR PLACES

Figure 4.1 Lucky Cheng's restaurant (formerly the Club Baths).

"This is Lucky Cheng's, *an Asian restaurant with drag waiters. But Lucky Cheng's isn't really Lucky Cheng's. To me, Lucky Cheng's is still is the Club Baths, a bathhouse chain that had baths in every major city. When I first moved into my apartment I used to say I lived right between the Club Baths and St. Mark's Baths, which is now Kim's Video, a video store I use on East Eighth Street. I frequented both baths a lot. At the Club Baths there was shag carpet everywhere. St. Mark's was much more cushy, streamlined, and had younger guys. There was a whole thing going on: orgies, anonymous sex, and when AIDS arrived, I was in a group of men who all assumed they had been put at high risk. One of these places will be the place where I caught HIV."*

"So, well, here it is: my brother's apartment building, right across the street from Lucky Cheng's and just round the corner from mine and also a fifth-floor walk-up. Jon was three years older than me, gay. Actually, I got him the apartment. A friend of mine died there from AIDS and afterward my brother ended up moving in. And then my brother died from AIDS."

Figure 4.2 John Vasquez and Jon Greenberg's old apartment building.

My brother actually died in the hospital but this is where he was for the couple of months before. There was a lot of vomiting, a lot of diarrhea. He lived in apartment twenty-five, I'm almost certain. How do you forget things like that? And his friend Risa lived across the hall. First my friend died in that apartment, and then when my brother moved in, he died too. This is my path to the subway station. Very often I'll pass right by here. And I almost always glance over to see if I'm passing his building and very often I'm not. I've already passed his building by . . ."

"My brother had this weird discrepancy and probably contradiction in his own mind. . . . He wanted a public funeral without being political. He wanted us to burn him in the street and for people to eat his flesh. His friends wanted to try and come up with a public funeral that was as close to his wishes as was possible. And the closest thing that would cover his wishes was that the body should be visible and that it should be public. The funeral started somewhere near here. . . . It was Friday, July 16th, and people congregated by the park by the subway station. His body was in a van because it is illegal to do something like this in New York. It was a nonviolent political action, it was peaceful. Then four or five of us took my brother out of the van and carried the coffin up First Avenue."

Figure 4.3 First Avenue: The route the body was carried.

Figure 4.4 Tompkins Square Park.

"At Tompkins Square Park the coffin was set on a stand and my brother was dressed in a flowered halter top, which was chosen by his friend Risa. People sat down here and watched and we went up to speak one at a time. Somebody did a Jewish prayer, and it really touched my parents that somebody would do that. Actually, my brother Jon would have liked that too. People talked about him, somebody said something hyper-political and somebody came up and said this wasn't a political thing. I can't walk by there without being reminded of my brother. When I first met my current partner, we went for dinner at a place on Seventh Street and then we took a walk and we ended up sitting in the park, and it was a wild thing on our first date to be in Tompkins Square Park. And I couldn't be there with this guy on a first date without thinking that right over there was where my brother's funeral was."

"Afterward, we loaded the coffin back into the van and they drove it back to the funeral hall and then it was cremated. Then what happened to the ashes is another story! We ate part of the ashes as per his wishes. It felt . . . I don't know what it felt like. I

mean, I can tell you that there were little pieces of bone left that crunched and were the consistency of a pretzel. Which is shocking, but you know, it's just ashes, there's nothing unhealthy about eating it as far as I can tell. . . . Then we went back up to Risa's and we had potato salad and we found out she had put some ashes in the potato salad. So the people who chose not to eat ashes ended up eating the ashes . . ."

Figure 4.5 Redden's "Home for Funerals."

EMERGENT ETHNOGRAPHY

The above journey around the Lower East Side, attempts to bring to life the realms of emotion, memory, and expression that form people's lived experiences of their local and habitual surroundings. These were generated and articulated in a particular kind of performative fieldwork context and in response to Frank's questions and comments. The resulting narrative is not only subject to varying levels of personal disclosure, self-censorship, and the act of recording but also by the limits of linguistic expression, memory, and recollection. As previously noted, not all thought processes take place in language and routinely incorporate nonlinguistic, nonpropositional, imagistic, and inchoate modes of thinking that operate beyond the threshold of language. Accordingly, Neil's words are best regarded as partial and distorted representations of the subjective lived experiences, emotions, and memories that emerged in dialogue with Frank as part of a performative journey around the neighborhood.

Whereas our being-in-the-world is experienced as an assemblage of perception and sensation—in which the copresence of thought, emotion, memory, and movement combine to create our embodied lived experience of the moment—language is largely linear in its structure and unfolds over time: what is experienced simultaneously across different cognitive, sensory, and emotional modalities is expressed verbally in a sequential fashion. It means that emotions experienced conjointly as part of an undifferentiated amalgam at the level of the body are separated out at the level of language and expressed in terms of bounded categories such as love, loss, grief, regret, and so forth. Neil's narrative therefore only offers a partial representation of a wider range of corporeal, sensory, and emotional experiences, of which many aspects are difficult to grasp, define, or articulate, and reinforces how lived experience often exceeds that which can be expressed or understood, including by the persons experiencing it themselves, through linear forms of speech and language.

Although certain realms of experience are destined to remain incipient or unarticulated, others coalesce into stable symbolic and communicable forms for narrative expression to oneself and others. This means that while Neil's testimony revolves around those realms of experience and expression that can be communicated within a public and highly performative encounter—and thus cannot claim to provide anything more than a fleeting and partial understanding of the complexity and diversity of his lifeworld—we nevertheless gain a sense of Neil's embodied experience of his neighborhood which emerges in the moment as he moves around its streets and buildings. The performative journey Neil and Frank take us on around the Lower East Side is embedded in their shared social circumstances and life histories and uses their agency, intentionality, and interaction to craft a specific fieldwork site through movement and dialogic interaction, building on Victor Turner's definition of performance as transcribed by Richard Schechner and Willa Appel: "Performance is a dialectic of 'flow,' that is, spontaneous movement in which action and awareness are one, and 'reflexivity,' in which the central meanings, values and goals of a culture are seen 'in action,' as they shape and explain behaviour. A performance is declarative of our shared humanity, yet it utters the uniqueness of particular cultures" (1990: 1).

As Neil walked around different parts of his neighborhood, thoughts, memories, and experiences emerged and were communicated to Frank and myself in a performative and storied form. The communication of subjective experience, memory, and emotion to other persons not only requires the establishment of relevance (Sperber and Wilson 1995) but also relies on storytelling to create a sense of codwelling and "space of shared *inter-est*" (Jackson 2002: 11). This necessitates the mediation of different personal experiences and moral understandings—in this case, in relation to events beyond human control, such as the deaths of friends and family—which are couched in a storied form in ways that speak to the existential human condition. This reinforces how acts of storytelling are "never simply a matter of creating either personal or social meanings, but an aspect of the 'subjective in-between'" (Jackson 2002: 11) and highlights how the readers of this chapter are part of the story-telling process, given how Neil had to make his narrative relevant not only to the three of us but also to an imagined audience and readership he has never met.

Neil's narration of his neighborhood demonstrates how we are not fully in control of our own thoughts and memories, and are instead at best partial agents in shaping our thought processes. Sometimes a thought, event, image, memory, or dilemma repetitively comes into consciousness, unwanted and unbidden. The person may want to be thinking about something else and actively tries to change the content or character of their lifeworld, but the thought or memory keeps returning no matter how hard they try. Some thoughts may be recurrent and ongoing to the extent that they define a sense of personal or collective experience (or both)—that may be common to many persons with HIV/AIDS—while others are destined to remain formless, unspoken, or impossible to articulate. This reinforces William James' notion of how the spectrum of consciousness ranges from barely graspable and transitory forms of thinking and being that exist on the periphery of consciousness, bodily awareness, and understanding to those more defined, purposeful, and stable forms that are easier to articulate and that enable persons to establish a sense of self and continuity, including amid radically changing conditions, crisis, or disruption. Certain moods and modes of consciousness may persist for hours, days, or weeks to create an experience of a world seemingly "shot through with regularities" and "essentially bound up with the way in which one moment in our experience may lead us toward other moments" (James 2000: 90).

Nowhere is this more obvious than when Neil walks to the subway station on First Avenue and Houston Street. To do so, he must walk past Lucky Cheng's—where he most likely caught HIV—as well his dead brother's apartment building: an act that usually brings forth the deep memory of the past. On those occasions when Neil walks along First Avenue and does not think about his brother's death—or his ex-partner John Vasquez, who died in the same apartment—he feels guilty about his lack of remembrance. On some days he simply does not want to engage with the emotional immediacy and intensity of walking down First Avenue; he walks the long way around the block or uses another subway station, thereby avoiding both Lucky Cheng's and his brother's apartment. However, taking the "long way around" elicits other qualities of thought and emotion, which for Neil accord a lack of respect to Jon and John's lives, and as a consequence he mostly chooses the direct way, both to acknowledge his brother and former lover but also as a personalized daily ritual and existential test of his moral fortitude and capacity for remembrance.

This illustrates how even the simple act of turning right or left when leaving an apartment building presents multiple possibilities for engaging with and experiencing the neighborhood. A person's daily movements through the neighborhood create many different emotional contexts for shaping thought and experience as well as remembering and forgetting, insofar as certain streets and buildings in the neighborhood have the capacity to elicit depths of personal experience, emotion, and memory, while other streets are much less defined in relation to personal history and offer the possibility of deadening the past or at least making the neighborhood less emotionally active. A person's daily movements help shape the empirical content and character of their *sensus interior* and establish different possibilities for being and expression from moment to moment. By deciding to walk down one street rather than another, by staying inside or choosing to go out, by going to a friend's house or sitting in his local park, Neil's movements actively create his sense of self and embodied, sensorial experience of the neighborhood.

Such choices are made on an hourly, even minute-by-minute basis and continually redefine the experience and meaning of living with HIV/AIDS. The radically different moods that emerge demonstrate what is at stake by *being-here* rather than *being-there* (Casey 1993), sensitizing the person to how life and history are made and manifested within the moment. The modes of thinking and being that are generated by walking in Tompkins Square Park or down First Avenue and past Lucky Cheng's, show what is at stake in people's quotidian movements and how different places have the capacity to generate realms of experience and emotion that are qualitatively different from being elsewhere. Although Neil's account of walking around his local neighborhood reveals the impossibility of entirely removing oneself from the emotional and mnemonic power of place, it demonstrates how people's lived experiences of the moment are continually generated through everyday movement whereby people shape their experience of the present and assign it new meanings and functions through their daily routines and actions.

Martin Heidegger employs the term *ausserlichkeit* (outwardness, externality) to describe the superficial appearances of routine actions and concerns, and "everydayness" to describe "the pallid lack of mood that dominates the grey everyday through and through" (1962: 395). Heidegger is not assigning a negative character to everyday life but instead is arguing that our perception and understanding of the world are never neutral or free-floating, insofar as the world is only disclosed through a specific mood and state-of-mind (1962). People's engagement and interaction with familiar objects and places are thus always intertwined with emergent modes of being, belief, and body, including those of health, illness, and emotion, which combine to define the character of dwelling from moment to moment. Neil's performative recreation of his everyday experience of walking around his local neighborhood continually moves between different moods and registers of expression: from loss, regret, and tragedy to humor, irony, and philosophical commentary. No matter how entrenched a particular perception may *seem*, it does not reveal an immutable reality or experience of the neighborhood but one that remains labile and whose mood can be reshaped and reworked through words and movement. This means the account of the neighborhood Neil produced for this chapter, like every ethnographic encounter, does not represent a static perception or mode of dwelling but a specific and situated lifeworld that was generated and expressed through action, dialogue, and movement.

Neil's testimony reveals how intense, often recurring, moments of thinking and being emerge through his everyday engagement with his neighborhood. The intensity of Neil's relationship with familiar objects, buildings, and streets, suggests that Heidegger mistakenly conflates the routine performance and collective expression of ordinary, everyday activities—or *sensus communis*—with people's situated, and sometimes intensely felt, experiences of everyday life. By making inferences based on outward appearances, Heidegger ascribes a lack of mood to people's routine activities rather than the intense emotions, feelings, and dilemmas that Neil so movingly recounts in his public expressions of the neighborhood. This holds important anthropological implications in that it cautions against theorizing and representing anthropological subjects or their social practices without taking account of the ongoing streams of consciousness and ever-changing reality of their inner lifeworlds. Grounding anthropological truth claims in people's emergent experience of the world and according it a more active role in shaping ethnographic accounts not only offers a more realistic understanding and representation of social life but also implies an anthropological responsibility for accurately reporting on people's inner lives in anthropological texts in ways that avoid theoretical overdetermination or reification and enable people to recognize their own experience in the text.

DEEP MEMORY

The emotional and mnemonic resonance of the neighborhood illustrates how memory is involved in every stage of the production of ethnographic knowledge, from fieldwork to field notes to final publication. Johannes Fabian even goes so far as to argue that every social interaction or articulation of knowledge is memory mediated, and that fieldwork and ethnography are largely activities aimed at getting people to remember: "The ethnographer must be able to catch memory at work and he must document this by means of texts. Ordinarily, the ethnographer does not find such texts; they must be made by means of recording communicative-performative events that become protocols when they are transcribed and translated. Thus, work—hard work—is required before memory work can be presented and interpreted" (2003: 492).

Fabian stresses how the production of memory is a practical activity carried out in the field and calls into question the anthropological emphasis upon integrative, normative, and symbolic functions of shared and collective memory at the expense of situated acts of remembering, whose empirical content is generated by specific persons in the field and subject to discrepancies and differences: "Not only could memories have critical effects: what I found was that in remembering in the sense of producing memory that could be narrated, exhibited, performed, in short, shared, required critical work. Such work had to be carried out in a field of tensions between positing and negating" (2003: 490).

This chapter can be seen as an attempt to inscribe the theoretical dilemmas of the anthropology of memory—as explored by Paul Antze and Michael Lambek (1996)—directly into the field and uses people's intentionality and moral agency to carry out the "work" of exploring how situated acts of remembering relate to the social and material environment. Memory is an embodied capacity, partially formed through repetition, and is inherently unstable right down to the proteins and molecules in the brain, meaning that even long-term, repetitively embodied memories enter a labile and unstable state every time they are retrieved before being repatterned back into the brain and body (Rose 2003). Moreover, as both the process of retrieval and repatterning take place in relation to the specific emotions inherent and active in the moment of remembering (Nader 2003; Walker et al. 2003), each time Neil walks by his brother Jon's old apartment, he is not only retrieving and revisiting a complex chain of memories, feelings, and associations about his brother's life and death but also these are subtly transformed by each and every act of recollection. During the process of remembering, memory enters an indeterminate state in which past events and episodes are intertwined with a complex assemblage of emotions to constitute a person's current mode of being—be that happiness, sadness, or boredom—before being reconsolidated. This means that every occasion of walking past Jon and John's apartment has the potential to refashion or add new layers and qualities of experience to the past that are then incorporated into being and body, recalling how truth and meaning are not fixed properties but are located "in future time" (Peirce 1998: 340). For Pierce, reality is not fully coterminous with perception and does not inhere in the moment but is subject to revision in light of future evidence, events, and experiences.

Beyond individually embodied memory and cognition, there are also various forms of shared memory that define people's collective experience and understanding of the neighborhood. Jon's public funeral is now part of the Lower East Side's local mythology and continues to shape the social landscape. I have met many people living in the neighborhood who still remember Jon's funeral, even though they were not there. *"Oh yeah,"* one person told me, who never met him and didn't witness the funeral, *"I know Jon Greenberg. He had that public funeral that blocked off the whole of First Avenue and speeches were read out."* Another friend, who lives close to Jon's old apartment but did not know him personally, told me that once he found out about Jon's corpse being publicly carried along First Avenue, he realized that people continue to have a political responsibility even in death and made a decision to politically choreograph his own funeral.

It seems that memories, like politics and disease, are also contagious. Jon's life, death, and public funeral continue to be part of the Lower East Side's present, especially now that photographs and recollections of Jon's funeral can be found on websites more than twenty years after his death. Consequently, Jon Greenberg maintains a kind of presence in many different people's lives that extends far beyond those that personally knew him. In establishing a type of *being-in-absentia* (see Sartre [1943] 1996), Jon is now part of the Lower East Side's social, political, and emotional fabric and collective memory.

Figure 4.6 Jon Greenberg's dead body blocking traffic and being carried along First Avenue.

Neil's words describe a personal and collective history of the Lower East Side and speak of such things as loss, contingency, and the politics of disease so as to offer a portrait of the Lower East Side shared by many other people in the neighborhood. However, Neil's narrative also describes a *specific* social and cultural history of places and buildings that is unknown to many of the neighborhood's inhabitants. The Lower East Side combines traces of its immigrant, artistic, and ghetto past with its recent gentrification to reinforce how—like the self—a neighborhood's emotional and mnemonic constitution can never be fixed or mapped as it only ever comes into being through the activities of its inhabitants over time. The content and character of any given neighborhood needs to be understood as incorporating the simultaneous copresence of many people's subjective and emergent lifeworlds that range from the ordinary to the extraordinary in any given moment, and often encompasses both.

The commonalities and discrepancies that exist among the local population's collective experiences and understandings of the Lower East Side exposes the foundational diversity that lies at the heart of all neighborhoods, meaning that Neil's experience coexists alongside countless other experiences of the very same shops, restaurants, buildings, and streets. The Club Baths and St. Mark's Baths are long gone, but their past still resonates for many locals in the sites they occupied, until they were taken over by Lucky Cheng's and Kim's Video Store (which have themselves given way to a BBQ restaurant and an amusement arcade). The Club Baths and St. Mark's Baths were closed in the mid-1980s under a citywide public health order so as to prevent the spread of HIV/AIDS. Tellingly, as we walked past the St. Mark's Baths, Frank remarked that a number of bath houses located in Harlem escaped the ban and remained open: an oversight (or otherwise) that reflects the wider political, racial, and economic realities, different life expectancies, and unequal exposure to risk across New York's neighborhoods and the United States more generally.

Neil and Frank are from a generation who came of age after decriminalization but before HIV/AIDS. Both were diagnosed in their mid-twenties in the 1980s and survived to tell the tale, while vast numbers of their friends and contemporaries did not, as signified by the photographs in Neil's apartment, which became untended memorials. Neil tried to salvage some meaning from the deaths that surrounded him by using the life stories of his friends as inspiration for his extraordinary award-winning dance production, *Not about AIDS dance*. The dance is based on a diary that Neil kept throughout 1993: his idea was to create and choreograph a dance based on whatever life events happened to him that year.

Neil had little idea when he embarked on the diary that one entry would describe his brother Jon's death. One of the most powerful scenes in the dance is when Neil tries to recreate his brother's facial expression in the moments before his death. Neil's face is both a site of family resemblance and human vulnerability that communicates the borders of life and death. At this point in the dance, Neil has already informed the audience that he himself is HIV+; Neil's expression effectively asks the audience to imagine his own impending demise. Thus, while seemingly about AIDS, Neil entitled the piece *Not about AIDS dance* because it describes the shared existential dilemma that all humans face—that is, of how to live a life in the knowledge of death. The dance met with great critical acclaim and won a number of prestigious prizes. Neil attributes its success to the dance's ability to communicate beyond the specifics of AIDS to a broad audience about the human condition of finitude. However, when I pressed Neil to describe his work as a politically motivated piece, he repeatedly insisted that it wasn't. Instead, he asserted that it was an *ontological protest.*

Figure 4.7 Neil tries to recreate his brother's facial expression in the moments before his death.

POSTSCRIPT: *PART THREE (LUCK)*

This chapter has attempted to develop an ethnographic approach to researching the emergent realms of thinking and being that mediate familiar urban spaces, by rethinking Kant's *Anthropology: From a pragmatic point of view* ([1798] 2006). Kant himself differentiated between mere knowing or being acquainted with the world (*die Welt kennen*) and the knowledge that emerges from continually acting in or having a world (*Welt haben*), arguing that "the one only *understands* the play (*Spiel*), of which it has been a spectator, but the other has *participated* (*mitgespielt*) in it" (Kant, quoted in Wood 2003: 41). Consequently, the aim has been to find a means of forming socially inclusive dialogues and moral collaborations with persons who are accorded an equal role in shaping the research rather than present an abstract or philosophical account of how memory and place shape people's senses of being when moving in urban space. The ethnographic content of the field emerges in real time, as Neil moves around his neighborhood in response to questions rooted in Frank's own embodied experience of HIV/AIDS, so as to bring to life and dramatize the past of the Lower East Side rather than recover or memorialize it.

In early September 2001, a few days before 9/11, I was sitting directly beneath the World Trade Center as I watched Neil Greenberg and his dance company on the Plaza Stage, performing his latest dance, *Construction with varied materials*, to a broad audience of dance fans, tourists, office workers, and passersby. When I heard about the two airplanes striking the Twin Towers, I couldn't stop thinking about how I had been sitting there just a few days before, watching Neil's performance. I recalled many conversations I had with Neil in which we discussed the contingency of life, whereby Neil would say that he might not die from AIDS but could be run over by a bus like anyone else. After the planes struck, it reminded me of another of Neil's dance pieces, *Part three (Luck)*, from 1998. The title, *Luck*, contains a double meaning that derives from how chance is fundamental to the shaping of existence. In Neil's case, it simultaneously refers to the "bad" luck of catching AIDS in his mid-twenties and the "good" luck of surviving—unlike his brother and his friends, whose photographs adorn his apartment and whose luck ran out before the arrival of antiretroviral medications. As such, it seemed to me that the events of 9/11 and the seeming permanence of the Twin Towers emphasized how cities, selves, and human histories are continually being rewritten—at the same time as neighborhoods are being walked—in relation to the twin forces of chance and contingency.

CHAPTER FIVE

A disintegration of the senses

The reduction of the sensorium into five senses was first determined by Aristotle, perhaps for neat numerological reasons rather than physiological ones; but Galen said there were six, Erasmus Darwin thought there were twelve, and Von Frey reduced them down to eight. . . . Recent authorities calculate there are seventeen senses.

—Anthony Synnott, *The body social* (1993: 155)

Clouds swirl along the blue ridges. You can sit for days watching the light play on the shadows of the mountains, which is maybe why William Burroughs, who drank the hallucinogen yage prepared by the Indians in the foothills of the Andes at Mocoa, in the Putumayo region of Colombia, in 1953, talks so much about blue throughout his life's work from his first book to his death. . . . Amongst other things, he notes a blue face, a blue wall, and plants growing out of genitals. No wonder he felt the room shaking. In the pharmacological appendix to the book, Burroughs assures us: "Blue flashes in front of the eyes is peculiar to Yage intoxication."

—Michael Taussig, *What color is the sacred?* (2009: 62)

You say to the boy open your eyes
When he opens his eyes and sees the light

You make him cry out. Saying,
O Blue come forth
O Blue arise
O Blue ascend
O Blue come in

—Derek Jarman, *Blue* (1993)

Figure 5.1 *Empire chair in the gloaming*, by John Dugdale, 1994. Cyanotype. *Reproduced by permission from the artist.*

Light is fundamental to lived experience. The human body exists and is immersed within different qualities of light that continuously act on the nervous system and elicit physiological transformations. Accordingly, this chapter attempts to offer a better understanding of the phenomenology of light and vision, as shaped by the possibilities and constraints of the human eye and body, with a special focus on the senses, montage, and lived experience. It considers how disruptions to people's embodied capacities caused by viruses, accidents, and violence can bring about new forms of imaginative, aesthetic, and ekphrastic practice. By observing how the senses can become fragmented during episodes of illness and crisis, it examines how the human body, like a landscape, is something that is inhabited and reinhabited over time. In doing so, a key aim is to move away from notions of embodied knowledge as a stable property of bodies and persons to a more fluid concept that considers how body and world are constituted in relation to the task-at-hand, a montage of the senses and a future that always lies "further on."

Ordinarily, a habitual integration of mind, body, and the senses is forged through people's ongoing practical activities whereby a seeming continuity of person, body, and action is maintained over time and across different environments. Nonetheless, models of habitual unity can also be criticized for presupposing a degree of existential and bodily stability that is not shared across the population. Illness disrupts the habitual embodied rhythms of daily life and is in part a future related activity directed toward recovery and restoration of well-being; if this is not possible, one develops strategies and modes of action to mediate illness and decline. People often need to relearn previously taken-for-granted practices and rehabitualize their bodies during and after periods of illness in order to maintain social and existential continuity, which generates new modes of sensing, knowing, and understanding the world (Irving 2005).

This chapter discusses how the acting body is assembled and reassembled within a continuous sensory exchange between body and world by documenting the sensory and corporeal transformations that take place during episodes of illness and crisis. It pays special attention to the interaction between the different sense organs and changes in the visible environment, including how the particular quality of light that emerges after sunset but before night has descended—known as *the gloaming*—introduces phenomenological uncertainties into the nervous system that transform the relationship between a person's *body* and a person's *surroundings*. Beginning with an outline of how people's actions in the world produce a form of *living montage* that creates continuous juxtapositions of sight, sound, smell, touch, and taste, I then provide an ethnographic account of the bodily and sensory transformations that take place during the gloaming hour, including the ways in which diminishing amounts of available light and visual impairment shape people's possibilities for practical action and ekphrastic expression.

EXPLORATIONS IN SENSORY MONTAGE

To a certain extent, montage is already prefigured in movement and the lived body. When people walk, as has often been noted, they are like film directors who stroll the streets, perceive images, and mentally record their visual experiences. People create movies in their heads by way of the images they encounter, including all the various cinematic techniques of looking, including close-ups, long shots, flashbacks, fleeting or lingering gazes, cutaways, and editing, alongside the use of the different kinds of sensorial effects, incidental music, ambient sounds, and voices that are encountered as one moves around the city. As such, the moving body continuously generates complex juxtapositions of sound, image, texture, taste, and aroma within the flow of everyday life. By deciding to walk down one street rather than another, by visiting a neighborhood park or shopping in a crowded mall, people actively shape their lived and sensory experience of the present through a creative act of *poesis*.

Maurice Merleau-Ponty ([1945] 1992) highlights how, in ordinary life, the lived body weaves together the different senses so as to create a unity of experience that underlies our perceived reality by way of a preconscious synthesis of information. A particular object—for example, this book—is not experienced as two different objects (i.e., as a book that exists in sight and another in touch) but is experienced as a single object that possesses different sensory dimensions. Likewise, an environment—for example, the room in which the book is being read—is not experienced as many different rooms according to its visual, haptic, acoustic, and aromatic properties but as a single environment that is brought into alignment through the body's capacity to process and integrate different kinds of sensory information.

However, closer ethnographic attention to the way experience is formed reveals the uncertain grounds for making holistic or overarching claims about sensory experience and understanding—be that visual or otherwise—given how perception and attention are weighted according to people's intentions and actions (see Howes 2004, 2006; Howes and Classen 2014). On the trivial end of the scale, this might be seen in the different realities that are generated by a bottle of milk, in that when we take the bottle from the fridge it may *look* fine although when we *smell* it we realize the milk has spoiled. In this case, the truth of the nose gains precedence over the truth of the eye. However this might be immediately reconfigured in the following action, when fruit smells good but is disappointing when bitten into, thereby illustrating the situational character of truth and perception. Given that a typical day encompasses thousands of sensory interactions, it is highly problematic to accord any one sense a privileged relationship to truth—say, in relation to a particular culture or historical era—without grounding these claims across the range of people's lived experiences and practices.

On a less trivial level, a house or building might be infused with the smell of a person who once lived there but has recently died. The conflicting realities that are experienced when entering a room in which someone's smell is tangibly present and alive but the person can no longer be seen, heard, or touched creates a disorientating and morbid montage of dissonant sensory information. The person still exists and seems so alive to consciousness within some sensory registers, but is not present in others. Equally disorientating is when a dead body appears to be sleeping but is cold to the touch, thereby indicating a different truth than initially suggested by the eye. Such experiences of milk, fruit, and bodies suggest that while the senses of sight, hearing, taste, touch, and smell often work in combination to confirm a single "whole-body" reality, as suggested by Merleau-Ponty, we must be aware that the senses can also oppose, destabilize, and juxtapose conflicting realities. This can create complex montages of sensory information whose consequences need to be addressed in order to understand how the senses establish the basis for perception, action, and interpretation. The copresence of different kinds of sensory information has a number of important repercussions for claims about the sensory character of different social, cultural, and historical contexts.

1. It demonstrates how each sense possesses a specific ontological relationship to the world. Because sensory realities are situational, it is problematic to accord a status of truth to any particular sense outside of specific actions, purposes, and situations.

2. It suggests that sensory attention is in a continuous process of formation. While certain senses are better for particular tasks and purposes in particular

moments, any hierarchical structures that are established between the senses are
fluid, contextual, and liable to be reformulated on an ongoing basis.

3. It calls into question attempts to define any culture or historical era in terms
of a dominant visual or sensory hierarchy, given how different senses are used for
different situations and purposes in people's daily lives.

4. It highlights how theoretical claims of bodily unity or holism only apply to
certain sensory contexts and thus need to be ethnographically grounded rather
than merely asserted.

Erwin Straus (1963, 1966) extensively documented the manner in which sensory
data is encountered within the flow of daily life, including how the body's sense
organs reveal and generate different kinds of knowledge about the world. For
example, whereas the visual world consists of the 180 degrees in front of the eyes
and locates objects precisely in space, the world of sound and smell is less localized and can encompass the person: consider the way it is easy to avert one's eyes
or look away from something but less easy to escape ongoing noise or an unpleas-
ant smell just by moving the head. For Straus, the evolution of human beings into
the upright posture led to a fundamental reorganization of the senses, in which
the importance of smell was reduced in favor of the eye. Vertical posture not only
freed vision from the ground: after humans were no longer on four limbs, the
hands were released, which offered new possibilities for hand-eye coordination,
communicative gestures, movement, and technology. The combination of the perpendicular body and bipedal movement thus created a distinctly human way of
sensing, experiencing, and interpreting the world, a legacy we still live with today.

When lying on an analyst's couch, Straus observed, the body loses its upright
posture and becomes more passive. In the cinema, a person's body also plays a
less active role in shaping its sensory environment because the world comes *to*
the person rather than vice versa. When watching a film, the body's nerve cells
register ever-changing combinations of sound and image, which sometimes
leap across centuries or oceans in a few seconds but are nevertheless rendered
meaningful within the flow of the film by the cognitive capacity to tie information together in consciousness. Here, the construction of complex montages of
time and space within film are not restricted to editing and cinematic technique
insofar as they are predicated on everyday experience and activity, displacing the
distinction between art and life.

Regardless of whether sensory information is encountered through people's everyday movements or when watching film, its interpretation relies on

the nervous system's ability to rapidly coordinate complex juxtapositions of sensory information in a manner whereby meaning is not closed off but left open for further revision and evaluation. In doing so, the nervous system's capacity for processing and interpreting different modes of sensory data troubles the boundaries of art and life, as indicated in Gilles Deleuze's summary of "seeing" Francis Bacon's paintings: "The levels of sensation would really be domains of sensation that refer to the different sense organs; but precisely each level, each domain would have a way of referring to the others, independently of the represented object they have in common. Between a colour, a taste, a touch, a smell, a noise, a weight, there would be an existential communication that would constitute the 'pathic' (nonrepresentative) moment of *the* sensation. In Bacon's bullfights, for example, we hear the noise of the beast's hooves" (2005: 30).

Deleuze's model of sensation returns us to earlier understandings of *aesthetics* and *aesthesis*, which were not so much concerned with art or disinterested contemplation but instead embodied life and perception as constituted through the interplay between different sense organs. This is the idea of aesthetics as a discourse of the body and complex assemblages of perception and feeling (Buck-Morss 1992). As Terry Eagleton puts it, aesthetics is "nothing less than the whole of our sensate life together—the business of affections and aversions, of how the world strikes the body on its sensory surfaces, of that which takes root in the gaze and the guts and all that arises from our most banal, biological insertion into the world" (1990: 13).

One consequence of being a body in the world is the continuous formation and juxtapositions of sensate and aesthetic experience—sometimes complementary and seamlessly intertwining, on other occasions discordant or jarring—that are generated through the body's sense organs and nervous activity. Walking around New York continually creates different cross-cuttings and juxtapositions of subject matter, tone, scale, rhythm, motion, sound, volume, contrast, and association, akin to the classic techniques of montage from Sergei Eisenstein to Luis Buñuel. The lived montage of the city is generated across all the different sensory registers: the raw meat in the butcher's shop contrasts with the human flesh displayed on magazine racks; the lively commotion coming out of a bar mixes with the sound of church bells where people pray and seek redemption. The city provides endless sounds, smells, images, and textures day and night: a highly cinematic representation of crowded streets, neon lights, and social contrasts in which conspicuous wealth and brutal poverty are on public display and generate conflicting and exacerbating images of difference with a simple flick of the head or minimal movement of the eye.

Although lived montage precedes cinematic montage, cinema has now become fundamental to perception and experience. Prior to the advent of film and sound recording it would have been nonsensical to define music, a play, or a sports match as a "live" event because it is only through the subsequent development of cinema and television that such insights have become thinkable or possible. The contemporary understanding and appreciation of "liveness" is thus partially a consequence of modern technology, which illustrates how the invention of film and its associated techniques have produced new ways of thinking, not just in relation to cinematic representation but also noncinematic experience. Analyzing cinematic techniques—such as montage—therefore provides theoretical and practical ways of thinking about how people's lived experiences and sensory realities of the world are shaped in movement and action.

INTO THE GLOAMING

I now want to offer a shift in focus by presenting an ethnographic exploration of visual and sensory perception in order to consider how light shapes lived experience. The body always exists within different qualities of light that bring about material changes in the body throughout day. When a person encounters the disappearing light of *the gloaming*, a subtle but significant reconfiguration of their sensory organs and nervous system takes place that alters the way the external world is perceived, and thereby affects the basis upon which many actions and responses are carried out, including haptic sensitivity, hand-eye coordination, proprioception, movement, and the quality and range of the human voice. The gloaming does not wholly belong to the visibility of day or darkness of night, but mediates the two by retaining traces of daylight and a presentiment of the darkness to come (or vice versa); when a person enters the gloaming, the sensory organization of their body is shaped by a past already gone and a future yet to arrive.

As the day ends, the largest and heaviest sense organ of all, the human skin, becomes much more sensitive as light diminishes and the diurnal arrangement of the senses becomes realigned in accordance with the human organism's anticipation of nighttime. The skin is generally less than 2 mm thick and connects directly to a network of underlying nerve terminals that continuously relay information about the external environment to the brain (Jablonski 2008). Insofar as the skin is sensitive to light, it can be said "to see," but unlike the eye and other sense organs—such as ears, nose, and tongue—the sensitivity of the skin is distributed across the entire body surface rather than being localized in one part, with nerves that are particularly concentrated in areas such as the face and fingertips.

At the same time, as the sensitivity of the skin increases in response to the decrease in light, the eye becomes less effective and smell and hearing become more acute. The eye's retina, which can be understood as an important extension of the brain, plays a key role in configuring spatial knowledge and establishing the body's relationship to its surroundings by way of retinocentric perception—i.e., the coordination of the position of eye and body relative to other objects in the environment so as to enable movement and allow objects to be acted upon effectively (Ward 2011). During the gloaming, retinocentric and other forms of visual perception become less precise: objects, materials, and shapes take on uncertain forms, people's distinguishing features and expressions become less clear, which makes their intentions and actions more difficult to discern. Even familiar rooms, streets, and buildings can become ambiguous spaces of reverie and possibility, demonstrating the frequency with which physiology and imagination meet within people's ability to perceive and give attention to their surroundings. Such shifts in sensory perception, receptivity, and activity are part of the body's wider capacity to reorganize its intentional and attentional abilities when encountering different qualities of stimuli, including the intensity of available light and other kinds of visual and sensory information. The brain continuously selects, fills in, and edits information about the external environment to the extent that for every nerve pathway that conveys information for visual processing, there are many others going the other way (R. Gregory 2005). This demonstrates how neither the external reality *nor* the perceiving body are stable insofar as they are both in a continuous process of transformation throughout the day: reinforcing how people's perceptions are not direct reflections of reality but are instead hypotheses about the world, formulated by brain and body and open to imaginative intervention.

There is, moreover, an interesting ethnographic correlation between the physiological and imaginative reconfigurations that occur during the gloaming hour and those experienced by persons during the onset of blindness. In fact, the metaphor of *the gloaming* was first suggested to me by John Dugdale—a photographer from New York with whom I began working in the 1990s—to describe his descent into blindness. John was a successful fashion and design photographer whose clients included Ralph Lauren and Martha Stewart and who gradually began losing his ability to see in his early thirties as a consequence of HIV/AIDS. Although John's commercial work in fashion was well paid, his long-standing ambition was to earn a living making fine art. Even as a child, his greatest aspiration was to have a photograph exhibited in the Metropolitan Museum of Art, but this dream was largely relinquished once he started down the commercial path. John's success in the fashion and design industry meant he was able to live in a farmhouse in the country and also rent an apartment in the city. One morning in 1993, he woke up, had some tea and toast for breakfast, and then left for the city where he had an appointment for a photo shoot. After reaching the city, John began feeling disorientated, lost consciousness, and collapsed onto the concrete sidewalk. He was taken to the hospital where it was discovered he had undergone an HIV/AIDS-related stroke. Consequently, John never arrived at his appointment and instead spent the following months in hospital. From now on, John would never see, touch, or move amid the world's surfaces and textures in the same way again.

Once in the hospital, John's condition rapidly deteriorated and over the following weeks and months he suffered six more strokes and also contracted viral meningitis and pneumonia. In addition to the intense pain he suffered, John was too weak to get out of bed and he experienced the severe fatigue that takes over the body when lying down for days on end: having one's habitual perpendicular posture removed and having one's flesh continually press down on a bed without being able to get up or move around, alongside the associations of infantilization that accompany being in such a state. Recall Straus' observations on upright posture: John's sensory experience of the world was transformed due to his horizontal confinement plus also the wider moral associations of being an upright and independent human being who could not *be* upright. Moreover, John had by point lost control over many of his bodily functions and had to wear diapers, which his mother, brother, and sister would come in to change, as he was too weak to change them himself. Here was a man who had just turned thirty-three: a man supposedly in the prime of life, who was too weak to stand or get out of bed and who was almost wholly dependent upon nursing staff and his family for his most basic needs.

After a while, John noticed that parts of his visual field had begun to disappear. Where he once saw the world, he now saw nothing but blackness in some areas, while other parts seemed covered by a heavily mottled veil. As time passed, more and more of his visual field diminished and, most disconcertingly, the center of his vision began to disappear. Humans' bifocal eyes placed on the front of the head take in a panorama of nearly 180 degrees, which encompasses almost everything in front of the shoulders, although less than 1/1000 of the visual field is actually in focus while the vast majority remains vague and blurry (McCrone 1999). This is why our eyes are in constant motion, by way of saccadic movements that occur, on average, three to five times per second to ensure that dramatic variations in focus and acuity are not noticed (R. Gregory 2005). Moreover, much like a film edit between scenes, visual information is "switched off" between eye movements so as to avoid the potential disorienting and nauseating effects that are also found when watching unsteady or frenzied camera movement.

John, who had learned to see through his culture and profession, now had to use the increasingly weak awareness on the periphery of his visual field because he no longer had sight in the center. He would move his head and eyes in an attempt to "look around" the blackness, but the blackness would follow and smother the object of his attention. Slowly, John had to learn a new way of co-ordinating eyes, head, and world in order to see and interact within his environment. Tests had revealed that John had cytomegalovirus (CMV) retinitis. CMV is a common DNA virus that is part of the herpes family and is carried by the vast majority of adults. Whereas healthy immune systems keep CMV at bay, for persons with HIV/AIDS whose immune systems are compromised, the virus can cause substantial cell death across the body. Unfortunately for John, CMV had entered his eye and had begun eating away the light receptor cells in the retina. After a few months, John had lost over 50 percent of his sight, although other aspects of his health had begun to stabilize and he was able to sit, walk slowly, and perform some basic functions unaided.

On one occasion, a close friend visited John in the hospital. They were sitting and talking in the hospital corridor when she went to get them some coffee. When she returned she noticed John was bent over, sobbing heavily, and her first reaction was to drape herself over and hold him in her arms. While she was getting the coffee, John had been informed that neither surgery nor medication would be able to stop his sight from deteriorating and that most likely it would continue to deteriorate until he was blind. The months that followed were akin to a slow and extended gloaming, and like a craftsman desperately trying to work at the end of the day, John tried to make the most of the remaining light. Should he look at his dog, an encyclopedia of the world's great paintings, at his own work? He actively scrutinized the world more intensely than he ever had as a photographer, drinking up colors, faces, patterns, textures, flowers, and storing them up for when he became blind. John studied the face of his mother, her hairline, every slight discoloration and wrinkle, her mannerisms and expressions, her face while smiling, while talking, and when at rest. He looked at his brother, his sister, at the woodiness of wood, at red and blue, the transparency of glass, and the reflection light makes on ceramic surfaces. John's actions reinforced the notion that memory is not simply a property of the past but also of the future insofar as our actions in the present create the memories and knowledge we will have access to in our forthcoming life. In choosing where to look, John undertook an active creation of his memory, scrutinizing the present to create what he would remember in a blind future. Most of all, John wanted to remember what he himself looked like, he wanted to create an image of himself at thirty-three years old that he could retain but also update in future years as he aged. It was not, however, a photographic image that he strived for but a cinematic one, couched in movement.

By the time he left the hospital, John had lost all his sight in one eye and was almost completely blind in the other, except for a tiny, heavily obscured crescent through which he could vaguely discern amorphous shadows and a degree of light and dark. John's brother took him to the farmhouse and away from the speed, chaos, traffic, and intolerant pedestrians of New York's crowded streets. This was where John was going to learn to reinhabit his body and renegotiate the world. Several months had passed since he awoke that fateful morning to leave for the city; as he felt and made his way around the farmhouse, he found the empty tea cup that he had drunk from that day and next to it his fingers found the plate and the remainder of the toast that had hardened over the intervening months. Little could John have imagined while eating his breakfast that morning that he would not return until many months later—almost completely blind—his life undermined and career as a photographer in ruins.

Unsurprisingly, John found the once familiar creaks and noises in the farmhouse disconcerting, especially after months of hospital noise in which machinery, footsteps, conversation, and the sounds of work dominated. In the hospital, John's senses existed in an environment where the human body meets biomedical technology: a complex montage of antiseptic aromas, metal trolleys, commodes, whirring sounds, overcooked food, plastic sheets, and staff banter. Now in the farmhouse, he was confronted with the absence of such sounds and smells, and was also set the task of reinhabiting and reacquainting himself with the sensory properties of his once familiar house. Most immediately, John had to learn how to orientate himself in the house by touch, texture, sound, and smell, and he had to learn how to create new associations between sense and space. He kept banging into things, grazing his shins, falling over, and hitting his head. He went outside where there was no furniture, doors, or walls to act as obstacles but lost his balance on uneven ground, slopes, and ditches, bashed his face, got black eyes, and stumbled into a thorny, unforgiving hedge. Scratched, bruised, bloody, covered in mud, he went back inside and headed to bed. As he could no longer read, he decided to put a book over his face and lie there crying while smelling the warm pages, which were now mixed with his tears: a book whose very purpose was to be looked at but now experienced through scent, the texture of paper on one's face, and the memory of what words look like.

As a photographer, when John lost the vast majority of his sight he also lost his livelihood and capacity for work. As a human being, John was facing further illness and most likely an early and painful death. Consequently, John saw few possibilities for the future and very little purpose in living. He began to plan his own death—in fact, many deaths—but there was one death in particular that he kept returning to: namely, the idea of committing suicide in the bath clutching a letter, with his arm hung over the side. More specifically, it was Jacques-Louis David's painting of the radical journalist and medic, Marat, lying murdered in the bath, which haunted John's imagination. Marat would frequently spend long hours in the bath and would work and even receive friends, colleagues, and visitors while bathing. It was one of these visitors—a young, French woman named Charlotte Corday, who asked to meet him to discuss political affairs—who murdered Marat in his bath with a knife she had bought that day and hidden under her clothes. David portrays Marat laying slain in the bath, arm draped over the side, clutching his assassin's letter.

In envisioning his suicide, John planned for his body to be found in his bath in the same position as Marat, his arm dangling, by whoever entered and found him. It is a scene that immediately juxtaposes two images: first, the image of John laying lifeless in the bath in an instantly recognizable and iconic pose; second, the image then cuts to a close-up of the face and reaction of the person who found him—no doubt a close friend or family member—most likely his mother. The intensity and vividness of the expression that John imagined on the face of his mother—a face that he had actively studied during his personal gloaming and remembered so well—as she found her son dead in the bath, was matched in scale and intensity by the realization that even though John was

Figure 5.2 *The death of Marat*, by Jacques-Louis David, 1793. Oil on canvas. *Reproduced by permission from Royal Museums of Fine Arts of Belgium.*

now nearly completely blind, he still possessed an aesthetic imagination and therefore could still create images of the world in his mind's eye.

Soon after, John began to earnestly create new images in his mind and imagination. These were often informed by the painful and degrading experiences of illness in hospital—only recast as a series of dramatic and beautiful enactments—or else they depicted quotidian acts and pleasures that are informed by the simple fact of being alive when one should be dead. So, for example, the moment when John was told in the hospital corridor that he was going to lose his sight and his friend comforted him was transformed into an image in John's mind in which the moment is reenacted with John naked and his friend draped over him (see fig. 5.3 below, *My spirit tried to leave me*). John's experience in the hospital of being emaciated and unable to get out of bed to urinate—he instead had to use an overflowing plastic container—was recast as a highly stylized recreation of a man at the height of physical health about to urinate into an antique porcelain chamber pot. If in these examples we can discern not a continuous film take but a constant back and forth between images of disease, degradation, incapacity, and their opposites, then we are also reminded that human beings are never fully directors of their own lives.

John now employs an assistant, Dan Levin, who operates John's antique nineteenth-century camera. John creates images in his mind and describes what he sees to his assistant, who looks through the camera and describes back to John what he can see. Through a process of descriptive verbal negotiation, the two images come closer together and when the images are more or less the same, the picture is taken. In order to understand this process better, John suggested he photograph me; he created a series of images that allowed me to observe the working process not only from the outside but also as the subject of the photograph. The images John formed in his mind's eye were an attempt to represent the ongoing dialogue we shared over the course of many months, where we would meet, ostensibly, to discuss the relationship between terminal illness and perception but would end up spending hours talking about many varied subjects, from Emily Dickinson to Henry Fox Talbot. John explained how the image he constructed of me in his imagination had formed gradually in response to the ideas we discussed, the expressions I used, and the tone of my English accent. This then informed the series of tableaus he created, which began with me sitting naked and in profile on a wood chair facing John across a wood table.

The process relies heavily on the ekphrastic dialogue that is created between John and his assistant, Dan. *Ekphrasis*, coming from the Greek *Ek* (out) and *phrasis* (to speak), relies on the translation of one form into another, which in our case can be understood as the verbal representation of a visual phenomenon. In constructing an artwork, John is required to translate the image he forms in his mind's eye into language, which he describes to Dan, who then constructs an image out of John's words. Dan then looks through the camera and puts into words what he can see through the lens, at which point John translates Dan's words back into a visual image and compares it to the image he already has in his imagination. The process continues until the image of the world in John's mind and the image Dan sees through the camera are more or less equal. John would continually ask Dan about certain distinguishing features, such as what my face was communicating, what I looked like in profile, from the front, and so forth, and would adjust the image in his own mind, while Dan would move and manipulate the camera in order to represent John's inner vision. The ekphrastic dialogue created by John and Dan brings into being a series of images, first by rendering into language what John sees in his mind's eye and then by making this manifest in the visible and material world. Here language forms a bridge between inner vision and external world, in which information travels back and forth so as to create a series of associative montages that seek to strengthen and stabilize the relationship between mind and world rather than destabilize it.

Because of the difficulty in translating visual images into written or verbal language, the images John creates are necessarily, even radically, simplified. For while a quick glance can take in a vast amount of visual information about the world—say a crowded street—to accurately describe the people, shapes, colors, actions, and everything else one sees in the street in detailed, coherent language would be an enormous, impossible task. John is thus required to reduce the image held in his mind down into its essential lines and materials; his photographs are characterized by an elegant simplicity that has emerged as a consequence of the damage to his retinas.

When asked to describe his art, John said:

> I realized that my vision has remained intact and how this has little to do with the fact that I can no longer see through my eyes. When people come to sit for the nude portraits, I also take my clothes off regardless of whether I am also going to pose in the shot or not, partly because clothing now seems so ridiculous after spending so much time in the hospital. In many of my photographs, people are naked because to me it seems like you're closer to each other, to God, to the cosmos, or even to the ground.

In the same year that John started going blind, in an uncanny coincidence, British filmmaker and artist Derek Jarman—who was HIV+ and lost his sight to CMV retinitis—was making his final film, *Blue* (1993). *Blue* consists of a

Figure 5.3 *My spirit tried to leave me,* by John Dugdale, 1994. Cyanotype. *Reproduced by permission from the artist.*

simple blue screen juxtaposed with a complex narrative that describes the effects of going blind. It is perhaps yet another coincidence that Jarman uses a similar shade of blue in his film that John uses in his photographs. Here, Jarman recounts the relationship between his condition and the color blue in an excerpt from his film's narration:

Figure 5.4 Screenshot from *Blue*, by Derek Jarman, 1993.

My sight seems to have closed in. The hospital is even quieter this morning. Hushed. I have a sinking feeling in my stomach. I feel defeated. My mind bright as a button but my body falling apart—a naked light bulb in a dark and ruined room. There is death in the air here but we are not talking about it. But I know the silence might be broken by distraught visitors screaming, "Help, Sister! Help Nurse!" followed by the sound of feet rushing along the corridor. Then silence:

> Blue protects white from innocence
> Blue drags black with it
> Blue is darkness made visible
> Blue protects white from innocence
> Blue drags black with it
> Blue is darkness made visible

Even as we witness a simple montage of the blues found in Jarman's film and John's photographs—or indeed between the two artists' experiences of CMV retinitis—we have no way of knowing whether there is a more elemental correlation between the blue they encounter in their mind's eye. Instead, we must rely on their images and accounts of what they see and experience during blindness.

One of the most insightful and detailed accounts of what blind people see is to be found in the diaries John Hull kept throughout the 1980s. Hull, who was a professor of religious education at the University of Birmingham, kept a daily record of his descent into blindness. It is interesting to read through Hull's diaries in order to trace the decline of his visual perception and journey into blindness. During the initial phases of his blindness, he describes experiencing intense, random, and often extreme montage-like sequences in the form of vivid visions and hallucinations, which are caused because the brain's visual pathways are no longer getting visual information from external sources and so the brain starts producing its own images. Hull (1992) then documented his descent into what he calls "deep blindness"—which is different in quality from the type of blindness that John Dugdale describes—in that his mind's eye has also become blind, leaving no visual stimulation at all. Here are some of John Hull's diary entries for June 1983:

How long do you have to be blind before your dreams begin to lose colour? Do you go on dreaming in pictures forever? I have been a registered blind person for nearly three years. In the past few months, the final traces of light sensation have faded. Now I am totally blind. I cannot tell day from night. I can stare into the sun without seeing the faintest flicker of sunshine. During this time, my dreams have continued to be pictorial. Indeed, dreams have become particularly enjoyable because of the colourful freedom which I experience when dreaming. (June 1, 1983)

It distressed me considerably when I realised that I was beginning to forget what Marilyn and Imogen looked like. I had wanted to defy blindness. I had sworn to myself that I would always carry their faces hidden in my heart, even if everything else in the gallery was stolen. I am beginning to lose the category itself. I am finding it more and more difficult to realize that people look like anything, to put any meaning into the idea that they have an appearance. (June 21, 1983)

What Do I Look Like? I find that I am trying to recall old photographs of myself, just to remember what I look like. I discover with a shock that I cannot remember. Must I become a blank on the wall of my own gallery? To what extent is loss of the image of the face connected with loss of the image of the self? (June 25, 1983)

Whereas John Hull lost all traces of his sight, including that of his mind's eye, John Dugdale continues to see and construct the world though his imagination.

John Dugdale trained and works as a visual artist; he actively continues to work in the visual realm despite his blindness. It is not clear whether that plays any role in John Dugdale retaining his inner vision while John Hull lost his. In 1978, French painter Hugues de Montalembert was staying in New York City when he was attacked after he interrupted two men robbing his apartment. In the ensuing struggle, one of the men threw paint remover into his face, which burned into his eyeballs, which by the next day had rendered him totally blind. De Montalembert relates the experience of blindness in his autobiography, *Eclipse* (1987), which was made into an outstanding film, *Black sun*, by Gary Tarn (2006). Tarn places random as well as intentional images against de Montalembert's voiceover, thereby producing a series of chance juxtapositions, associations, and tangential montages to astounding effect. In describing his initial days of blindness (in his book), de Montalembert writes:

> I am afraid that the memory I have of the visible world is disappearing little by little, to be replaced by an abstract universe of sound, smell, and touch. I force myself to visualize the bedroom with its metal furniture, its window, the curtains. I bring to mind paintings, Rembrandt's Polish cavalier, Francis Bacon's portraits of Innocent X [see below]. My ability to create images absolutely must not atrophy. I must remain capable of bringing back the world I looked at intensely for thirty-five years. By contemplating in my memory the volcano of Lombok or the perfect harmony of a building designed by Michelangelo, I continue to receive instruction and knowledge from them. (de Montalembert 1987: 32–33)

In *Black sun*, de Montalembert describes how he developed the ability to sense objects in space by way of "face-vision": a phenomenon that is a widely reported ability in blind people (see Kells 2001 for a comprehensive survey of object detection by face-vision in medical studies). As de Montalembert underwent rehabilitation, he had to learn to walk in a straight line, at first under controlled conditions and then outside on the street with guidance. He was then shown how to orientate himself through the sound and airwaves that traffic produces, as this forms a "sonic edge" that allows people without sight to orientate themselves and navigate in a straight line. Later on, unbeknownst to de Montalembert, a blackboard was placed halfway along a corridor he was asked to walk down. He stopped abruptly inches from the blackboard, and when the instructor asked why he stopped, de Montalembert said that he could sense that there was an object in his way. He tells the instructor that he can go around it, over

Figure 5.5 *Study after Velazquez's portrait of Pope Innocent X*, by Francis Bacon, 1953. Oil on canvas. © *The Estate of Francis Bacon.*

it, or under it, after which the instructor confirms and informs him the object is a blackboard on an easel, which had been placed there to test his face-vision.

Hull, too, developed a sophisticated face-vision, to the extent that he could accurately navigate across a park while walking to work. He could even detect specific individual trees through the tactile air currents that registered on his face, which illustrates how the loss of one way of sensing and relating to the environment generates new forms of body-world interaction. From another of Hull's (1992) diary entries, we read:

> I first noticed that walking home over the campus in the quiet of the evening I had a sense of presence, which was the realisation of an obstacle. I discovered that if I stopped when I had this sense, and waved my white cane around, I would make contact with a tree trunk. This would be no more than three, four or five feet from me. The awareness, whatever it was, did not seem to extend beyond this range, and sometimes the tree would be as close as two feet. It was through sensing these trees, and verifying their exact location with my stick, that I gradually realised that I was developing some strange kind of perception. I learned that I could actually count the number of these trees which I would pass along the road leading down to the University gate. The sense did not seem to work on thin objects like lampposts. It had to be something about as bulky as a tree trunk or a human body before I sensed it. As the months go past, sensitivity seems to be increasing.
>
> Not only have I become sensitive to thinner objects, but the range seems to have increased. When walking home, I used only to be able to detect parked cars by making contact with my cane. These days I almost never make contact with a parked car unexpectedly. The experience itself is quite extraordinary, and I cannot compare it with anything else I have ever known. It is like a sense of physical pressure. One wants to put up a hand to protect oneself, so intense is the awareness. One shrinks from whatever it is. It seems to be characterised by a certain stillness in the atmosphere. On one of my walks, I pass beside a five-foot-high fence made of vertical metal bars. This gives way, at a certain point, to a solid brick wall. I find that if I pay attention I can tell when I have left the fence and am going along the wall. There is, somehow, a sense of a more massive presence. I gather from conversations that this experience is essentially acoustic and is based upon awareness of echoes. (July 14, 1983)

As Oliver Sacks (2004) observes, it is not currently possible to establish from a neurological perspective why some persons, such as John Hull, enter into the realm of "deep blindness" and cease to have the ability to produce images in the mind's eye, whereas others, such as John Dugdale and Hugues de Montalembert, continue to dwell in a visual world and create intricate and powerful visual images. But even if the neurological evidence remains unclear, it is still possible to consider how viruses, degenerative conditions, and acts of random violence that result in the loss of sight have the potential to effect radical transformations in sensory being that necessitated bodies and landscapes to be reinhabited in new ways. The experiences of John Dugdale, Derek Jarman, John Hull, and Hugues de Montalembert provide an empirical basis from which to consider how the disintegration of people's sensory lifeworlds generate different ways of visualizing, sensing, and moving in the world.

CONCLUSION: OSTRANENIE IN ACTION

Many actions and practices have a language-like or syntactic quality. This is not to say their performance depends on language. Rather, it is to use the situational and sequential qualities of language to understand how actions and practices unfold in process. In other words, there is a syntax of practices that places the body in time. As illness progresses, previously routine practices become increasingly explicit in terms of how each constituent part is ordered into a syntactical chain of action and embedded in one's surroundings. For example, *brushing-teeth* involves an extended chain of action, and whenever people enter periods of decline it becomes apparent that brushing-teeth involves *animating-the-body*, *raising-one's-head-off-the-pillow*, *getting-out-of-bed*, *walking-to-the-bathroom*, *opening-the-door*, *standing-unsupported*, *leaning-over-the-sink*, *administering-toothpaste*, *brushing*, *and walking-back*. Simple tasks become fragmented and their constituent parts are "made present" by an inability to perform, revealing facets and temporalities that were previously hidden in an embodied memory once naturalized through practice but now degraded through illness and disruption. Persons become more conscious of the entire chain of action involved in previously taken-for-granted practices. The syntactic chain can be strategically modified and adapted, while certain parts can be discarded according to current physical condition. However, some facets must be retained and the ability to perform a task may lie with a single key component. If this cannot be renegotiated, the practice is jeopardized regardless of its importance or pragmatic need.

Blindness, as a mode of being-in-the-world, reveals how habitual, seemingly taken-for-granted activities have a narrative quality that can be likened to the way film scenes are assembled, sequenced, and edited. This is not to say the performance of these practices possesses a formal syntax or grammatical structure, but rather it is to use the narrative characteristics of language and film to understand the procedural and disruptive possibilities of familiar, everyday activities. It is not normally recognized that something as commonplace as *drinking* involves eyesight, walking, and navigation. However, whenever John Dugdale offered me some tea, it became apparent that it involved an entire chain of action based in strategic planning, movement, and recollection, from establishing the precise angle to traverse the living room, reaching out for the entrance to the kitchen, locating the whereabouts of the strategically placed tea, milk, kettle, cups, teapot, and tray, then walking back by way of deliberate steps rooted in his proprioceptive memory of the room.

When immersed in action, people are not always fully cognizant of their movements or how these are embedded within the world. For example, when *walking*, most people are not consciously thinking about lifting one foot off the ground, coordinating their eyes, lungs, and legs, or synchronizing their thigh, flexing the knee, moving the leg forward, placing the sole back on the ground, and so forth. Likewise, when *talking*, people do not explicitly concentrate on making the relevant facial and labial movements or coordinating their accompanying body postures and hand actions, but are instead focused on the conversation they are having. In such moments, the body "disappears" from conscious awareness, sometimes for quite extended periods, insofar as the human body has evolved to give attention where it is most needed—i.e., to the world rather than itself—in what is known as the body's primary "from-to orientation" (Leder 1990).

However, during the onset of blindness, the modes for giving attention to the world are recast as part of people's wider adaptation to the new conditions of sensory perception. When *talking*, for example, words, ideas, lungs, mouth, tongue, lips, hands, air, and sound waves ordinarily merge into seamless action. Here, the body's coordinated activity that enables speech is familiarized and naturalized through the ongoing practices of daily life in ways that are often absent to consciousness. In such moments there are few conscious boundaries between person and world and instead there is an unbroken continuity, a moving-together, coherence, or confluence of human action within the world (Parkin 1985). By contrast, Dugdale's body *is* present to consciousness when talking, in that he actively practices and deliberately performs a sighted person's head movements and facial expressions when responding to other people's words, so as to ensure he does not lose the facial and gestural expressions that signify sociality, hearing, and comprehension. He continually reminds himself to respond to different topics and themes of conversation by moving his head, hands, and body in such a way that is appropriate to the emotional tone and subject being discussed. Likewise, Hull and de Montalembert's development of "face-vision" demonstrates another way in which the relationship between body and world becomes present to consciousness when walking, in the form of sensing air currents, the sonic edges formed by traffic, subtle variations in temperature, the echoes of different substances or materials, and other forms of sensory information that allow persons to establish the relative position of objects in space and facilitate movement.

For John Dugdale, like many people living with HIV/AIDS or other conditions, habitual modes of dwelling, moving in, and knowing the world are disrupted on an ongoing basis and they have to repeatedly *reinhabit* their bodies during and after periods of illness. People learn to continually "test out" their bodies at strategic times and within different contexts for different purposes, recalling the etymological origin of "experience" wherein *ex* signifies "out of," while *peira* means "attempt, trial, test," reinforcing Edward Casey's suggestion that "Places, like bodies and landscapes, are something we experience . . . and to have an experience is to make a trial, an experiment, out of living. It is to do something that requires the proof of the senses" (Casey 1993: 30).

Living with HIV/AIDS, like negotiating blindness, means that being a body-in-the-world is subject to potential disruption and self-conscious reflection. Even when there is minimal disruption, people plan, strategize, and legislate for the possibility of future needs and develop modes of action that are necessary for social and bodily continuity. Becoming blind necessitates becoming conscious of the various constituent parts of many previously routine actions that were embedded in embodied memory and naturalized through years of habit. Ordinary actions become transformed through a kind of *ostranenie-in-action* in which the normal becomes disrupted and defamiliarized, akin to the way common words and images are taken from ordinary life and are "made strange" through techniques such as poetry and montage.

Dugdale, Jarman, Hull, and de Montalembert each describe how they experienced their bodies and surroundings as different, obstructive, and disjointed, and how their interactions with familiar persons, places, or objects demand new kinds of awareness and attention. Rather than a seamless flow of mind, body, and world conjoined in action, objects that once barely registered in conscious awareness take one unawares in unexpected places. Surfaces, layouts, and textures take on new practical and aesthetic meanings and are made present. Nevertheless, as their experiences illustrate, once the world falls apart it is remade anew, and the constitutive elements of daily life are recombined and reassembled into new chains of action. The physiological and sensory reorganization of the body amid the gloaming hour and onset of blindness reinforces how "truth" and "reality" are not fixed to any particular sense organ but are ever-changing properties of our current purposes, actions, and circumstances. John Dugdale still wakes every morning and tests out the relative position of his body by moving around the house before going outside. Nowadays, he has come to an arrangement between himself and the environment whereby he cedes to its power each morning before reclaiming the rest of the day for himself.

CHAPTER SIX

The eternal return

The transformation of waste is perhaps the oldest preoccupation of man. Man being the chosen alloy, he must be reconnected—via shit, at all cost. Inherent with(in) us is the dream of the task of the alchemist to create from the clay of man. And to recreate from excretion of man pure and then soft and then solid gold. All must not be art. Some art we must disintegrate.

—Patti Smith, "25th floor (& high on rebellion)"

The desire for money takes the place of all genuinely human needs. Thus the apparent accumulation of wealth is really the impoverishment of human nature, and its appropriate morality is the renunciation of human nature and desires—asceticism. The effect is to substitute an abstraction, *homo economicus*, for the concrete totality of human nature, and thus to dehumanise human nature. In this dehumanised human nature man loses contact with his own body, more specifically with his senses.

—Norman O. Brown, *Life against death* ([1959] 1970: 211)

If my own activity does not belong to me, if it is an alien, coerced activity, to whom, then, does it belong?
To a being *other* than myself.
Who is this being?
The *gods*?
—Karl Marx, *The economic and philosophical manuscripts of 1844* ([1844] 1988: 79)

When Patti Smith sings the words above, she reminds us that we are never far away from magic, alchemy, and waste, including how human beings—like art and life—are something created, have a value placed on them, and can be discarded. This chapter continues this story to investigate how human lives, art, and value, might be connected within the social, political, and economic wastelands of America. It begins with a quote concerning the relationship between life and art, by Maurice Merleau-Ponty in his essays on painting and perception: "Although it is certain that a person's life does not explain his work, it is equally certain that the two are connected. The truth is that *that work to be done called for that life*" (Merleau-Ponty 1994: 70, italics in original).

I would like to ask what kind of life is it necessary for someone to live in order to conceive and produce the painting below, and whether it is possible to discern traces of that life within the artwork itself?

The painting is by New York–based artist William Cullum, who—after getting a tattoo with a large + sign on his shoulder to display his HIV+ status to the world—began working on a series of paintings he imagined would be the final paintings he would ever make. I worked with Bill over the summer of 1999. What began as an attempt to understand the artistic productions and imaginative lifeworlds of someone living with a radically unstable body and future, ended abruptly when I lost track of Bill the following year. He no longer answered his door, responded to emails, or picked up the phone. I no longer saw him around the neighborhood or at events, and each time I called by his apartment or studio he was not there. Bill had seemingly disappeared from the face of the earth and I presumed him to be dead. I was thus shocked to rediscover Bill twelve years later, in the summer of 2011, after more than a decade of unexplained absence. I was equally surprised to find him fit, healthy, and obsessively working on a new series of paintings whose sole subject matter was endless packets of processed mackerel.

Bill's paintings of mackerel provide evidence of his continued existence in the world. Traces of his body, elbow, and brushstrokes can be found in each painting, alongside a series of artistic and aesthetic decisions about color, style, and subject matter. But beyond the reference to pop art, the intentions behind these paintings or the reasons for their presence in the world remain unknown. Interpretation and understanding are further complicated when art is understood *as an act of making* rather than the finished product, or following Claude Lévi-Strauss (1966), when the meaning and value of an artwork are located less in the final outcome than in the process of making it. Indeed, why would

Figure 6.1 *Fresh catch*, by William Cullum, 2012. Oil on canvas. *Reproduced by permission from the artist.*

a person dedicate months of precious life, especially when framed by brevity, illness, and uncertainty, painstakingly painting packets of mackerel in an era of digital cameras and smartphones?

The transformation of light, matter, and color into art draws on an object or material's capacity to simultaneously encompass properties of substance and

Figure 6.2-6.3 Comparison with packet: Left: Oil on canvas of packet of mackerel (2012), by William Cullum. Right: Photograph of packet of mackerel (2012), by William Cullum. *Reproduced by permission from the artist.*

sign, recalling the religious origins and development of painting. Andy Warhol's work explicitly plays on the religious aura of art by according a reverence and importance to Campbell's soup cans and other industrially manufactured objects—including Brillo Pads, Heinz Tomato Ketchup, Kellogg's Corn Flakes, Del Monte canned peaches, and Coca Cola bottles—to transform cheap mass-produced goods into works of art and veneration. All art, to some degree, involves a similar act of transubstantiation, which according to Jean-Paul Sartre, is rooted in the workings of the human imagination. For Sartre, the imagination is not simply a variant of perception—given that objects are apprehended differently in the imagination than in perception—but a distinct form of consciousness that encompasses both the act of imagining *and* the diverse worlds that the imagination brings into being. Sartre continues: "When I look at a drawing I posit in that very look a world of human intentions of which that drawing is a product [and for] the image to appear, the cooperation of my consciousness is necessary, but the artist knows this, counts on it; the artist solicits this cooperation" ([1940] 2004: 35).

Sartre contends the shared capacity of imagining brings together the respective worlds of artist and audience. And yet, Bill's paintings of mackerel remain highly ambiguous because we do not know what type of cooperation he is trying to elicit or who his intended audience might be. Doubt and uncertainty emerge concerning how intentionality and material substances intertwine, and whether it is possible for the imagination to bridge the artist and audience's respective lifeworlds. Rather than providing material evidence as to Bill's life experience, it seems his endless paintings of processed mackerel only raise further questions and his intentions and actions remain uncertain and ambiguous.

An alternative approach, following Martin Heidegger, would be to begin with the ontic presence of the artwork itself and build from there. For Heidegger, a material thing does not make sense or possess meaning in its own terms but through its use and relationship to the world. A hammer, famously, possesses little purpose in and of itself insofar as its design, shape, and materials only make sense in relation to the nail. However, the hammer and nail have no more meaning or value in combination than the hammer in isolation because they also need wood and an understanding of intentionality, future-orientated action, and the phenomenal world—for example, hammering a nail into wood to make a roof, which in turn reveals an understanding of how the human organism needs to be protected from the elements and provide care for itself and others. Beginning with the hammer, it becomes possible to expand out, via people's practical activities, to gain an understanding of how persons and things are related and engage with the world through particular moral understandings. This leads us to ask, what does the world have to be in order for a person to spend weeks on end painting packets of processed mackerel—especially when there are so many other things to give attention to—and what might Bill's paintings of mackerel reveal about such things as care, shelter, and wider society?

BRIEF HISTORY OF BILL AND ME

I first got to know Bill in the late 1990s when I was trying to understand the imaginative lifeworlds of people close to death, including the transformations in people's perceptions, practices, and worldviews when confronting mortality. One research method I employed was to juxtapose people's artworks alongside their life histories in an attempt to trace the trajectory of people's perceptions and experiences through the works they produced during periods of stability, uncertainty, illness, and crisis. I also adapted Friedrich Nietzsche's ([1883]

1974b) idea of "eternal return" and turned it into a question to generate insights and conversation while carrying out people's life histories. For Nietzsche, if time and space are infinite, then repetitive events and patterns are liable to emerge and reemerge in the structure of the universe. The more time passes, the more likely a thought, action, event, or roll of the dice is likely to repeat itself. On a quotidian level, this can be used to think about the habitual forms and repetitive patterns and practices of everyday life, such as commuting, the working day, one's lifestyle choices, and social relations. This can even be extended into a kind of thought experiment whereby—under conditions of eternity—the specific configuration of atoms and molecules that constituted a specific moment might return so that we live this precise moment over and over again: an eternal recurrence back to the same point in time and space. All our pains, hopes, desires, joys, and errors will have to be lived through again and again.

Whether it does or not is less relevant to Nietzsche, who is not presenting eternal return as an empirical fact but as a conceptual possibility in order to think about the moral quality and value of life as it is lived. For Nietzsche, we need to go beyond the conventions and habits of social life, many of which he sees as empty and banal, to think about the unique potential of each moment. If we apply this as a kind of practical philosophy to our lifeworlds—for example, when watching a bad soap opera, stuck in the daily traffic jam, munching through meaningless bureaucracy, or otherwise frittering life away—it is painful to go through these just one more time, but imagine eternally returning to them over and over again.

As a practical appraisal of existence, we can consider the various activities that make up our life and imagine what it would be like to return to them eternally—both good and bad—so as to identify and create a meaningful existence. It is indeed extraordinary to think that this very moment in which these words are now being read is the moment to which the whole of eternity refers to insofar as everything that has ever happened, including the whole of history and whole of the past, has resulted in this particular moment in time. Likewise, everything that is *going to happen* in the future comes out of this moment. As such, each and every moment in which we are dwelling is the vital point to which the whole of eternity refers to and is the culmination of the past and gateway to the future. Of course, it is impossible to be cognizant of the unique potentiality of each moment given the practical demands of everyday life, and consequently the existential significance of each moment usually fades into the background. However, when placed in the context of people whose lives are framed by terminal illness, the temporality of being and potential for action are made tangible on a day-to-day, even moment-to-moment basis.

Under such circumstances Nietzsche's idea takes on a different hue and complexion and the question of what someone does or does not do with their lives—including the choices they make, the demands they are willing to submit to, and the justifications they give to themselves and others—is concentrated in the face of finitude and reveals new possibilities for practical and moral person-hood. How would you respond if you were told you had six weeks, six months, or six years to live? Would you spend this time engaged in religious activities and working toward an afterlife? Would you spend as much time as possible with friends and family? Would you create a bucket list and travel to see all the places you wanted to see? Would you continue to go to work and try to carry on as normal? Would you spend all your savings?

Bill was confronted with such a set of questions after he was tested for HIV/AIDS in the 1980s. At the time, the term AIDS had only recently been coined and those in the scientific community were still at a loss to explain why so many young, healthy gay men were falling sick and dying. Bill thinks he got "it" during one particularly memorable orgy that involved twenty other men, which he saw as much as a political act as a sexual act for a Southern boy. If Bill did not catch it that evening, he "damn well should have," given the personal and political significance of the night.

Following diagnosis, Bill always imagined he would be dead in eighteen months, a settled expectation of death that he described as his "horizon of exist-ence." The fact that Bill survived into the 1990s did not make it any more likely that he would survive. In fact, the opposite was the case because having already lived longer than he should have, Bill was ever more convinced he was going to die at some point within the next eighteen months; he lived and planned life accordingly. The arrival of antiretroviral medications might have ordinarily altered his eighteen-month horizon of existence, except for the fact that Bill was among the significant minority of persons for whom medications only had a limited effect and caused life threatening side effects so severe that Bill had to be hospitalized.

As a long-time atheist, Bill did not believe in salvation or an afterlife, mean-ing death represented the furthest extension and limit of his being. Initially, Bill decided to spend the remainder of his life in a state of intoxication by taking lots of drugs, mainly crystal meth, and entering into death high. Crystal meth offers intense euphoria but is highly addictive and dangerous insofar as it leads to brain damage, premature aging, lung, kidney, and liver problems and is also accompanied by a rapid decline in social functioning. The risk of addiction, overdosing, and danger to his long-term health meant little to Bill given his circumstances and eighteen-month expectation of death. Nevertheless, by the time I met Bill he had largely stopped using meth in order to dedicate what remained of his life to painting. Rather than spending his time high or traveling the world or working out at the gym or any of the other alternatives that presented themselves, Bill locked himself away in a tiny art studio on East 14th Street. He stopped going out at night, rarely spent money, and almost never saw people. Instead, from Monday to Friday he worked obsessively and lived, ate, and slept in the studio, only venturing out for cigarettes and food or to walk his dog, Caleb. Come Friday afternoon, he would lock up the studio and return to his normal social life, spending time with his partner and socializing with friends, until Monday morning when he would return to the studio. In doing so, Bill accorded a value and significance to spending his time painting in the context of imagining he only had eighteen months left on the planet.

The first time I met Bill, we had arranged for me to spend a whole Friday in the studio before he went back to his apartment for the weekend. This meant Bill had been cooped up all week long, alone with his paintings and barely speaking to anyone but himself and his dog. A flood of ideas about art, life, politics, and much else besides came spilling out after five days of self-imposed confinement. Thereafter we met every Friday for the next three months. Starting from Nietzsche, our conversations over the summer covered everything in Bill's life and worldview. It covered his personal history, his Southern upbringing, his training and original aspiration to be a concert pianist, his life as a sexual outlaw and male prostitute—which he gave up not because he was HIV+ insofar as he told me "there's a market for everything," but because it distracted from his painting—it covered his artistic ambitions, drug companies, Southern table manners, sex with politicians and CEOS, his "relatively sympathetic view of science," Rauschenberg, postmodernism, Mozart, money, literature, and the Enlightenment works of philosopher John Locke.

At this stage in his life, Bill imagined that the painting he was currently working on was going to be his last and wanted to cram as much as possible into it. His paintings are chaotic, troubled, and they attempt to challenge the linearity of time by putting everything he ever wanted to express onto a single canvas. As such, Bill started "in the middle of each painting" as the immediacy of time meant he did not have time to waste on preparatory work, drawing sketches, or conducting research. When he embarked on a painting he would often have little sense of how it would turn out. If he made a bad brush stroke, got the color wrong, or something did not look right, Bill would simply leave it in the painting, as he did not have the time to correct mistakes. Instead, they were left to play upon the eye and to irritate.

Figure 6.4 *Red*, by William Cullum, 1995. Wax, oil, pigment, laser print, plastic paper, resin, wood. *Reproduced by permission from the artist.*

There is a morbid intensity and compression of dark symbols in Bill's paintings that connects the works to Bill's life and worldview. In our conversations, Bill often intimated there was something universal in the paintings, due to the circumstances in which they were painted and how they touched on a shared human awareness of mortality. I disagreed and argued that they were better understood as being representative of a specific state of mind that was a product of a specific social and historical understanding of death rather than one that pertained to all human beings. Bill agreed there was some truth in this but argued there were frequently elements found in art, including some of his own, which could not be so conveniently reduced to or explained away by theories of social construction. He said the encounter with mortality was not as neatly tethered

Figure 6.5 *Green*, by William Cullum, 1995. Wax, oil, pigment, laser print, plastic paper, resin, wood. *Reproduced by permission from the artist.*

to social and cultural context as many theorists, including myself, would have us believe.

Because I would soon be traveling to Uganda, where I had previously carried out extended periods of fieldwork, I decided to take slides of Bill's images with me. While in Uganda, I asked a good friend of mine, Lillian Nabulime—one of Uganda's leading artists, who lectures at Makerere University's School of Industrial and Fine Art, and whose husband died of HIV/AIDS—if she would let me teach a couple of her classes. I divided the students into two groups. I asked one group to leave and come back in an hour, and showed to the remaining group slides of works by Bill and other artists with HIV/AIDS. I introduced the artworks to the group as being by artists who were living with or had died from HIV/AIDS and recounted their life stories before I opened up a class discussion about the works. After an hour we swapped groups, and I showed the exact same artworks to the other group, only this time I did not reveal the artists' HIV status and simply said they were works by New York artists. When it came to Bill's work, both groups were unanimous that "they were painted by a man whose mind was full of death." To this extent, Bill was correct that his work touched on something universal. But in another regard, Bill's paintings revealed a different story in that certain of the devices that Bill used to evoke a sense of foreboding in his paintings—for example, the consistent use of abandoned buildings—were reinterpreted as representing God's mercy and a welcome destiny of peace and paradise that someone finds after a difficult death. For, according to these students at least, in paradise the buildings are large, spacious, have a decent roof and are not made out of mud and straw.

Shortly after Bill completed the two paintings shown above, he had a severe reaction to the antiretroviral medications he was taking, which culminated in a massive heart attack while he was out walking Caleb. Although only in his thirties, the combination of medications and steroids used to treat his HIV had the effect of raising the triglycerides in his blood to dangerously high levels. Up until his heart attack, Bill described his worldview (as discerned by the Ugandan students) as one overshadowed by his impending death. However, after his heart attack and finding himself "up close to death," he came to see death "as something totally natural, as though it was like being born." After he left the hospital, Bill found death no longer held the same fear or intensity and he was no longer able to paint the same types of painting or feel the driving urgency that underpinned his work. He sent me images of his new works, which consisted of soft, rounded, and fluffy shapes painted in pastel shades. Bill told me he wasn't sure if the paintings were any good or not. Indeed I wasn't very sure myself.

Then he disappeared.

FIELDWORK RETURN

I returned to New York in the summer of 2000 and I called around to see Bill in order to tell him about the comments that people in Uganda had made about his artworks, but he was nowhere to be found. He no longer answered his door, responded to emails, or picked up the phone, and he was never in his studio. He had seemingly disappeared from the face of the earth. Almost every year I returned to New York to continue my fieldwork and looked up Bill, but he was nowhere to be found:

Bill is not there in 2000.
Bill is not there in 2001.
Bill is not there in 2002.

Bill is not there in 2003.

Bill is not there in 2004: It is now the era of Google and I still can't find Bill.

Bill is not there in 2005.

Bill is not there in 2006: I presume Bill is dead.

Bill is not there in 2007.

Bill is not there in 2008.

Bill is not there in 2009: It is now ten years since I saw Bill. I am certain Bill is dead.

Bill is not there in 2010.

I found Bill in 2011 . . .

Bill had been in prison, serving an eight-year sentence for dealing crystal meth.

The Drug Enforcement Administration (DEA) had caught Bill in a sting operation. When I had last seen Bill in 1999, his health had stabilized and he was able to go on an ARV regimen without any major reactions and he was mostly clean. He was dedicated to his art career, was represented by a gallery, and was working intensely in his studio on his paintings while experimenting with new styles and searching for new modes of expression. His art was being written about in magazines and his destiny as a painter looked promising. However, in the end it seems that Bill was never quite able to kick his drug habit. His addiction, which had its roots in not having to worry about the long-term consequences of taking crystal meth or its dangerous physical and cognitive side effects, had become a daily part of his life and was eating up his money. Bill had started small-scale dealing in order to support his own habit. A friend of Bill's asked if Bill would come in with him on a big deal he had lined up, which would be worth up to thirty thousand dollars.

Bill, who had mostly been dealing in terms of small, one hundred dollar fixes said yes, and saw this as his opportunity to finally act on a plan he had been harboring of leaving New York to get away from drugs, kick his addiction, and return to his painting. His plan, which in the final instance might have only been a junkie's promise, was to live somewhere remote, out of the city—maybe a cabin in the Bahamas—where he could recreate his studio, live frugally for a year, and get back to his art. What Bill did not know at the time was that his friend had already been caught by the DEA, which had been actively targeting drug use by gay men; the deal was part of a sting operation. The DEA had made Bill's friend an offer, namely giving up his contacts and setting up a couple of undercover narcotics busts in exchange for a short sentence. Bill's friend arranged a meet

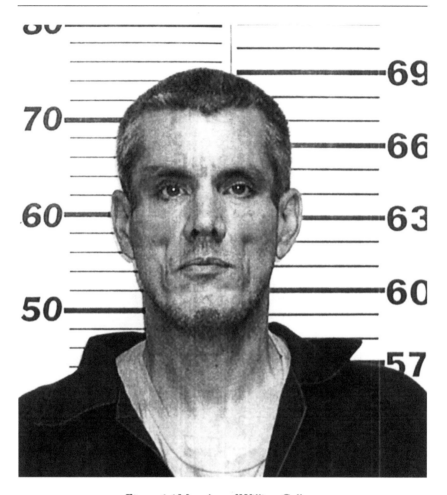

Figure 6.6 Mug shot of William Cullum.

in order to make the deal. When Bill arrived, his instincts told him something was not quite right about the two guys in his friend's living room, but he also had a junkie's head on and was thinking about the possibility of thirty thousand dollars. The two people he met were undercover DEA agents. Instead of going to the Bahamas, he got over seven years in federal prison.

Bill's arrest also coincided with a new policy that was being carried out by the DEA, targeted at gay men, for which hundreds of posters of dealers—with their names and photographs—were posted around the neighborhoods in which the dealer lived or was caught. The ethics of this even made the *New York Daily News*, the *Associated Press*, and *Newsday*.

United States Attorney
Southern District of New York

FOR IMMEDIATE RELEASE   CONTACT: U.S. ATTORNEY'S OFFICE
OCTOBER 28, 2004   HERBERT HADAD, MEGAN GAFFNEY
                                                PUBLIC INFORMATION OFFICE
                                                (212) 637-2600

**U.S. ATTORNEY ANNOUNCES INITIATIVE OF PUBLIC POSTERS
OF CONVICTED CRYSTAL METH DEALERS TO DETER TRAFFICKING**

DAVID N. KELLEY, the United States Attorney for the Southern District of New York, announced today the sentencing in Manhattan federal court of WILLIAM M. CULLUM to 87 months in prison on five counts of distributing methamphetamine in Manhattan and one count of conspiring to distribute more than 50 grams of methamphetamine, commonly known as "Crystal Meth."

Mr. KELLEY also announced an initiative of the public display of posters of convicted crystal meth dealers in the neighborhoods where they plied their drug trade.

According to the Indictment and a criminal Complaint, over the period July 2003 through October 2003, CULLUM was involved in distributing crystal methamphetamine on approximately five separate occasions in Manhattan. On at least two occasions, CULLUM sold approximately one ounce of crystal meth to an undercover special agent of the Drug Enforcement Administration ("DEA"), at a price of $2,800 per ounce. CULLUM pled guilty to all of the charges contained in the six-count Indictment on June 10, 2004.

Figure 6.7 US Attorney announcement.

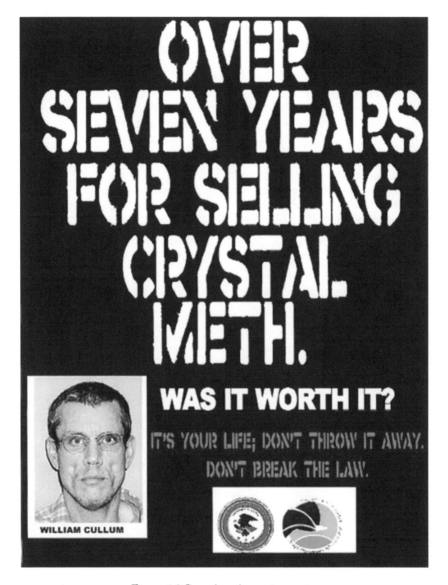

Figure 6.8 Crystal meth warning poster.

Gay activists angered by poster
by the Associated Press
November 2, 2004, 2:37 PM EST

A public awareness campaign featuring posters of convicted
methamphetamine dealers has drawn an angry response from gay
activists.

Last week, federal prosecutors in Manhattan unveiled the posters, which have the defendants' names, mug shots and warnings like, "Over seven years for selling crystal meth. Was it worth it?"

They planned to plaster them in gay neighborhoods that have been ravaged by the highly addictive stimulant.

Activists responded on Tuesday by accusing authorities of needlessly vilifying gay men who were caught selling small amounts of crystal meth. They also argued the campaign could undermine efforts within the gay community to treat addicts and discourage potential users.

"Gay men telling other gay men that crystal is dangerous is one thing," said Peter Staley of the Crystal Meth Working Group. "It is quite another thing for government, especially law enforcement agencies, to threaten gay men with what look like 'wanted' posters."

Activist Dan Carlson also criticized prosecutors for not consulting with gay leaders about the campaign, and said he still hopes to convince them to drop it.

"Rule No. 1 is that you enlist the community," Carlson said.

U.S. Attorney David Kelley said he had agreed to meet with activists to discuss their objections. He declined further comment.

Kelley announced the campaign following the sentencing of a Manhattan artist, William Cullum, 46, to more than seven years in prison. The defendant was arrested last year after selling 1 ounce of crystal meth to an undercover agent for $2,800.

Activists say most crystal meth dealers in gay neighborhoods like Chelsea and the West Village are nonviolent addicts who sell to support their habits.

Rather than deter dealing, the posters would "heighten homophobia both within our community and outside it," said psychologist Bruce Kellerhouse. "Gay men need to be informed about drug laws and sentencing, but they don't need another reason to beat themselves up."

The cruel irony of ending up incarcerated in federal prison after his self-imposed confinement in his studio furnishes a sense of tragedy and absurdity to Bill's story. In the next section, Bill is going to provide an ethnography of the US federal prison system as an insider and as a body, as for many years he was subject to its regimes and mechanisms of power. These are Bill's observations . . .

FROM THE INSIDE: AN ETHNOGRAPHY OF PRISON

The first thing that happens when you're arrested is you are handcuffed and shackled and put on a bus and driven out to Brooklyn, to a concrete facility, and put into an elevator. And then you are taken down into the bowels of the building. Then all of us are ushered out onto a ramp, the shackles are taken off our bodies, our clothes are removed, and we're given jumpsuits. At this time, we're also given numbers. These numbers are the numbers that we have to use whenever we're spoken to, from that point on. Mine was 55552054. This is all part of the prison system's policy of dehumanization, of reducing you to a number. It has the effect of making it absolutely clear from the very beginning that you don't count as an individual. It is also very effective and makes it very difficult to fight against. At the same time, it immediately sets up

(i)   A set of social and moral expectations;
(ii)   Subsumes you into common identity with all of your fellow prisoners;
(iii) Introduces a punitive mode of addressing the staff.

After receiving your number, everyone is ushered into different holding cells and is processed. Then, ultimately, we end up in a cell in the prison. This creates and sustains the idea that you are part of an us-against-them system, whereby all inmates, regardless of socio-economic status, are part of one unit: a "we" who are opposed to "them": a complex disciplinary administration that comprises the guards, the counselors, and all of the people involved in running the prison.

There are several orders of people who are in federal prison: there are white-collar criminals who are generally white and college-educated and some of whom have come from a high economic status and who generally enter into the prison system with a sense of entitlement, which they are disabused of very quickly because they don't get special privileges because of their status. Then there are the rest of the people, most of whom are there on drug charges. The prisons in which I was incarcerated were about a third white, a third Latino, and a third black.

For the first few years I was in a high-security prison. In the higher-level security institutions you are allocated ten-minute moves. This means that for every hour there are ten minutes where you can move from one place to another. Then you have to stay in that place for fifty minutes before you are allowed move again. Beyond that is the temporal structure of the particular prison, where there is a certain time and procedure whereby, for example, you are herded to meals or chow, which is allocated and you are called by your building. Your building left en masse and you had to go in line and you ate whatever was given to you. And it became my life. In the end, it turned out that it was actually kind of comforting to have that kind of ritual, that kind of surety. There is no decision to be made. It was as it was.

Because prisoners are not allowed to have money, one thing that develops in the prison is that the population is divided into two recognizable groups, which are central to the social structure. One group has people on the outside—for example, friends, parents, siblings—who send money, and the other group is not sent money. The group that has no money sent in has to find ways to make money in order to operate in the prison system, for example, by doing odd jobs for other prisoners that would earn some sort of an income so they can get necessities from the commissary. However, because prisoners are not allowed money in itself (that is, cash in hand), money is not a tangible item but a number that is deposited into a commissary account. The commissary is the prison store that sells toiletries, food items, snacks, clothes, and so forth. The prison provides to you a jumpsuit, four pairs of socks, four pairs of underwear, four T-shirts, and a pair of steel-toed boots. And that was all you got. So it was necessary to have some sort of an income while you were there. If you wanted anything, you had to have money in a commissary account to buy it from the commissary store. The only way that people who weren't sent money were able to get things from the commissary was by doing chores for the inmates who had money in their accounts.

As a form of currency and substitute for money in material form we used packets of mackerels. There were two kinds of mackerels—money macks and eating macks—a money mack was a packet of mackerel that had been passed around so often that the fillets had broken up into mush and were not fit to eat. When the commissary ran out of mackerel, which it did from time to time, we would use tuna as a substitute. But mackerel was always the go-to substance for commerce. When macks were scarce, we would also occasionally use stamps; in some prisons stamps are the regular currency but in a large number of prisons it is mackerels. Interestingly, the company that makes the mackerels tried to make them for the general population but no one would buy them, and so they're actually made specifically for the prison system. The prison system is the only place where you can buy or obtain these packets of mackerel.

I smuggled one out when I left so that I could make paintings of it.

So, say you wanted your laundry done. Your laundry could be done once a week for three mackerels, or your cell could be cleaned for five mackerels, then another mackerel for doing the floor. Mackerel, or "macks" can be used to get a haircut, your clothes pressed, can be exchanged for pieces of fruit, sexual favors, legal advice, or used as poker chips. A cigarette cost one mackerel. A haircut cost two macks. These were people's jobs. They would do these jobs, be paid in and collect the mackerels, then they would sell the *mackerels to gamblers, who in exchange would then buy commissary items for them. It was a kind of complicated system but it worked, and it worked well. In the end, and I suspect it is still true—inflation sort of took place—because when I got there the going exchange rate for mackerels was around a dollar. When mackerel cost $1 on the commissary it was easy to make the conversion so that anything that would cost $1 could be paid for by mackerel without having to work it out. By the time I left they were $1.40. So you were paying $1.40 for a product that would only allow you a dollar value. You weren't getting a cigarette and a half, or rather 1.4 cigarettes, for your mackerel, you were still only getting a cigarette. I suspect that if it gets to $2, some sort of change will take place, but I don't know about that—and I don't want to know about that.*

Prisoners with lots of mackerel are called "mackonnaires." There are also instances of violence in terms of people collecting a large number of macks and other people trying to steal them but that's not really anything that's different from the outside world. Conditions exist in prisons in the same way they exist outside. You're walking down the street and you get mugged because the person doesn't have money and you do.

Prisons are also really important to the economy of the area in which they are placed. There is a national census every ten years, and in the census the prisoners incarcerated in the prison are counted as citizens of that particular county or district. A primary purpose of the census is to establish representation in government. For instance, my particular prison had seven hundred inmates and so that was an extra seven hundred citizens for this particular rural county that would increase their representation in congress and in the state legislature and in the distribution finances. There is a move to change that now, whereby prisoners will be counted in the next census as being from where they were arrested rather than the area where their prison resides. Back in 1991, there was a big push in the system to build prisons in the rural areas, mostly by the Republican Party, so they would provide jobs and census numbers. So they're really important to these particular rural areas, which were unrepresented before and now have an extra legislature.

I was moved around a lot, spent time in many different prisons, started out in high security for the first years and then ultimately ended up in a "camp," which is the lowest intensity prison available in the US system. In the camp, as opposed to the high security prison or regular prison, there are no fences and you have freedom of movement and can pretty much come and go as you please with certain exceptions. One of my favorite things to do was to wake up before the sun came up and then I would go out to a particular nook where the guards couldn't see me, and I would smoke cigarettes and drink coffee and watch the sun come up. One of the most remarkable things is that I had lived in New York City for a long time and wasn't really aware of nature, and this camp was in the middle of a thousand acres of hayfields. So I was able to watch the sun come up every morning and see the rotation of the Earth, and just how far it goes was kind of remarkable to me. That was one of the lovely things about it.

It took a good while for the prison system to sort out my antiretroviral medications. It's also a mistake to think of antiretrovirals as this kind of Lazarus drug that's going to give you a normal lifespan, although that's how they are sold and marketed by the medical profession. The fact is that they are still new drugs and we don't know what the long-term effects are. At any point I could have another heart attack and people on antiretrovirals get all sorts of weird cancers and things and die. I have degenerative arthritis in my spine and it's most likely from the drugs and I could develop some kind of cancer and I'll die. So the point is, I still don't see my lifespan as a normal one—I don't expect to be seventy, for instance. I might be, but generally I still work on the eighteen-month plan. I think it's entirely possible that something will happen; I'll have a heart attack, I'll have some kind of cancer.

THE MACKEREL ECONOMY: A CONFUSION OF RELATIONS

Prisoners in the United States are banned from possessing cash. Instead, money exists as an electronic balance in a commissary account that allows inmates to buy goods, such as snacks, ramen noodles, spice, pens, toiletries, and underwear from the commissary store. When federal prisons banned cigarettes and smoking in 2004, the same year Bill started his prison sentence, prisoners were required to find a new item to use as a currency substitute for the dollar, to reestablish their own prison economy. For decades, cigarettes had been the main currency. Afterward, and after trying out various options, mackerel emerged as the new currency. Since the smoking ban, Global Source Marketing Inc., which supplies the US prison system with mackerel, has seen a massive growth in the sale and distribution of processed mackerel, which now accounts for half of their entire sales, outstripping their lines in canned tuna, crab, chicken, and oysters (Scheck 2008).

There is a lot more that circulates with money than the goods and services it buys: it distinguishes persons, conveys social status, and is used for a broad range of purposes, including establishing relationships, emotional bonds, and social distances in the communities and contexts in which it is used (Hart 2005). As such, the use of mackerel in prison, as with other currencies, cannot be reduced to a fixed utilitarian value. Instead, it is embedded within a network of unfolding social relations and operations of power that help define people's moral identities and categories of personhood (Zelizer 1997). Mackerel exists alongside, or perhaps more expressively, below the official commissary economy and gives access to goods or services and helps create social ties, obligations, and relationships that are not possible through the commissary. If the official commissary account can be thought of as legitimate state-backed prison currency, or what Chris Gregory (1997) terms the *superalternate* money of the system and its "masters" and "landlords," then macks are the *subalternate* currency of the "slaves" and "tenants," which operates and circulates in the hidden spaces and margins of the prison.

Mackerel economics in the prison is not isolated from the outside world. There are numerous factors that affect the mackerel economy, including fluctuating fish stocks, global warming, and the housing market. When the dollar weakened during the global economic crisis of 2008, macks proved to be a more stable currency. The exchange rate for macks rose from $1 to as high as $1.40 during the time Bill was inside, exceeding the Euro and approaching the British Pound, which was around $1.48. Macks, as a subalternate currency, are also more flexible than commissary dollars as they can buy homemade alcohol, drugs, sex, and a whole range of services that can't be paid for on the official account. As a result, prisoners stockpile macks, although accumulation presents its own problems insofar as trading, plus the prison authorities do not allow stashing macks, and people's personal reserves have to be hidden from guards who make regular checks. Moreover, macks have little value on the outside and prisoners are not allowed to take macks with them when they finish their sentence. This creates further distortions and fluctuations in the local mackerel economy because prisoners approaching their release have to spend or give away their stockpiles of macks to fellow prisoners.

The ability to assign a shared social value to substances accorded the status of *money* means the materiality of money is often of less importance than the ability to invest material objects with value. Anthropologists working around the world and in different contexts have shown that many different materials, often with little practical utility in and of themselves, such as shells, clay, teeth, stones, beads, small bits of metal, and paper, can be brought to life by the capacity of the imagination to invest meaning into certain materials and accord them the status of *being valuable*.

"Money," Norman O. Brown suggests, is "dead matter which has been made alive by inheriting the magic power which infantile narcissism attributes to the excremental product" ([1959] 1970: 245). Such an activity presupposes a faith and belief in substance as well as sociality and culture, as summarized by George Santayana's discrimination between properties of objects as they exist independent of perception (*existents*) and the essence that is attributed to an object by the capacity of the human mind (*subsistents*). As we can never be certain the attributed essence actually inheres in the substances themselves—whether they are worthless or not—doubt and skepticism emerge, but this uncertainty must also be balanced by the type of pragmatic "animal faith" that is necessary to live, act, and survive. For Santayana: "All knowledge, being faith in an object posited and partially described, is belief in substance, in the etymological sense of this word; it is a belief in a thing or an event subsisting in its own plane, and waiting for the light of knowledge to explore it eventually, and perhaps name or define it" ([1923] 1955: 182).

Once named, *money*, as Georg Simmel (1950) pointed out, reflects and encourages a type of thinking that, like art, is simultaneously based in substance and sign, in the objective world and mental abstraction. It is a type of thinking that is impersonal, quantitative, and promotes strategic rationalities that temper the excessive appetites and desires of the body in favor of the ascetic accumulation of specific material substances that would otherwise be worthless. Money, rather than being the ultimate expression of secular reason and rationality, is therefore rooted in a community of faith and collective imagining, which is to say that like art, money is fundamentally *religious* not simply in its origins but in its various incarnations (Brown [1959] 1970).

The transubstantiation of mackerel into money requires the collective imagination and cooperation of the prison body to assign shared value, meaning, and significance to specific material forms. This does not mean all prisoners accord the same value or status to mackerel—for value is precisely constituted by the differences and play between objects and signs—but there nevertheless exists a shared economy within which relative values of oily fish emerge and become negotiated. According to the enlightenment philosopher John Locke, whose ideas Bill and I had discussed so long ago in his studio, "Mankind having consented to put an imaginary Value upon Gold and Silver by reason of their Durableness, Scarcity, and not being very liable to be counterfeited, have made them by general content the common Pledges, whereby Men are assured, in Exchange for them to receive equally valuable things to those they parted with" (Locke 1714: 12).

Macks are turned into money, on the one hand, through the specific conditions of incarceration in the federal prison system, and on the other hand, via a process of imagination, animism, and alchemy carried out by the collective prison body, whereby fish can be transformed into prison hooch, bread, spices, sex, and services. It is a magical, and not just rational, transubstantiation that speaks less to economic theory than the intricacies of the human mind. Locke himself inspired a line of philosophical thought in which the impossibility of describing, let alone understanding, the complexity of the human mind shifted the focus of explanation from definition to function, that is to say, not asking *what mind is* but rather observing *what mind does.* This removes us from considering the nature, essence, or ontology of human thinking and instead invites an empirical investigation into observable behavior, function, and action. Robin Collingwood developed Locke to summarize how such a study of mind involves two methodological renunciations: "First, it renounces with Locke all 'science of substance.' It does not ask what mind is; it asks only what mind does. . . . Secondly, it renounces all attempt to discover what mind *always and everywhere does*, and asks only *what mind has done* on certain definite occasions" (Collingwood [1942] 1992: 61).

When Locke extended his analysis from *mind* to *money*, he sided against ascribing an essential materiality to money and argued that the material body of money was for most purposes worthless and irrelevant. As such, the nineteenth-century economist Francis Amasa Walker was largely following Locke's line of reasoning when he argued that social theorists should not investigate what money *is* and instead proclaimed that "money is what money does" (quoted in Ingham 2004). And *what money does* is serve as "a medium of exchange, store of value, means of unilateral payment (settlement), and measure of value (unit of account)" (Ingham: 2004: 19). By focusing on the observable social conventions of exchange, Walker set the tone for twentieth-century philosophers, economists, and anthropologists to abandon the metaphysics of money in favor of observations and descriptions of function. Monetary value is seen as self-evident, visible, and can function through any substance that can be stored, passed on, exchanged, given away, and whose value is negotiated in economic contexts from the Kula ring to Wall Street.

Like many functional approaches, this leaves many of the most interesting questions unasked and unanswered. Because macks are not an officially sanctioned currency, their circulation must be unobserved and invisible. To be seen trading macks or caught with a large reserve can lead to the loss of privileges, being moved to a worse cell, or being sent to "the hole," which ensures that macks and the mackerel economy remain hidden. Outside the prison, money also tends to be "put out of sight" (Marx [1867] 1999: 9) and on those occasions when we catch a glimpse of money being exchanged for services and commodities, it soon escapes visibility and disappears into pockets, tills, and banks and enters into a virtual realm of exchange and algorithms where there is no gold standard, material resting place, or guaranteed value. For Marx, a commodity may have a price without having value or else might shift its shape or conceal its value: "A commodity . . . must quit its bodily shape, must transform itself from mere imaginary into real gold, although to the commodity such transubstantiation may be more difficult than to the Hegelian concept, the transition from necessity to freedom, or to a lobster the casting of his shell, or to Saint Jerome the putting off of the old Adam" (Marx [1867] 1999: 63).

Transubstantiations of matter and value involve a form of *modus vivendi* whereby rationality and irrationality—alongside other irregularities, inconsistencies, and confusions—do not rule each other out but sit side by side. Global Source tried selling their mackerel on the outside but found no one wanted it and there was no market for their fish. Mackerel's transformation into a valuable and much desired substance inside of the prison, while remaining worthless outside, is representative of a reversal and confusion of relations concerning the moral and ethical values accorded to different kinds of body. In prison, this means living, feeling, incarcerated human bodies are reduced to and addressed by a number (in Bill's case, 55552054) and take on the status of waste, while the dead bodies of mackerel, even those that have been handled so often to have been turned into "mush macks" are given a value. Such a drastic reversal of value, in which death is privileged over life, is symptomatic of a deeper-seated uncertainty about the value of human bodies vis-à-vis money whereby knowledge, faith, and belief in the substance of humanity is called into question.

To quote Norman O. Brown, "What the elegant laws of supply and demand really describe is the antics of an animal which has confused excrement with aliment and does not know it, and which like infantile sexuality, pursues no real aim. Having no real aim, acquisitiveness, as Aristotle correctly said has no limit. Hence the psychological premise of a market economy is not, as in classical theory of exchange that the agents know what they want, but that they do not know what they want" ([1959] 1970: 227). Moreover, "The desire for money takes the place of all genuinely human needs. Thus the apparent accumulation of wealth is really the impoverishment of human nature, and its appropriate morality is the renunciation of human nature and desires-asceticism. The effect is to substitute an abstraction, *homo economicus*, for the concrete totality of human nature, and thus to dehumanise human nature. In this dehumanised human nature man loses contact with his own body, more specifically with his senses" (1970: 211).

Here lies a deep-seated uncertainty about the moral and ontological status of lives, bodies, and substances, which often plays out with tragic consequences both inside and outside the US prison system, whereby certain human beings are surplus, unnecessary, and unneeded—including nonwhites, gays, undocumented migrants, the homeless, and people struggling with addictions or certain kinds of disease—while other kinds of persons who enriched themselves by gambling with client pensions and savings, such as high frequency traders and subprime mortgage brokers, remain free to move in society, including rarefied political circles. Incarceration is but one way of attempting to restrict and control the movement of bodies, of defining how people are classified, and ascribing their moral and economic value. Recalling Bill's allowance of being permitted to move for ten minutes per hour, the control over *how*, *where*, and *when* a person moves, not only attempts a moral definition of "who" the person is but also "what" they are, and is enforced through a nexus of regimental power and institutional categorization that determines the relative status and value of the person in ways that displace the distinction between the inside and outside of the prison. In other words, certain types of human body, like money, are accorded the status of waste.

However, there is more, as by coincidence I was also arrested and thrown in jail during the summer of 1999, the same summer I started working with Bill at his studio. Here is an extract from my field notes, written after I got out:

Field notes: August 1999. *What follows is the sorry tale of my arrest and subsequent trial during the s-s-sweltering summer of 1999 in New York City. It speaks of crime and negligence and how these are played out on a routine, everyday basis. . . . It exposes c-c-corruption and a casual disregard for law. . . . It contains truths that some would prefer to remain hidden . . .*

. . . so it goes that during the summer of '99, I was walking back from my good friend Albert Velasco's place in the East Village and decided to cut across town to West Fourth Street to take the A train uptown. When I arrived at the station and swiped my ticket, the turnstile jammed and so I swiped it again and then again. Seeing that everyone else has decided to jump over, I did the same. Less than a minute after I had done so, I was accosted by two guys who pressed me up against the wall and demanded to know who the hell I was and what the hell I thought I was doing. Admittedly, I

couldn't resist telling them I was King Tut, but even so it seemed that it was with indecent haste that I was cuffed in chains and thrown in the back of a police car. A Hispanic guy called Ernesto was already in there and was also handcuffed. Then the cops t-t-turned to me and my fellow con and asked if we knew of any criminal activity in the area. This being near Washington Square, Ernesto gestured to the various guys lined up on the corner and sarcastically said "yeah, he's a dealer, the one next to him is a dealer, so is the one next to him as well . . . in fact, they're all dealers." The cop replied, "Tell us something we don't know," to which Ernesto said, "Well, you asked." But the cops obviously couldn't be bothered or were being paid off to look the other way and so Ernesto and I were driven down to Chinatown and thrown in some jail near Canal Street.

. . . then the fun really started . . .

The initial booking was meant to be done by the two cops that arrested us . . . but by some once-in-a-lifetime miracle the computer was *down . . .* which meant that we couldn't be processed *and also meant that our names couldn't be run through the computer and checked against the database of known felons on the run. Thus, by some equally miraculous coincidence this meant that the arresting cops couldn't go back out on the streets to continue their work policing the city and making it a safer place but were instead forced to stay inside and play cards and drink coffee for the entire duration of their shift. The cops weren't all cut from the same cloth, and one guy who seemed to be working in another part of the office on something else came over and said I was the politest prisoner he had ever known. When you get taken to the cell, they take everything off you. He asked me if I had anything with me when I arrived. When I said a bottle of wine and an original artwork, he said, "Well, you might not see those again."*

Eight hours later, at the end of their shift, when it was time to go home rather than go back out and work the streets, the computer miraculously started working again. I was in awe about how an inanimate machine could be so considerate as to not work for the precise duration of their shift—meaning they had to stick around the jails playing cards while they waited for it get back online rather than pounding the streets—and how at the very moment the cops ended their shift and were due to go home it started working again . . .

First off, it is important to note that I had a valid ticket and had already told the cops as much at the station. "Go ahead, check it, you'll see it's valid but the turnstile doesn't work." But the cops weren't interested in my ticket or whether it was valid and just wanted to cuff me and get me into the car so that they could take me down to the jail and get on with their card game. The ticket was confiscated with my other stuff

*and so I couldn't even show it . . . but the chief who was in charge wasn't interested.
. . . As I languished in the cell, I started getting b-b-bored and after a couple of hours
I started to speak loudly to Ernesto by recounting the plot of Kafka's Trial and how it
was funny that the country's values on freedom were so easily undermined by a bunch
of lazy cops and how this wouldn't happen in my country as the cops were professionals who went about their business in a thorough and systematic manner. Of course, I
wasn't really talking so much to Ernesto (though he became quite interested in how
Kafka's Trial ended) but was really talking to the cops in the corner playing cards—
who he could see were getting distracted from their game—until one came over to my
cell and started chewing off my ear about how cops in England all secretly carry guns
and that I should be grateful as New York was so much safer now than in the '80s
because of the work the cops were doing. I said that the only danger I'd ever been in
while in New York was from lazy cops and that I certainly didn't feel safer knowing
they were playing cards and making up false arrests rather than getting their ass out
onto the street. This seemed to rile one of the other cops who came up to me to ask "what
my problem was," to which I replied that my problem was that I had a valid ticket
and had now been banged up for nearly eight hours. "What the fuck do I care about
that," came the answer. . . . The same cop then went along the cells baiting people until
he found a guy with learning difficulties who he kept baiting until he got him to moo
like a cow and howl in confusion.*

*I imagined myself as Jimmy Cagney as he pressed his face up to the c-c-cold metal
bars of his prison cell in* Each dawn I die. *In the film, we see Cagney holding the
bars, face pressed up as huge white letters fly over the top of his head:* HOURS! DAYS!
MONTHS! YEARS! 1939! 1940! 1941! 1942!

*Another cop came in off the street and came over as I held the bars and looked out
of the cell. He told me he was ashamed of his colleagues, and that they did this every
week. How it worked, he said, is they pull a double shift. They work the first shift and
then for the second shift they arrest some poor mugs in the street, bring them back here
. . . lock them up . . . and effect a computer breakdown so that they spend the second
shift in the station playing cards. It's kind of like compensation for the dangers and
conditions of the job . . . the low pay and bad hours . . . so that the officials have to turn
a blind eye to it, because they know it's a dirty and dangerous job and have to keep cop
morale up and keep some slack in the system. But these guys abuse it, they're lazy cops.
It started with a policy brought in by [Mayor Rudy] Giuliani; the idea is simple . . . to
stop anybody who's doing any kind of infraction—jaywalking, dropping trash, absolutely anything—at which point you are allowed to ask for ID and run them through
the system and see if they had any outstanding warrants for crimes still on the books.*

If there's no warrants then they are supposed to let you go . . . but these cops abuse it. But also a blind eye gets turned because as a by-product it creates the illusion of higher clear-up rates, which is always good for statistics and reelection.

At one point, two young girls were brought in, around two a.m., who'd been out dancing and spent their money and jumped the barriers to get the subway home. "You should be ashamed of yourself," another cop said to the arresting officer, "Imagine if they were your kids, would you rather have them walk home at two a.m. through New York?"

Because of the computer glitch, it was now officially too late to release us and so we had to go into the system. So, around 2:45 a.m. we were bundled into another van and taken across town to Central Processing—a massive, half-windowless building on the edge of Chinatown. What's not apparent from the outside of the building is that it also extends downward, and it's into these bowels—full of airless cells with no light—that you get processed and held. First off, we were put into a long line to get our mug shots done. Thus it came that I'm now subject to the iconic image of holding up your crime number, facing the camera, having your image taken full on and in profile. However, not quite knowing the system, I asked the policewoman who was taking the shots how she wanted me to stand. "Don't smartass with me, you fuck," she said. I replied, "I was only trying to be helpful," and she proceeded to hurl further abuse.

What was interesting was that by this point it was clear the demographics down in the cells and bowels of Central Processing spoke a story of institutional police prejudice. Out of what I would estimate as around 150 or so of us in the cells, there were about four white people—the other three white people were all gay and had been cruising in a park—which tells its own sorry story. I noticed they managed to wind up the arresting officer by giving addresses in the Midwest. This apparently causes an administrative problem in terms of police procedure and bureaucracy insofar as they are out-of-state residents. The cop, clearly frustrated, put pressure on them to give a New York address, but they managed to maintain their Midwestern, wide-eyed, farm boy innocence, leading the cop to get more frustrated.

Once your mug shot is taken, you get thrown into a large holding cell, approximately twenty-five feet by twenty-five feet, into which it seemed around thirty or fifty prisoners were squeezed. This meant there was no room to lie or sit down for most of us; instead, all the newcomers had to stand. Gradually, as people got called from the holding pen and were transferred to the next pen, a little space of concrete floor would open up and if you were quick, this was the opportunity to grab a bit to sit on, and then when a bit more space opened up, lie down. The cold concrete floor seemed like luxury after standing for hours. Nobody wanted to lie down next to the toilet, which was an open metal toilet with no seat, exposed to everyone right smack-dab in the middle of the cell. The concrete floor around the toilet was free of bodies but not of piss. And only the desperate venture onto it. Not knowing the rules, I kept myself to myself and once I'd found my piece of concrete floor, although I didn't manage to sleep, I did manage to hear the conversations going on around me. The group immediately to my left had been caught with a stash of guns but they were just chewing the fat and not concerned. The guy who seemed to be the leader among the group said, "It's no problem, I'll call my man Derkowitz and he'll have us out of here by tomorrow or the next morning."

There was still humanity to be found among the cops in the dark bowels of Central Processing. One cop in particular was noticeable in the way in which he treated everybody with humor and dignity, making jokes that had a common theme of "doesn't life suck," which no doubt also referred to his own existence spent in the bowels. It was also his job to move people between the holding cells. As the night went on, we gradually moved from cell to cell down toward the far end. Each time I left the cell, the whole process was repeated. The newbies got to stand and after a while a piece of concrete would open up, before I was called to the next cell. By this time it's about 7 a.m., and we proceeded along the building and closer and closer to the end. By lunchtime, I was absolutely STARVING because the only food that was brought around consisted of some kind of ham sandwich; being vegetarian, I didn't touch it, and was told there were no alternatives on offer. The choice of ham is interesting for a number of reasons—mostly religious. Either way, I'd now missed what passed for breakfast and what passed for lunch and had been in the system and hadn't eaten for twenty-four hours.

Finally I reached the last cell, and my name was called out. It was at this point I got to see the lawyer on duty. A lawyer who, as far as I could ascertain, was assigned to Central Processing and was the first point of contact with any form of judicial representation. I was led into a small room to have my five minutes and explained my story. The lawyer responded, "This is typical. Clearly you should never have been arrested in the first place. You can prove you had a valid ticket and I can get you out of this place no problem."

"But there's a choice," she went on to say. "You can plead not guilty and I can get you off but you're gonna to have to go back into the system, meaning if you don't get seen by six p.m. today before the court closes, we will have to wait for tomorrow and you could be in here for another twenty-four hours. Or I can get you out of here within the hour. How that works is you plead guilty and we can arrange it such that as long as you don't commit another offense in the next three months everything will be *completely expunged from the record." She then explained some further technicalities but assured me there's no chance of it going wrong unless I was stupid enough to something else in the next three months and after three months everything would be wiped. So we cut a deal, I said I'd plead and about an hour later, twenty of us are standing in a line in front of a judge (bored out of his skull) and the public in the courtroom. Having pled guilty, we get a thirty-second lecture telling us not to do it again and then I was free. That was the trial. All told, I'd been inside for almost a day and a half. I was now an officially cleared up crime for Giuliani's statistics and the NYPD. Starving. I turned left out of the courtroom, walked past the bail bond shops into the first eating establishment I came across,* Jaya Malaysian *on Baxter Street, and ordered* roti canai.

AFTER PRISON

I later discovered that Bill was processed in the bowels of the very same building when he got caught. In his ethnography of the prison, Bill describes the enactments of substatus: the social rules, daily rituals, and customs; the structures of power, hierarchy, and relations with guards and other prisoners; being called for meals, and having one's movements restricted to ten minutes of movement per hour. However, like me, he also found a more human side, of people offering care rather than abuse and doing their best in the system, and Bill made many close friends. Another of the upsides of Bill's incarceration is that he is better read than any of us, having read the complete works of Fyodor Dostoyevsky in their first, second, and third translations, all nine volumes of Laurence Sterne's *Tristram Shandy*, and all seven volumes of Marcel Proust's *In search of lost time*. He also ended up an expert in German political history and Angela Merkel's style of leadership. After a period in a halfway house and a further two years of parole, Bill finally left the prison system. It goes without saying that Bill's current life can no more be understood as being fully outside the prison than his life inside was isolated from the world outside. Both are frameworks for understanding the other. However, the boundaries are not completely porous, and when Bill finally got out there was a whole new world of Google, Facebook, iPads, smartphones, Starbucks, kale juice, gluten-free products, and much else besides. He had not eaten mozzarella for eight years, and when he tasted it again he started crying in front of the whole restaurant.

When I finally found Bill again in 2011, he had just got out prison and was still serving his sentence insofar as any infringement of his release conditions would see him back inside. Bill and I attempted a number of experimental field-work collaborations as part of an art/anthropology project on inner dialogues I was carrying out at the time, not all of which were successful. We started by wiring Bill up to a radio microphone into which he spoke out loud the stream of his inner dialogue as he walked around New York and I followed about thirty feet behind, listening in. Bill walked from the halfway house into which he was released as a condition of his parole, across Central Park, and down to the West Side Highway, and finished up at the Drug Enforcement Administration building on West 17th Street, where the DEA agents who caught him in the sting were operating. As part of the project we tried to cleanse the experience by an act of methodological voodoo, whereby Bill walked anticlockwise around the DEA building three times while miked up, exteriorizing his thoughts. Then we ate in the same restaurant that Bill tasted mozzarella, and again he cried into his meal.

The meaning of Bill's most recent painting at the time of writing? That's an open question.

Figure 6.9 *Requiem for Lin Jun*, by William Cullum, 2015. Oil on linen. *Requiem* is William Cullum's most recent painting as of the time of writing. *Reproduced by permission from the artist*

You only live twice

The smallest number, in the strict sense of the word "number" is two.

—Aristotle, *Physics, Book IV*

You only live twice,
Or so it seems,
Once in your life,
And once in your dreams.

—Nancy Sinatra, "You only live twice"

The events and experiences that shape our lives are continually being relived and retold, reminding us that the art of life and death remains an unfinished story. The lives retold in this book draw attention to the fact that there is no such thing as a pure life experience. Instead, as Aristotle suggests, the smallest number is two, insofar as life is endlessly divided and differentiated: there is no light without dark, hot without cold, health without illness, or life without death. Life can only be understood and imagined in relation to the other states of being and the many possible lives one could have lived, recalling Clifford Geertz's assertion that "One of the most significant facts about us, is that we all begin with the natural equipment to live a thousand kinds of life but end up in the end having only lived one" (1973: 45).

The often radical discrepancy between the actual life trajectory someone lives and all the other equally possible but unlived lives they might have lived—including an everyday life with or without HIV/AIDS—exposes the fundamental contingency of our being-in-the-world and how it is played out across a series of social and practical contexts. The imagined life offers a framework of interpretation and a range of alternative perspectives through which people can understand and contextualize their thoughts and feelings concerning their circumstances and situation. It is precisely because this contrast is made explicit while living with HIV/AIDS, that imagining, daydreaming, or fantasizing about the alternative lives someone *could* be living is not an abstract or trivial enterprise but is constitutive of people's embodied experience and understandings of themselves, other persons, and the world. The strange distance between the different possible lives provides a comparative moral framework for interpreting one's daily practices and circumstances, meaning the reality and residue of one's life constantly mixes and merges with other lives.

For example, Bill's experience of life inside the prison can only be properly understood in relation to the life he would have been living at the same time outside the prison, *had* his friend not been caught, *had* the DEA not cut a deal, *had* Bill followed his momentary instincts and not fallen for the sting. This means that to understand people's lives and experiences, it is necessary to consider not only people's current situation but also the many other lives they could, and do, live through their inner dialogues, dreams, fantasies, and imagination. I would even go as far to say that that we cannot carry out an ethnography and life history of persons without accounting for the many different possible lives someone could have lived.

For many people in New York, life is carried out in relation to dominant cultural narratives concerning the promises of capitalism and its predictions of the future. The city's streets offer an ever-present reminder of the rewards of a life lived according to the straight lines of the grid. The persons on these pages did not fit this narrative and were thrown out of the world. Education, work, health, and pensions were all closed off. However, the future—like all futures—remained unwritten. In New York alone, many tens of thousands of persons who faced and prepared for death now live in a future they never thought they would see and have resumed careers and experience the world through healthy and stabilized bodies. They are learning to live again as HIV/AIDS is gradually transformed from an acute into a chronic disease in many parts of the world.

For many hundreds of thousands of people, the future is now encountered under different circumstances. Death may no longer pose the same threat or feel so immediate, but life is not what it was either: it is now informed by the type of knowledge that emerges out of extraordinary experiences. It is not surprising that many people find it impossible to return to their previous lives. The life stories on these pages are but a few small examples of how people created their own context for experiencing illness, which now informs how they want to spend the rest of their life. Despite being thrown back into the grid of capitalism, these people no longer dwell or relate to it in quite the same way as before they were diagnosed with HIV.

There are various possibilities inherent in every moment, but choosing a particular path excludes other possibilities, if only because the corporeality of the human body grounds us in time and place (Merleau-Ponty 1968). A person cannot take both a right and left turn at the same time, and life involves making choices that open up certain possibilities while simultaneously closing off others. The passage of time means that some possibilities are irrecoverable. On this reading, *The art of life and death* is not purely a product of happenstance or agency but the broad diversity of embodied actions though which mortal beings live amid conditions of consistency and contingency. It is a mode of being that is predicated less on a script than improvising and acting in relation to the ongoing and changing circumstances of the world and the different possible futures this opens up.

The *modus vivendi* of HIV/AIDS encompasses deep-seated, often irresolvable, tensions. These are given a tangible form in the decisions someone makes about how to live and act in a world of social and existential possibility, shared moral attitudes about disease, death, and dying, and broader social, political, and economic forces. Many institutions through which society, culture, and morality operate—not least law, government, bureaucracy, education, medicine, and the media—routinely classify and effect judgments upon persons through the inscription and overdetermination of certain analytical tropes and processes of categorization, including those of social identity, context, and habitus. In contrast, *The art of life and death* is firmly committed to the idea that the meaning and value of human life rests less on the circumstances of where a person is born, lives, socializes, works, prays, or has sex than the existential fact of their belonging to the human race and their capacity to act with and alongside others.

The art of life and death involves negotiating the inexact grounds for human existence and the practice of getting by in an uncertain world that is shaped by power and contingency. The first, and often most enduring contingency is that of the body itself, including the kind of body one is born with, the land of one's birth, its position in the global-political economy, the economic status of one's parents, and one's health. It is worth reiterating that there is no necessary onto-logical relationship between the value of someone's life and the land on which they were born. It is a completely arbitrary relation. But in the current global-political climate, the correlation between body, nation, gender, desire, health, and the value of life is maintained through an erroneous yet politically powerful and pathological identification of a human being's worth with the land where they (or their ancestors) were born.

Being born on the wrong soil or without money or without the right kind of sexual desire or bodily characteristics does not prohibit people from imagin-ing a life of health and existential possibility they *could* lead if it were not for the circumstances of their birth; on too many occasions they are unable to *live* that life. When placed in a global comparative perspective, people living with HIV/AIDS originating from all parts of the world can actively imagine a dif-ferent kind of life—and thereby transcend categorical, social, economic, legal, or national borders—but their bodies, dreams, and desires are not legitimated or are designated as other. This finds its official expression in the criminalization of certain diseases, desires, and ways of being but also finds expression across a range of other forms. Social, legal, and institutional anxiety about engaging with persons with HIV/AIDS as fully equal citizens extends out into the topography of the world and is translated into international borders, boundaries, and regula-tions designed to allow money, goods, and certain persons to cross but prevent the bodily movement of others. In doing so, difference becomes mapped onto the structure of law itself insofar as who has rights and access to health, educa-tion, security, and so forth remains rooted in the contingencies of birth, national identity, and gender rather than according to need or the notion that human beings are equal.

Closer attention shows how it is not only bodies and identities that are categorized though such processes but also the content of people's thoughts, characters, and imaginings in a restrictive and erroneous conflation of people's moral lifeworlds with, for example, their skin color, gender, sexuality, wealth, or homeland. The control over how, where, and when persons live, move, and express themselves—vis-à-vis the judicial, categorical, spatial, and customary borders that are enforced through state power, law, and classification—reflects the moral value attached to different kinds of persons. This legally enforced restriction of life and movement provides an ongoing and frequently macabre commentary on a world in which the negative effects are rarely confined to an individual body but instead extend into the lives of friends, families, and communities.

From a global perspective, the subsequent development of effective, life-saving medications for HIV/AIDS or other diseases has reinscribed bodily differences on national and economic lines. This means many families in non-Western countries still confront illness and death in the knowledge of cures that are freely available elsewhere in the world but are still denied them due to their national, ethnic, or economic identities, as etched in law, custom, and practice.

At heart lies a deathly confusion between persons, land, and identity in which the contingencies of birth, body, and gender have become so reified as to perpetuate unequal access to health, educational opportunities, social mobility, and sexual life. The needs and rights accorded to humans, as a species, are repeatedly subordinated to an irrational faith in categorization and differentiation—in terms of the entitlements of persons, wealth, law, etc.—that has the effect of substituting the moral rights of the totality of the human species for those of the few. This represents a renunciation and impoverishment of the very idea of the *human* and is a means of perpetuating difference by distinguishing between different kinds of persons. In this dispersed, differentiated, and de-humanized form, humanity loses its unity as a species, resulting in a hierarchy based on the idea of different categories of human being, a confusion that is played out with tragic consequences across a world in which certain types of human body are accorded the status of surplus or as expendable.

This illustrates how it is not just labels and categorical identities that are attached to people's bodies but also capacities for enduring risk, suffering, hardship, and discrimination according to nationality, wealth, sexuality, and gender. In the 1980s, the Reagan administration accorded a radically different value to the lives of people with HIV/AIDS, which affected their access to equal health care and treatment. People with HIV/AIDS were considered expendable in a way that was not simply a moral judgment about sexual and other practices but also a judgment about the right to life itself. Men and women, categorized according to a medical condition, found themselves on the wrong side of the law and social convention, including most notably gay men: a group who are often economically and educationally privileged but socially marginalized. HIV/AIDS became a site of anxiety across numerous political, religious, and legal arenas, and in doing so made visible the processes of classification at work, alongside institutional attempts to contain persons within prescribed national, ethnic, legal, and economic life pathways. The active reinforcement of these categories was not only directed toward keeping prescribed persons within prescribed limits and life possibilities but was a means for managing and controlling the chances of witnessing or coming into contact with the sexually transgressive or economically unviable bodies of others.

When Ronald Reagan said he believed in family values, what he really meant was fuck the gays, single parents, the homeless, and the marginalized; when he said he believed in the United States, what he really meant was fuck Latin America, Nicaragua, El Salvador; and when he talked about public health, what he really meant was fuck healthcare and treatment for people with HIV/AIDS, leading to extensive and high-profile campaigns by groups such as GMHC and ACTUP, which were necessary and effective. Nevertheless, if Karl Marx taught us anything it is that society is not static, and this is exemplified by how HIV/AIDS treatment, reproductive rights, working legislation, and so forth have been fought for by persons who challenged the legitimacy of the governing bodies in question.

This leaves the problem of how we might go about answering the question of *The art of life and death* in ethnographic terms in ways that do not presuppose or impose a knowledge of persons based on such limiting categorizations but instead addresses people as subjects of their own life experience. This is more an ethnographic and methodological problem rather than a theoretical one. I argue it needs to be based on collaboration and face-to-face modes of investigation with persons so as to establish mutually defined areas of interest and concern, shared research objectives, and joint methodological projects aimed at understanding people's lived experiences. This not only provides a necessary check on anthropological claims but also challenges us to find collaborative methods, including literary, imaginative, and cinematic ones, to research and represent people's lifeworlds as part of a process of shared understanding.

The spirit of anthropology remains in the face-to-face encounter. Here, the other person—as famously prefigured by Martin Buber ([1923] 1970)—is not referred to as *he, she, they, elite, working class, gay, sick, healthy, English, African, informant*, etc. but as **you**, which places them in a second-person position, thus mediating the dualism of first-person subjectivity and the objective categorization of the third-person position. In this reciprocal address of *you*, the grounds for mutual and embodied interaction are established that allow the possibility for a type of moral awareness and appreciation, which even if it can only be termed a method manqué, provides a practical basis for engaging with, learning about, and responding to the lived experiences of other people. The moral appreciation of human difference that emerges through face-to-face interaction generates a series of existential viewpoints that continually signify the presence of other perspectives. This exposes the provisional, finite, and bodily basis of perception, knowledge, and moral practice, and simultaneously indicates how a perspective can be taken upon oneself by others, including the questioning or verification of one's own existence, moral values, and beliefs.

If this constitutes a method, then we must also admit that we can never actually succeed in defining *The art of life and death*. Personhood, truth, and failure are all contextualized within the face-to-face encounter and the attempt to open up an imaginative, empathetic, and practical means through which people attempt to reach an understanding in the field. Nevertheless, as any artist or anthropologist knows, failure is necessary to all forms of representation—including ethnography—and we might add that failure is also necessary to learning about people's lives, entering new social worlds, and the ethnographic project. The failure of people to understand each other confirms our limits as finite, mortal beings, and suggests mutuality and understanding are not guaranteed by human phylogeny alone. They are only generated through ongoing processes of interaction, identification, and dialogue through which people negotiate and respond to others. Diversity, difference, and otherness are therefore not the opposites of shared understanding but the conditions that bring it into being as people engage with each other's emotions, motivations, and actions within the flow of everyday life: a kind of quotidian methodological activity aimed at generating new knowledge or casting old knowledge in a different light.

This does not require movements across vast distances or radical renunciations of previous ways of being; it is sufficient for the movement to be any activity (purposeful or otherwise) that reveals the contingency of habitual thoughts and actions. Or in Jean-Paul Sartre's terms, "the small movement which makes of a totally conditioned social being someone who does not render back completely what his conditioning has given him" (1974: 45). *The art of life and death* is therefore the province of the small movements of the finite, mortal human being who can live in, act in, and imagine the world otherwise.

References

Al-Mohammad, Hayder. 2016. "Never quite given: Calling into question the relation between person and world in postinvastion Iraq." In *Living and dying in the contemporary world: A compendium*, edited by Veena Das and Celia Han, 463–75. Berkeley: University of California Press.

———. Forthcoming. "What is the 'preparation' in the preparing for death?: New confrontations with death and dying in Iraq." *Current Anthropology.*

Alderson-Day, Ben, and Charles Fernyhough. 2015. "Inner speech: Development, cognitive functions, phenomenology, and neurobiology." *Psychological Bulletin* 141 (5): 931–65.

Antze, Paul, and Michael Lambek, eds. 1996. *Tense past: Cultural essays in trauma and memory.* New York: Routledge.

Appadurai, Arjun. 1988. "Introduction: Place and voice in anthropological theory." *Cultural Anthropology* 3 (1): 16–20.

Aristotle. 384–22 BC. *Physics, Book IV.* Translated by R. P. Hardie and R. K. Gaye (1930). Oxford: Clarendon Press.

Astuti, Rita. 2017. "On keeping up the tension between fieldwork and ethnography." *HAU: Journal of Ethnographic Theory* 7 (1): 9–14.

Augustine of Hippo. 354–430. *Confessions.* Translated by Albert C. Outler (1955). http://faculty.georgetown.edu/jod/augustine/conf.pdf.

Austen, Jane. 1833. *Emma.* London: Colburn and Bentley.

Bachelard, Gaston. 1971. *On poetic imagination and reverie.* Dallas: Spring Publications.

Bakhtin, Mikhail. 1986. *Speech genres and other late essays.* Translated by Vern W. McGee. Austin: University of Texas Press.

Banks, Marcus. 2001. *Visual methods in social research.* London: Sage Press.

Barratt, William. (1958) 2011. *The irrational man: A study in existential philosophy.* New York: Doubleday.

Bateson, Gregory. (1936) 1958. *Naven: A survey of the problems suggested by a composite picture of the culture of a New Guinea tribe drawn from three points of view.* Stanford, CA: Stanford University Press.

———. 1972. Steps to an ecology of mind: Collected essays in anthropology, psychiatry, evolution, and epistemology. Chicago: University of Chicago Press.

Bauby, Jean-Dominque. 2008. *The diving bell and the butterfly.* London: Harper Perennial.

Bauman, Zygmunt. 1992. *Mortality and immortality.* Oxford: Polity Press.

Becker, Ernest. 1997. The denial of death. New York: Free Press.

Becker, Gaye. 1997. *Disrupted lives: How people create meaning in a chaotic world.* Berkeley: University of California Press.

Berger, John. 1972. *Ways of seeing.* London: BBC Books.

———. 1982. *Another way of telling.* New York: Pantheon.

———. 1997. *A fortunate man.* New York: Vintage International.

Birth, Kevin. 2012. *Objects of time: How things shape temporality.* New York: Palgrave Macmillan.

Bloch, Maurice, and Jonathan Parry, eds. 1982. *Death and the regeneration of life.* Cambridge: Cambridge University Press.

Bourdieu, Pierre. 1990. *In other words: Essays toward a reflexive sociology.* Stanford, CA: Stanford University Press.

Breckenridge, Carol, and Candace Vogler. 2001. "The critical limits of embodiment: Disability's criticism." *Public Culture* 13 (3): 349–58.

Brodkey, Harold. 1996. *This wild darkness: The story of my death.* London: Fourth Estate.

Brown, Norman O. (1959) 1970. *Life against death.* London. Sphere Books.

Buber, Martin. (1923) 1970. *I and thou.* New York: Scribners and Sons.

Buck-Morss, Susan. 1992. "*Aesthetics and anaesthetics*: Walter Benjamin's Artwork Essay Reconsidered." *October* 62:3–41.

Burrows, Edwin, and Mike Wallace. 2001. *Gotham: A history of New York City to 1898.* New York: Oxford University Press.

Butler, Judith. 1999. *Gender trouble: Feminism and the subversion of identity.* New York: Routledge.

Canguilhem, Georges. (1943) 1991. *The normal and the pathological.* New York: Zone Books.

———. 2008. *Knowledge of life.* New York: Fordham University Press.

Carr, David. 1986. *Time, narrative and history.* Bloomington: Indiana University Press.

Carruthers, Peter. 2002. "The cognitive functions of language." *Journal of Behavioural and Brain Sciences* 25:657–726.

Casey, Edward. 1991. *Spirit and soul: Essays in philosophical psychology.* Dallas: Spring Publications.

———. 1993. *Getting back into place: Toward a new understanding of the place-world.* Bloomington: University of Indiana Press.

Céline, Louis-Ferdinand. (1932) 1983. *Journey to the end of the night.* Translated by Ralph Manheim. London: John Calder.

Churchland, Paul. 1989. *A neurocomputational perspective: The nature of mind and the structure of science.* Cambridge, MA: MIT Press.

———. 2004. "Knowing qualia: A reply to Jackson." In There's something about Mary: Essays on phenomenal consciousness and Frank Jackson's knowledge argument, edited by Peter Ludlow, Yujin Nagasawa, and Daniel Stoljar, 163–79. Cambridge: MIT Press.

Clare, Eli. 2001. "Stolen bodies, reclaimed bodies: Disability and queerness." *Public Culture* 13 (3): 359–66.

Clark, Andy. 2008. *Supersizing the mind: Embodiment, action and cognitive extension.* Oxford: Oxford University Press.

Collard, Cyril. 1993. *Savage nights.* London: Quartet Books.

Collingwood, Robin. (1942) 1992. *The new Leviathan; or, Man, society, civilization, and barbarism.* Oxford: Oxford University Press.

———. (1940) 2002. *An essay on metaphysics.* Oxford: Oxford University Press.

Condran, Gretchen. 1995. "Changing patterns of epidemic disease in New York City." In *Hives of sickness: Public health and epidemics in New York City*, edited by David Rosner, 29–35. New Brunswick, NJ: Rutgers University Press.

Conigrave, Timothy. 2010. *Holding the man.* London: Penguin.

Connerton, Paul. 1989. *How societies remember.* Cambridge: Cambridge University Press.

Connor, Steven. 2004. *The book of skin.* London: Reaktion Books.

Cox, Rupert, Andrew Irving, and Christopher Wright, eds. 2016. *Beyond text: Critical practices and sensory anthropology.* Manchester: Manchester University Press.

Crapanzano, Vincent. 1992. *Hermes' dilemma and Hamlet's desire: On the epistemology of interpretation.* Cambridge, MA: Harvard University Press.

———. 2004. *Imaginative horizons: An essay in literary-philosophical anthropology.* Chicago: University of Chicago Press.

———. 2015. "Half disciplined chaos: Thoughts on destiny, contingency, story, and trauma." In *Genocide and mass violence: Memory, symptom, and recovery,* edited by Devon Hinton and Alexander Hinton, 157–74. Cambridge: Cambridge University Press.

Crapanzano, Vincent, and Michael Jackson. 2014. "Thinking without a banister." *Journal of the Royal Anthropological Institute* 20 (4): 774–81.

da Col, Giovanni. 2017. "Two or three things I know about ethnographic theory." *HAU: Journal of Ethnographic Theory* 7 (1): 1–8.

da Col, Giovanni, and David Graeber. 2011. "Foreword: The return of ethnographic theory." *HAU: Journal of Ethnographic Theory* 1 (1): vi–xxxv.

da Col, Giovanni, and Caroline Humphrey. 2012. "Subjects of luck: Contingency, morality, and the anticipation of everyday life." *Social Analysis* 56 (2): 1–18.

Das, Veena. 1996. *Critical events.* Oxford: Oxford University Press.

Das, Veena, and Clara Han, eds. 2016. *Living and dying the contemporary world: A compendium.* Berkeley: University of California Press.

Davies, Douglas. 2006. "Inner-speech and religious traditions." In *Theorizing religion: Classical and contemporary debates,* edited by James Beckford and John Walliss, 211–23. Aldershot: Ashgate.

Davis, Christopher. 2000. *Death in abeyance.* Edinburgh: Edinburgh University Press.

de Certeau, Michel. 1986. "Practices of space." In *On signs,* edited by Marshall Blonsky, 122–45. Oxford: Blackwell.

Deleuze, Gilles. 2005. Francis Bacon: The logic of sensation. London: Continuum.

de Montalembert, Hugues. 1987. *Eclipse: An autobiography.* London: Sceptre.

Desjarlais, Robert. 1997. *Shelter blues: Sanity and selfhood among the homeless.* Philadelphia: University of Pennsylvania Press.

———. 2012. *Counterplay: An anthropologist at the chessboard.* Berkeley: University of California Press.

———. 2016. *Subject to death: Life and loss in a Buddhist world.* Chicago: University of Chicago Press.

Desjarlais, Robert, and Jason Throop. 2011. "Phenomenological approaches in anthropology." *Annual Review of Anthropology* 40:87–102.

Dostoyevsky, Fyodor. (1886) 1995. *Crime and punishment.* London: Penguin.

Eagleton, Terry. 1990. *The ideology of the aesthetic.* Oxford: Blackwell.

Elliott, Denielle, and Dara Culhane, eds. 2016. A different kind of ethnography: Imaginative practices and creative methodologies. Toronto: University of Toronto Press.

Evans-Pritchard, E. E. 1969. *The Nuer.* Oxford: Clarendon.

Ewing, Katherine. 1990. "The illusion of wholeness: Culture, self, and the experience of inconsistency." *Ethos* 18 (3): 251–78.

Fabian, Johannes. 1983. *Time and the other: How anthropology makes its object.* New York: Columbia University Press.

———. 2003. "Forgetful remembering: A colonial life in the Congo." *Africa* 73:489–504.

Flaherty, Robert. 1950. "Robert Flaherty talking." In *Cinema 1950*, edited by Roger Manvell, 10–29. London: Pelican.

Fernyhough, Charles. 2008. "Getting Vygotskian about theory of mind: Mediation, dialogue, and the development of social understanding." *Developmental Review* 28:225–62.

———. 2016. *The voices within: The history and science of how we talk to ourselves.* London: Profile Books.

Fink, Eugen. 2016. *Play as symbol of the world and other writings.* Bloomington: Indiana University Press.

Fischer, Michael. 2009. *Anthropological futures.* Durham, NC: Duke University Press.

Foucault, Michel. 1994. "The art of telling the truth." In *Critique and power: Recasting the Foucault/Habermas debate*, edited by Michael Kelly, 139–48. Cambridge, MA: MIT Press.

Geertz, Clifford. 1973. *The interpretation of cultures.* New York: Basic Books.

Gell, Alfred. 1996. *The anthropology of time.* Oxford: Berg.

Guibert, Hervé. 1995. *To the friend who did not save my life.* London: Quartet Books.

———. 2015. *Cytomegalovirus: A hospitalization diary.* New York: Fordham University Press.

Good, Byron. 1994. *Medicine, rationality and experience: An anthropological perspective.* Cambridge: Cambridge University Press.

Gregory, Chris. 1997. *Savage money: The anthropology and politics of commodity exchange.* London: Routledge.

Gregory, Richard L. 2005. *Eye and brain: The psychology of seeing.* 5th edition. Oxford: Oxford University Press.

Grimshaw, Anna. 2001. *The ethnographer's eye: Ways of seeing in anthropology.* Cambridge: Cambridge University Press.

Grosz, Elizabeth. 2008. *Chaos, territory, art: Deleuze and the framing of the earth.* New York: Columbia University Press.

Hacking, Ian. 1990. *The taming of chance.* Cambridge: Cambridge University Press.

Hallam, Elizabeth, and Jenny Hockey. 2006. *Death, memory and material culture.* Oxford: Berg.

Haraway, Donna. 1991. *Simians, cyborgs and women: The reinvention of nature.* New York: Routledge.

———. 1992. *Primate visions.* London: Verso.

Hart, Keith. 2005. "Money: One anthropologist's view." In *Handbook of economic anthropology*, edited by James Carrier, 160–75. Cheltenham: Elgar Press.

———. 2008–9. "Towards a new human universal: Rethinking anthropology for our times." *Radical Anthropology Journal* no. 2: 4–10.

———. 2010. "Kant, anthropology and the new human universal." *Social Anthropology* 18:441–47.

Heidegger, Martin. 1962. *Being and time.* New York: Harper Row.

———. 1977. *The question concerning technology.* Translated by W. Lovitt. New York: Harper and Row.

———. 2000. *Introduction to metaphysics.* New Haven, CT: Yale University Press.

Herzog, Werner. 1997. *Little Dieter needs to fly.* 80 min. Werner Herzog Filmproduktion.

Henley, Paul. 2009. *The adventure of the real: Jean Rouch and the craft of ethnographic cinema.* Chicago: University of Chicago Press.

Hogan, Susan, and Sarah Pink. 2010. "Routes to interiorities: Art therapy and knowing in anthropology." *Visual Studies* 23 (2): 158–74.

Hollan, Douglas, and Jason Throop, eds. 2008. "Introduction." In "Whatever happened to empathy?," Special Issue, *Ethos* 36 (4): 4.

Holloway, Marguerite. 2014. *The measure of Manhattan: The tumultuous career and surprising legacy of John Randel Jr., cartographer, surveyor, inventor.* New York: W.W. Norton.

Hooper, Edward. 2000. *The river: A journey back to the source of HIV and AIDS.* London: Penguin.

Howes, David, ed. 2004. *Empire of the senses: The sensual culture reader.* Oxford: Berg.

———. 2006. "Charting the sensorial revolution." *Senses and Society* 1 (1): 113–28.

Howes, David, and Constance Classen. 2014. *Ways of sensing: Understanding the senses in society.* London: Routledge.

Hull, John M. 1992. *Touching the rock: An experience of blindness.* London: Vintage.

Hulsker, Jan. 1996. *The new complete Van Gogh: Paintings, drawings, sketches.* 2nd edition. Amsterdam: John Benjamins Publishing Co.

Hume, David. 1739. *A treatise of human nature.* Bk. I, part IV, sect. VI. London: John Noon. https://www.gutenberg.org/files/4705/4705-h/4705-h.htm.

Hurlburt, Russell. 1993. *Sampling inner experience with disturbed affect.* New York: Plenum Press.

———. 2009. "Descriptive experience sampling." In *Oxford companion to consciousness*, edited by Tim Baynes, Axel Cleermans, and Patrick Wilken, 225–27. Oxford: Oxford University Press.

Ingham, Geoffrey. 2004. "The nature of money." *Economic Sociology* 5 (2): 18–29.

Ingold, Tim. 1992. "Editorial." *Man*, n.s., 27 (4): 693–96.

———. 2014. "That's enough about ethnography!" *HAU: Journal of Ethnographic Theory* 4 (1): 383–95.

———. 2017. "Anthropology contra ethnography." *HAU: Journal of Ethnographic Theory* 7 (1): 21–26.

Ingold, Tim, and Jo Lee. 2006. "Fieldwork on foot: Perceiving, routing, socializing." In *Locating the field: Space, place and context in anthropology*, edited by Simon Coleman and Peter Collins, 67–86. Oxford: Berg.

Irving, Andrew. 2002. "Life made strange: A comparative study of how HIV/AIDS affects perception." PhD thesis: University of London.

———. 2005. "Life made strange: An essay on the reinhabitation of bodies and landscapes." In *Qualities of time: Anthropological approaches*, edited by Wendy James and David Mills, 317–33. Oxford: Berg.

———. 2007. "Ethnography, art and death." *Journal of the Royal Anthropological Institute* 13 (1): 185–208.

———. 2011. "I gave my child life but I also gave her death." *Australian Journal of Anthropology* 22 (3): 332–50.

———. 2013. "Bridges: A new sense of scale." *Senses and Society* 8 (3): 290–313.

———. 2014a. "The suicidal mind." In *Mediating and remediating death*, edited by Dorthe Christensen and Kjetil Sandvik, 217–32. Farnham: Ashgate.

———. 2014b. "Freedom and laughter in an uncertain world: Language, expression and cosmopolitanism experience." In *Whose cosmopolitanism? Critical cosmopolitanisms, relationalities and discontents*, edited by Andrew Irving and Nina Glick-Schiller, 121–38. Oxford: Berghahn.

———. 2016. "Random Manhattan: Thinking and moving beyond text." In *Beyond text: Critical practices and sensory anthropology*, edited by Rupert Cox, Andrew Irving, and Christopher Wright. Manchester: Manchester University Press.

———. 2017. "The art of turning left and right." In *Anthropologies and futures: Researching emerging and uncertain worlds*, edited by Andrew Irving, Sarah Pink, Juan Salazar, and Johannes Sjöberg, 23–42. London: Bloomsbury.

Jablonski, Nina. 2008. *Skin: A natural history*. Berkeley: University of California Press.

Jackson, Frank. 1986. "What Mary didn't know." *Journal of Philosophy* 88 (5): 291–95.

Jackson, Michael. 1996. "Phenomenology, radical empiricism and anthropological critique." In *Things as they are: new directions in phenomenological anthropology*, edited by Michael Jackson, 1–50. Bloomington: Indiana University Press.

———. 2002. *The politics of storytelling: Violence, transgression, and intersubjectivity*. Copenhagen: Museum Tusculanum.

———. 2011. *Life within limits: Well-being in a world of want*. Durham, NC: Duke University Press.

———. 2013. *Lifeworlds: Essays in existential anthropology*. Chicago: University of Chicago Press.

———. 2015. "Afterword." In *Phenomenology in anthropology: A sense of perspective*, edited by Kalpana Ram and Christopher Houston, 293–305. Bloomington: Indiana University Press.

———. 2016. "Life and concept." In *Living and dying the contemporary world: A compendium*, edited by Veena Das and Celia Han, 449–62. Berkeley: University of California Press.

Jacobs, Brian, and Patrick Kain, eds. 2003. *Essays on Kant's anthropology*. New York: Cambridge University Press.

James, William. 1890. *Principles of psychology*. Vol. 1. New York: Holt.

———. 2000. *Pragmatism and other writings*. London: Penguin.

James, Wendy, and David Mills, eds. 2005. *Qualities of time: Anthropological approaches*. Oxford: Berg.

Jameson, Frederic. 1979. "Reification and utopia in mass culture." *Social Text* no. 1: 130–48.

Jarman, Derek. 1993. *Blue*. 79 min. London: Basilisk Communications.

Jay, Martin. 1991. "The disenchantment of the eye." *Visual Anthropology Review* 7 (1): 15–38.

Johnson, Galen. 1999. "Inside and outside: Ontological considerations." In *Merleau-Ponty, interiority and exteriority, psychic life and the world*, edited by Dorothea Olkowski and James Morley, 25–35. New York: SUNY Press.

Jonas, Hans. 1965. "Life, death, and the body in the theory of being." *Review of Metaphysics* 19 (1): 3–23.

———. 2001. *The phenomenon of life: Toward a philosophical biology*. Evanston, IL: Northwestern University Press.

Joyce, James. (1922) 2000. *Ulysses*. London: Wordsworth Classics.

Kant, Immanuel. (1800) 1963. *Introduction to logic*. New York: Philosophy Press.

———. (1798) 2006. *Anthropology from a pragmatic point of view*. Cambridge: Cambridge University Press.

Kastenbaum, Robert. 2011. *Death, society, and human experience*. Boston: Pearson.

Kaufman, Sharon, and Lynn Morgan. 2005. "The anthropology of the beginnings and endings of life." *Annual Review of Anthropology* 34:317–41.

Kells, Karolyn. 2001. "Ability of blind people to detect obstacles in unfamiliar environments." *Journal of Nursing Scholarship* 33 (2): 153–57.

Kiechle, Melanie. 2015. "Navigating by nose: Fresh air, stench nuisance, and the urban environment, 1840–1880." *Journal of Urban History* 42 (4): 1–19.

Kirmayer, Laurence. 2008. "Empathy and alterity in cultural psychiatry." *Ethos* 36 (4): 454–74.

Koolhaas, Rem. 1994. *Delirious New York: A retroactive manifesto for Manhattan*. New York: The Monacelli Press.

Kondo, Dorinne. 1990. *Crafting selves: Power, gender and discourses of identity in a Japanese workplace.* Chicago: University of Chicago Press.

Kuehn, M. 2006. "Introduction." In *Anthropology from a pragmatic point of view*, by Immanuel Kant, edited by Robert Louden, vii–xxxi. Cambridge: University of Cambridge Press.

Lambek, Michael, ed. 2010. *Ordinary ethics: Anthropology, language, and action.* New York: Fordham University Press.

———. 2015. "Living as if it mattered." In *Four lectures on ethics anthropological perspectives.* HAU Books Masterclass Series, vol. 3. Chicago: University of Chicago Press.

Langer, Susanne. (1941) 1979. *Philosophy in a new key: A study in the symbolism of reason, rite and art.* Cambridge, MA: Harvard University Press.

Leach, Edmund. 1982. *Social anthropology.* Glasgow: Fontana.

Leavitt, John. 1996. "Meaning and feeling in the *anthropology of emotions.*" *American Ethnologist* 23 (3): 514–39.

Leder, Drew. 1990. *The absent body.* Chicago: University of Chicago Press.

Leed, Eric. 1979. No man's land: Combat and identity in World War I. Cambridge: Cambridge University Press.

Lende, Daniel, and Greg Downey, eds. 2012. *The encultured brain: An introduction to neuroanthropology.* Cambridge, MA: MIT Press.

Lende, Daniel. 2013. "Our inner voices." *Plos* (blog), May 10, 2013. http://blogs.plos.org/neuroanthropology/2013/05/10/our-inner-voices/.

Levinas, Emmanuel. 1996. *The Levinas reader.* Oxford: Blackwell.

Lévi-Strauss, Claude. 1966. *The savage mind.* London: Weidenfield and Nicholson.

Lloyd, Geoffrey E. R. 1976. "Time in Greek culture." In *Cultures and time*, edited by Louis Gardet, 117–47. Paris: Unesco Press.

Lock, Margaret. 2004. "Displacing suffering: The reconstruction of death in North America and Japan." In *Death, mourning, and burial: A cross-cultural reader*, edited by Antonius Robben, 91–111. Oxford: Blackwell.

Locke, John. 1714. The works of John Locke, Esq.; in Three Volumes. London: John Churchill and Sam Manship.

Low, Setha. 1996. "The anthropology of cities: Imagining and theorising the city." *Annual Review of Anthropology* 25: 387–99.

Luhrmann, Tanya. 2012. *When God talks back: Understanding the American Evangelical relationship with God.* New York: Alfred A. Knopf.

MacIntyre, Alasdair. 1999. *Dependent rational animals: Why human beings need the virtues*. Chicago: Open Court.

MacKay, Donald. 1987. *The building of Manhattan*. New York: Harper and Row.

Malik, Kenan. 2015. *The quest for a moral compass: A global history of ethics*. London: Atlantic Books.

Mann, Thomas. 1999. *The magic mountain*. London: Vintage.

Martin, Emily. 1992. "Body narratives, body boundaries." In *Cultural studies*, edited by Lawrence Grossberg, Cary Nelson, and Paula Treichler, 411–19. New York: Routledge.

Marks, Harry. 2016. "Chemonotes." In *Living and dying the contemporary world: A compendium*, edited by Veena Das and Celia Han, 675–95. Berkeley: University of California Press.

Marx, Karl. (1844) 1988. *The economic and philosophical manuscripts of 1844*. Amherst, NY: Prometheus Books.

———. (1867) 1999. *Capital: An abridged edition*. Oxford: Oxford University Press.

Mattingly, Cheryl, Nancy Lutkehaus, and Jason Throop, eds. 2008. "Troubling the boundary between psychology and anthropology: Jerome Bruner and his inspiration." Special Issue, *Ethos* 36 (1).

McCrone, John. 1999. *Going inside: A tour round a single moment of consciousness*. London: Faber and Faber.

Merleau-Ponty, Maurice. (1945) 1992. *The phenomenology of perception*. London: Routledge.

———. 1968. *The visible and the invisible*. Evanston, IL: Northwestern University Press.

———. 1994. *The Merleau-Ponty aesthetics reader: Philosophy and painting*. Evanston, IL: Northwestern University Press.

Miller, Daniel. 2017. "Anthropology is the discipline but the goal is ethnography." *HAU: Journal of Ethnographic Theory* 7 (1): 27–31.

Mims, Cecil. 1999. *When we die*. London: Robinson.

Minh-ha, Trinh. 1982. *Reassemblage*. 40 min. SFS.

Mithen, Steven. 2006. *The singing Neanderthals: The origins of music, language, mind and body*. London: Weidenfeld and Nicolson.

Monette, Paul. 1997. *Borrowed time: An AIDS memoir*. London: Abacus.

Montaigne, Michel de. 2003. *The complete essays*. London: Penguin Classics.

Moore, Oscar. 1996. *PWA: Looking AIDS in the face*. London: Picador.

Morris, Gouverner, Simeon De Witt, and John Rutherford. 1811. *Remarks of the Commissioners for laying out streets and roads in the City of New York*. http://www.library.cornell.edu/Reps/DOCS/nyc1811.htm.

Moss, Mitchell, and Carson Qing. 2012. "The dynamic population of Manhattan." Report for Rudin Center for Transportation Policy and Management Wagner School of Public Service. New York: New York University. https://wagner.nyu.edu/files/rudincenter/dynamic_pop_manhattan.pdf.

Murphy, Robert. 2001. *The body silent: The different world of the disabled*. New York: Norton.

Nader, Karim. 2003. "Re-recording human memories." *Nature* 425:571–72.

Nagel, Thomas. 1974. "What is it like to be a bat?" *Philosophical Review* 83 (4): 435–50.

Needham, Rodney. 1978. *Primordial characters*. Charlottesville: University of Virginia Press.

———. 1981. "Inner states as universals." In *Indigenous psychologies: The anthropology of self*, edited by Paul Heelas and Andrew Lock, 65–78. London: Academic Press.

Nehamas, Alexander. 1998. *The art of living: Socratic reflections from Plato to Foucault*. Berkeley: University of California Press.

Nicolini, Kim. 1998. "The streets of San Francisco: A personal geography." In *Bad subjects: Political education for everyday life*, edited by Bad Subjects Production Team, 78–83. New York: New York University Press.

Nietzsche, Friedrich. (1882) 1974a. *The gay science: With a prelude in rhymes and an appendix of songs*. New York: Vintage.

———. (1883) 1974b. *Thus spake Zarathustra*. London: Penguin Classics.

———. (1888) 2003. *Twilight of the idols and the Anti-Christ*. London: Penguin Classics.

Obbo, Christine. 1998. "Who cares for carers? AIDS and women in Uganda." In *Developing Uganda*, edited by Bernt-Hansen and Michael Twaddle, 207–14. Oxford: J. Currey.

Parkin, David. 1985. "Reason, emotion and the embodiment of power." In *Reason and morality*, edited by Joanna Overing, 134–49. London: Tavistock.

———. 1999. "Suffer many healers." In *Religion, health and suffering*, edited by John Hinnells and Roy Porter, 433–58. London: Kegan Paul International.

Parry, Jonathan. 1994. *Death in Banaras*. Cambridge: Cambridge University Press.

Peirce, Charles. 1998. *The essential Peirce: Selected philosophical writings, Vol. 2 (1893–1913)*. Bloomington: Indiana University Press.

Pina-Cabral, João de. 2017. *World: An anthropological examination*. HAU Books Malinowski Monograph Series. Chicago: University of Chicago Press.

Pink, Sarah. 2009. *Doing sensory ethnography*. London: Sage.

Pinney, Christopher. 1995. "Moral topophilia." In *Anthropology of landscape*, edited by Eric Hirsch and Michael O'Hanlon, 78–113. Oxford: Clarendon.

Polanyi, Michael. 1969. *Knowing and being*. Chicago: University of Chicago Press.

Potter, Dennis. 1986. *The singing detective*. BBC TV Series.

———. 1993. "The last acre of truth." *Guardian*, February 15, 1993.

———. 1994. *Interview with Melvyn Bragg*. Channel 4 Television. United Kingdom, March 15, 1994.

Quine, Willard. 1960. *Word and object*. Cambridge, MA: MIT Press.

Raban, Jonathan. 1998. *Soft city*. London: Harvill Press.

Rabinow, Paul. 1994. "Introduction." In *A vital rationalist: Selected writings from Georges Canguilhem*, 11–25. New York: Zone Books.

Radley, Alan. 2009. *Works of illness: Narrative, picturing and the social response to serious disease*. Ashby de la Zouch: InkerMen Press.

Rapport, Nigel. 2000. "Writing on the body: The poetic life-story of Philip Larkin." *Anthropology and Medicine* 7 (1): 39–62.

———. 2008. "Gratuitousness: Notes towards an anthropology of interiority." *Australian Journal of Anthropology* 19 (3): 331–49.

Reason, Matthew, and Dee Reynolds. 2010. "Kinesthesia, empathy and related pleasures: An inquiry into audience experiences of watching dance." *Dance Research Journal* 42 (2): 49–75.

Reynolds, Dee. 2012. "Kinesthetic empathy and the dance's body: From emotion to affect." In *Kinesthetic empathy in creative and cultural practices*, edited by Matthew Reason and Dee Reynolds, 121–36. Bristol: Intellect.

Reynolds-Whyte, Susan. 1997. *Questioning misfortune: The pragmatics of uncertainty in Eastern Uganda*. Cambridge: Cambridge University Press.

Robben, Antonius. 2004. *Death, mourning, and burial: A cross-cultural reader*. Oxford: Blackwell.

Robbins, Joel. 2013. "Beyond the suffering subject: Toward an anthropology of the good." *Journal of the Royal Anthropological Institute* 19 (3): 447–62.

Rose, Steven. 2003. *The making of memory: From molecules to mind*. London: Vintage.

Rosen, Lawrence, ed. 1996. *Other intentions: Cultural contexts and the attribution of inner states.* Santa Fe, NM: School of American Research Press.

Rouch, Jean, and Edgar Morin. 1960. *Chronicle of a Summer.* 90 min. BFI.

Sacks, Oliver. 2004. "The mind's eye: What the blind see." In *Empire of the senses,* edited by David Howes, 25–42. Oxford: Berg.

Santayana, George. (1923) 1955. *Scepticism and animal faith: Introduction to a system of philosophy.* New York: Courier Dover Publications.

Sartre, Jean-Paul. (1940) 2004. *The imaginary: A phenomenological psychology of the imagination.* Translated by Jonathan Webber. London: Routledge.

———. (1943) 1996. *Being and nothingness.* Translated by Hazel E. Barnes. London: Routledge.

———. 1974. *Between existentialism and Marxism.* New York: Morrow.

Schechner, Richard, and Willa Appel, eds. 1990. By means of performance: Intercultural studies of theatre and ritual. Cambridge: Cambridge University Press.

Scarry, Elaine. 1987. *The body in pain: The making and unmaking of the world.* Oxford: Oxford University Press.

Sennett, Richard. 1991. *The conscience of the eye: The design and social life of cities.* New York: Alfred A. Knopf.

———. 1994. *Flesh and stone: The body and the city in Western Civilisation.* London: Faber and Faber.

Simmel, Georg. 1950. *The sociology of Georg Simmel.* Translated by Kurt H. Wolff. New York: The Free Press.

Scheck, Justin. 2008. "Mackerel economics in prison leads to appreciation for oily fillets." *Wall Street Journal,* October 2, 2008.

Sperber, Dan, and Deirdre Wilson. 1995. *Relevance.* Oxford: Blackwell.

Stacey, Jackie. 1997. *Teratologies: A cultural study of cancer.* London: Routledge.

Staples, James. 2003. "Disguise, revelation and copyright: Disassembling the South Indian Leper." *Journal of the Royal Anthropological Institute,* n.s., 9 (2): 295–315.

Steel, Eric. 2006. *The Bridge.* 95 min. IFC Films.

Stein, Edith. (1917) 1989. *On the problem of empathy.* Washington, DC: ICS Publications.

Steiner, George. 1978. *On difficulty and other essays.* Oxford: Oxford University Press.

Stocking, George. 1992. *The ethnographer's magic and other essays in the history of anthropology.* Madison: University of Wisconsin Press.

Stoller, Paul. 2005. Stranger in the village of the sick: A memoir of cancer, sorcery and healing. Boston: Beacon Press.

———. 2009. *The power of the between: An anthropological odyssey.* Chicago: University of Chicago Press.

Straus, Erwin. 1963. The primary world of senses: A vindication of sensory experience. New York: Free Press of Glencoe.

———. 1966. Phenomenological psychology: The selected papers of Erwin W. Straus. New York: Basic Books.

Sturken, Maria. 1997. *Tangled memories: The Vietnam War, the AIDS epidemic, and the politics of remembering.* Berkeley: University of California Press.

Synnott, Anthony. 1993. *The body social: Symbolism, self and society.* London: Routledge.

Tarn, Gary. 2006. *Black Sun.* 70 min. New York: Indiepix Films.

Taussig, Michael. 2009. *What color is the sacred?* Chicago: University of Chicago Press.

Taylor, Charles. 1979. *Hegel and modern society.* Cambridge: Cambridge University Press.

———. 1992. *Sources of the self: The making of the modern identity.* Cambridge: Cambridge University Press.

Throop, Jason. 2008. "On the problem of empathy: The case of Yap, Federated States of Micronesia." *Ethos* 36 (4): 402–26.

———. 2010. *Suffering and sentiment: Exploring the vicissitudes of experience and pain in Yap.* Berkeley: University of California Press.

———. 2015. "Ambivalent happiness and virtuous suffering." *HAU: Journal of Ethnographic Theory* 5 (3): 45–68.

Todd, Oliver. 1998. *Albert Camus: A life.* London: Vintage.

Toombs, Kay. 1992. "The body in Multiple Sclerosis: A patient's perspective." In *The body in medical thought and practice*, edited by Drew Leder, 122–37. Dordecht: Klumer Academic Press.

Turetsky, Philip. 1998. *Time: Problems of philosophy.* London: Routledge.

Turner, Victor. 1969. *The ritual process: Structure and anti-structure.* London: Routledge.

———. 1982. *From ritual to theatre: The seriousness of human play.* New York: Performing Arts Journal Publications.

Volosinov, Valentin. 1973. *Marxism and the philosophy of language.* Cambridge, MA: Harvard University Press.

Vonnegut, Kurt. 1987. *Bluebeard.* New York: Random House.

Vygotsky, Lev. (1934) 1986. *Thought and language.* Cambridge, MA: MIT Press.

Walker, Matthew, Tiffany Brakefield, J. Allan Hobson, and Robert Stickgold, eds. 2003. "Dissociable stages of human memory consolidation and recon-solidation." *Nature* 425:616–20.

Ward, Jamie. 2011. *The student's guide to cognitive neuroscience.* New York: Psychology Press.

Whitehouse, Harvey, ed. 2001. *The debated mind: Evolutionary psychology versus ethnography.* Oxford: Berg.

Whyte, William H. 1992. "Introduction." In *Works Progress Administration guide to New York City.* New York: New York Press.

Wilde, Oscar. 1992. *The picture of Dorian Gray.* London: Wordsworth Classics.

Wittgenstein, Ludwig. (1953) 2009. *Philosophical investigations.* Oxford: Blackwell.

Wood, Allen. 1999. *Kant's ethical thought.* Cambridge: Cambridge University Press.

———. 2003. "Kant and the problem of human nature." In *Essays on Kant's anthropology*, edited by Brian Jacobs and Patrick Kain, 38–60. Cambridge: Cambridge University Press.

Zelizer, Viviana. 1997. *The social meaning of money: Pin money, paychecks, poor relief, and other currencies.* Princeton, NJ: Princeton University.

Index

Selected Names

Hau Books is committed to publishing the most distinguished texts in classic and advanced anthropological theory. The titles aim to situate ethnography as the prime heuristic of anthropology, and return it to the forefront of conceptual developments in the discipline. Hau Books is sponsored by some of the world's most distinguished anthropology departments and research institutions, and releases its titles in both print editions and open-access formats.

www.haubooks.com

Supported by
Hau-N. E. T.
Network of Ethnographic Theory

University of Aarhus – EPICENTER (DK)
University of Amsterdam (NL)
Australian National University – Library (AU)
University of Bergen (NO)
Brown University (US)
California Institute of Integral Studies (US)
University of Campinas (BR)
University of Canterbury (NZ)
University College London (UK)
University of Cologne – The Global South Studies Centre (DE)
and City Library of Cologne (DE)
University of Colorado Boulder Libraries (US)
Cornell University (US)
University of Edinburgh (UK)
The Graduate Institute – Geneva Library (CH)
University of Groningen (NL)
Harvard University (US)
The Higher School of Economics in St. Petersburg (RU)
Humboldt University of Berlin (DE)
Indiana University Library (US)
Johns Hopkins University (US)
University of Kent (UK)
Lafayette College Library (US)
London School of Economics and Political Science (UK)
Institute of Social Sciences of the University of Lisbon (PL)
Ludwig Maximilian University of Munich (DE)
University of Manchester (UK)
The University of Manchester Library (UK)
Max-Planck Institute for the Study of Religious and Ethnic
Diversity at Göttingen (DE)
Musée de Quai Branly (FR)
Museu Nacional – UFRJ (BR)
Norwegian Museum of Cultural History (NO)
University of Oslo (NO)
University of Oslo Library (NO)
Princeton University (US)
University of Rochester (US)
SOAS, University of London (UK)
University of Sydney (AU)
University of Toronto Libraries (CA)

www.haujournal.org/haunet

CPSIA information can be obtained
at www.ICGtesting.com
Printed in the USA
LVHW07n1622080818
586379LV00001B/3/P

* 9 7 8 0 9 9 7 3 6 7 5 1 5 *